Don, So good to s[...]
all these years and you[...]

# Flying High
# Living Free

I hope you enjoy this book and
understand it is all true.

Thanks

# Flying High Living Free

## Chronicle of a Sky Diver

### Told As He Lived It
### Rocky Evans

CHB Media
Publisher

ISBN 978-1-946088-93-2
LIBRARY OF CONGRESS CONTROL NUMBER: 2018932631



CHB MEDIA, PUBLISHER

(386) 690-9295
chbmedia@gmail.com
www.chbmediaonline.com


First Edition
Printed in the U.S.A.

**Rocky Evans** is a National and World Champion skydiver, a highly skilled pilot, and a co-developer of the Accelerated Freefall Training Program. One of the early legends in skydiving, Rocky Evans is no choir boy, but when he's in the air he is as pure as they come. **This is his story, told in his own words.**

# CONTENTS

# CONTENTS CONTINUED

## ACKNOWLEDGEMENTS

WHEN I THINK OF GRATITUDE, two groups of people come to mind: those who helped make me who I am, and those who helped me complete this book, *Flying High, Living Free*. I would first like to thank my family—my parents Bob and Betty Evans, my brother Mike and sister Dawn. Thanks for the memories. There were many more people in my hometown of Three Rivers, Michigan, who didn't find their way into this book, but who I remember in the warmest way as if it was yesterday.

At the center of my gratitude to those who made me the man I am in my aviation career are Gary Dupuis and Bob Lee. They are very much part of this book. Special thanks also to Skydive DeLand and its owner, Bob Hallett.

To thank those who helped me complete this book I'll start with Bambi Knight and Georgia Outman, who helped me with my first book, *Truth*. As for this book, I first have to mention my editor and publisher Gary Broughman, and add in all those who had an important hand in preparing the manuscript for publication: Martha Scott, Marcia Tucker, and T.K. Donle. Also, my thanks to Kim for her motivation, and to Smitty of Sky Dive City. Finally, my heartfelt thanks to Saundra Emerson for her unique role in bringing *Flying High, Living Free* onto the market.

And, as always, my sincere and humble appreciation to God and this country for giving me the opportunity to share these stories with you, the reader.

— Rocky Evans

# INTRODUCTION

**WE AT CHB MEDIA ARE PROUD TO PUBLISH** *Flying High, Living Free*, Rocky Evans' latest book. As an editor I'm always looking for writers with a distinct voice that is engaging and tells you something about who they are before you even know their full story. When I read Rocky's first book, *Truth*, I knew he had such a voice.

As a publishing company CHB Media tends to specialize in what society might call common people, but the kind of common people whose courage pulls them through and allows them to accomplish something good and noble despite having to swim against the current along the way.

I hope you will agree with me that *Flying High, Living Free* is the kind of inspirational tale that leaves you feeling like things are possible if we just hang in and have faith.

> — Gary Broughman
> Publisher and Editor
> CHB Media

The Autana Experience: The BBC film crew tandem jumps onto the Venezuelan mountaintop and then rappels down into the cave running through the mountain.

Chapter One
## JUMPING ONTO THE LOST WORLD

DeLand, Florida. The year was 1983. A Brit by the name of Adrian Warren, along with a famous mountain climber named Don Whillans, also a Brit, came to the DeLand skydiving facility to do Accelerated Freefall (AFF) jump training. Don only did a couple of training jumps, but Adrian went through the full course. Both were great guys, and I missed them when they were gone.

Adrian worked for the BBC as a film producer. In 1985 he sent me a package with a picture of this giant monolith—an isolated flat-topped mountain in Venezuela called a *tepui*. It rose 4,300 feet above the Amazon jungle. An awesome sight. Cerro Autana—Autana Mountain. Adrian wanted to take a team of skydivers to jump onto the top of Autana and rappel down the side to explore the caves that were 1,200 feet below the summit. Members of the team would then climb back up, BASE jump off the top to the jungle floor, and hike to the Orinoco River. From there we would paddle dugout canoes to Puerto Ayacucho. The entire expedition would be filmed to produce a NOVA science documentary. This was right up my alley and I told him yes, count me in.

Adrian called with some bad news just a month and a half before we were to go. Carl, an important team member, was dead. He hit the side of a cliff in Norway while BASE jumping.

"Troll Wall," I said.

"Yes, how did you know?"

I told him that I had heard that Carl was going there.

"Now what?" I asked.

"Jean, Carl's wife, is going to fill the photography contract we had with Carl."

"Jean?" I questioned.

"Yes, she's going to fill the contract. That was part of the deal, and we don't have a choice."

Well, that didn't bother me too much. All she was going to do was take the freefall photos. Plus, I thought that she would have BASE jumping down pat. I'm not a male chauvinist, but this was no kind of trip for the meek and mild. I worried whether Jean could even pick up one of the tandem rigs. I only hoped her camera work was as good as Carl's.

Our team consisted of 12 people—five Americans, six British, and one Venezuelan special forces Major to monitor the expedition for the government. I knew only two people on our team well—Mitch Decoteau and Bill Booth. And when I say that, I was referring to their skydiving skill level and how they performed in the air.

Mitch was solid—a two-time world skydiving champion, a seasoned smoke jumper, and an expert at cargo drops. He had twenty-some years with the U.S. Forest Service and was still around. Yeah, I wanted him with me. Bill, acting as one of the tandem masters for our team, had recently begun selling tandem parachute rigs—a rig that allowed two jumpers harnessed together to fly and land under the same canopy.

Adrian originally wanted to use Strong Enterprises' tandem rig, but Bill's looked a lot cleaner at the time. Canopies on the Booth rig were made by Pioneer 375 High Lifters. Both the main and reserve. Reliable. And they had a real good flair. Not as many square feet as the Strong, but the tradeoff was the good lift at the end. I figured landing at 4,300 feet could be pretty windy, windier than at sea level.

Last minute details fell in place. We left for Autana in March. We flew to Orlando, then Miami, and then Caracas, Venezuela. Once in Caracas, I finally got to meet the other members of the team. We got our equipment organized, got a quick lesson in climbing and rappelling, and then Adrian and I went to see the DC-3 he had chartered. The Caracas regional airport was on top of a mountain at 6,000 feet. The hanger was beautiful—painted floor, everything in place. There was a P-51 Mustang, a P-3 Orion, and a perfectly restored Pitts B2. And there she was as pretty as the day she came off the production floor—a Douglas Super DC-3. I stood in awe. Never had I seen one exactly like her. Adrian poked me. "What do you think?"

"She'll do the job well," I said.

We had five tons of equipment and people. We gave this info to the pilot so he could determine his weight and balance— we were close to max. When we got back to the hotel we told the rest of the team about the plane.

Mitch and I went down to the bar that night and got drunk. The place was full of dolled-up women trying to get us to buy them drinks. Mitch and I blew them off as we discussed how to put the passenger DC-3 into a cargo configuration. I had gotten my A&P aircraft maintenance license a few years earlier and knew a lot about the airplane. Shit, I also had 2,000 jumps or more out of the DC-3.

Several team members and I loaded a great big two-ton truck with cargo and drove it out to the airport. We packed the cargo into the DC-3 and got it all tied in place. I asked the pilot if I could fly some of the way down to Puerto Ayacucho, the town where we would be based prior to our jump. He said sure. Three hours from Caracas. The flight down was really cool. I got to fly an hour or so in left seat. On the way down the pilot asked if I wanted to fly by Autana. I said, "Of course."

I was up in the cockpit probably 20 miles away when I saw it in the distance sticking up out of the green jungle— Cerro Autana. The closer we got, the more massive it looked. We were probably five miles out and this damn thing was way more impressive than I ever imagined. I went to the back of the plane—the rest of the team was crouched on their knees pasted to windows on each side of the plane. They couldn't see Autana yet because we were flying straight at it.

I went back to the cockpit. We were close now. The color stood out, so vivid. The monolith had long streaks of pink along the brown limestone faces. It didn't look like I thought it would look. The pictures were deceiving. It was one long and narrow rock with a tail on the end. From the side it looked like the top angled down at 45 degrees. But if you looked at it from the front, it jutted up to 4,300 feet—damn near straight up. On top there was a small hill that stuck up probably 300 feet. About 1,200 feet down from the top was a giant cave that went all the way through the mountain to the other side. As we flew by I noticed small rocks falling from the sides. The noise and vibration from the DC-3's powerful round engines and swirling props had rattled loose pieces of rocks that had laid motionless for millions of years. I watched them as they bounced their way to the jungle floor. *My God*, I thought, *this thing is impressive.*

I asked the pilot if he would fly across the top, but he said we'd better land. He was getting low on gas. I said okay and went to the back of the plane again. Never had I seen such humbled faces. Their expressions were pretty much all the same—all but Mitch, who was smiling as our eyes met. He gave me a big thumbs up. I returned the gesture. "Pretty impressive, 'eh guys?" I said, trying to break the stone cold silence of the truth the mountain had brought on.

At that moment everybody had something to say. Most of it was "what ifs." What if we miss when we land? What if someone gets hurt? What if we miss with the cargo drops? Too many questions too quick, all the questions directed to Adrian. I could hear him stumbling for answers.

I went back up front to watch for the airport in Puerto Ayacucho. I was amazed at how long the runway was. The strip was asphalt and probably 7,000 feet long, and the ground was red. Red clay, like the state of Georgia. We landed and taxied up, shut down. The airstair door worked just like it did when the airplane was new. We all piled out. As I walked down the stairs, I noticed a Cessna 207 taxi up and shut down. The plane slammed down on the tail. I laughed, "What the hell?" That damn airplane must have been packed full. *What kind of pilot was that,* I thought. I was glad he wasn't flying the DC-3.

We unloaded the cargo from the plane onto a big truck and took the gear to the motel. The motel was really nice. It had a large open outdoor area where we would have our meals. A small bar stood alongside. Fans dotted the ceilings. Wicker seats and chairs were everywhere. The rooms had beds made of bamboo and wicker. We got our equipment organized and packed into 3'x6' cardboard boxes ready for the cargo drops onto the top of Autana.

During the day the team went out to the airport for practice jumps. I was assigned to tandem jump with Gordon, the sound man for the BBC, and over the next three days we made several practice jumps. Mitch was jumping with Hugh, the BBC cameraman, and Bill was assigned to take the Venezuelan special forces Major.

My first jump with Gordon was his first jump ever. He had never even seen any skydivers except on television. On the first jump, Gordon and I did about a 15-second delay before I opened our parachute. He and I then did the steering together. Our tandem canopies had been custom-made just for this expedition. We came in and landed perfectly. I packed our parachute and we made another jump. This time the wind was light and variable. We came in and landed pretty hard. It knocked the wind out of us, but after I unhooked Gordon we both walked it off with no lingering injuries.

That night more cargo packing. I was starting to get worn down. Mitch said, "C'mon up to the room for a minute. I want to share something."

"OK," I said, still thinking about gear.

We got into the room and shut the door tight. Mitch brought out a little mirror and razor blade. I knew what he had in mind. We finished and went downstairs and continued packing till 4 a.m. The same the next night. Then came a day of rest and some kickback time. The film crew left early the next morning to take advantage of the good light to do some prep work for filming the DC-3 dropping the jumpers onto the top of Autana. This required two planes to fly in formation—the DC-3 and another plane carrying the film crew. I slept late.

About 10 a.m., a knock at my door.

"Come in." It was Adrian.

"How did it go?" I said.

"Terrible."

"Why?"

"These bush pilots don't know how to fly formation."

That made sense to me. "All they do is take off and fly into little runways cut into the jungle."

Adrian hung his head in his hands and said, "What are we gonna do?"

"Let me fly. I'll get you the shots you need."

"Can you fly formation?"

"Hell, yes, I can. I used to chase everybody in my Cessna 120, even 'Mr. Douglas,' the famous DC-3 used for jumping based out of DeLand. Gary Dupuis bought the plane in the early 1970s, and I spent a lot of hours practicing formation flying. When the DC-3 with a jump load would be taxiing out, I would already be in the air in my Cessna waiting for it. I would always be 500 feet higher than the DC-3 and close. My airspeed would build to 130 mph. As the DC-3 would climb, I would dive. My timing had to be right on. I would swoop in for a few seconds and would be a few yards from the big twin. My little 85 HP single engine was no match for the 600 HP engines on each side of the DC-3. But if you traded altitude for airspeed and got the right combination, formation flying was possible, and I could be there. But only for a moment. As I got into flying jumpers in the bigger Cessna 182s, 180s, and 185s, we would do a lot of formation flying. That way drop zones with smaller planes were able to take up a lot of jumpers to jump at the same time and make bigger circles of people called stars."

Adrian lowered his hands, raised his head, and looked at me.

I said, "Have that bush pilot fly from the left seat and I'll sit in the passenger seat and when it's time for the formation stuff, I'll fly."

Adrian knew what I was telling him would work.

Hell, I taught him how to skydive, and he knew I was no bullshit.

"I'll set it up for the morning," Adrian said. "I'll knock on your door at 6 a.m."

"OK, matey. I'll be ready."

I saw Mitch and he told me he was going to drop the cargo on top of Autana later that day. In the afternoon, Mitch came in and said, "OK, I put all five tons dead in the middle of the mountain." I slapped him five and said, "Of course, dude. I wouldn't have thought anything but."

Everything was in place except the aerial shots and the jump. We were all in the bar that night. I had my share of the local brew called Polar beer and retired at a reasonable hour. When I laid down for bed, I ran the flying part of my job over and over. *Piece of cake in a 206*, I thought as I faded to sleep, *it's got a lot more balls than my little 120.*

I was up at 4 a.m., took a shower and started to run through my head the way I wanted the DC-3 to make its run in to get the shots that Adrian and I discussed the night before in the bar. I had a good idea of how it needed to be flown. I just had to decide what position the two planes should be in to get that shot of the DC-3 with Autana in the background that Adrian wanted.

Hugh, Adrian, and I drove to the airport and met with the two DC-3 pilots. I gave the briefing. I talked about the radio frequency to be used, the speeds to be flown, and I also told the pilots, "Do not look at me. Focus on where you are going and your job, and I will fly the film crew where they need to be for the shots they want."

We met the Cessna 206 pilot, and I watched as he did the pre-flight inspection. Hugh and Adrian got their equipment in the plane and secured it, and then we were ready to take off. The DC-3 taxied down the runway. We followed in the 206. After we were off the ground, I told the 206 pilot, "My airplane." And that meant I was the pilot at that point in time. As the two planes headed to the mountain, I thought of those days in my Cessna 120. *This was going to be fun.*

As the DC-3 pulled into position, I pulled off to the left side and told the pilot to speed up. As the 3 started to increase its speed, the 206 started to drift into the prop wash from the 3. I knew from previous experience not to be in that position because control of the airplane then becomes difficult. As we started to drift into the 3's dirty air, I eased the 206 back in order to keep our plane in control.

When we got close to Autana, I turned around to look at Hugh. Adrian was helping him put on a special harness. To get the shots he wanted, Hugh had to get his huge camera completely out the door. I had removed the two clam shell cargo doors before we took off to give them maximum visibility for filming. The camera was strapped to him, and he was strapped to the seat with the special harness. I thought, *Good grief, too much shit for me.*

I asked Adrian, "Hey, you guys all set?"

Adrian replied, "Just about."

I said okay and told the DC-3 pilots to get ready for the first pass. One third of the way down from the top of the mountain was the big cave I mentioned earlier. The shot was for the DC-3 to roll by the mountain, pass by the cave, and then keep going until there was nothing but sky.

I looked back to Hugh and Adrian and shouted, "You ready?" and got the thumbs up.

I got on the radio and told the DC-3 pilot to start the first run. As the 3 started its run in, I told the pilot to slow down because he was pulling too far away from me. No response came back. "Slow down!", I repeated. I could see I was catching up. I had a ways to go, and I was afraid he was going to beat me to the shot. "Slow down!", I called again on the radio. I could see now that I was approaching him too quickly, and I was going to pass him. I reached over and dropped 10 degrees of flaps. The airplane wanted to climb but I didn't let her. I pushed the yoke in to keep her level with the 3. We were lined up. I started to ease in closer, closer, closer. My right wing was in behind the 3's left wing, three feet lower to stay in clean air. The 206 pilot reached for the yoke. I slapped his hand and yelled, "Don't touch that yoke!"

I held the 206 steady. The DC-3 was doing her job—flying slowly past the cave. My mind was on the shot. *Keep her close,* I said to myself as I flew alongside the 3. My right wing was five yards from the 3's door—no further. As we cleared the side of the mountain, I eased back on the yoke. I turn back to Hugh and shouted, "Did you get the shot?" Hugh screamed back, "Jesus Christ, you don't have to get that damn close!" I chuckled to myself, and I said "Okay. But don't think for one minute that I can't fly this goddamn airplane. Let's do it again."

"Everything was perfect," Adrian said, "except don't get that close!" Point taken. I called to the DC-3 to do another pass just like the first one and to hold her at 90 mph. "Roger that," the captain replied. I looked over to the 206 pilot. He looked at me, and I gave him a big wink and said, "We're gonna do that one again."

All in all, it was a good session. We got all the shots Adrian wanted including three or four low passes across the top. I kept the airplane good and slow on those passes as I wanted to see what was on top of the mountain. It was covered with yellow flowers that stuck up like a funnel—tight on the bottom with the top spread out. And there was the hill I saw in the pictures. It was covered with rocks, big giant rocks. Looked like someone sprinkled them out of a giant salt shaker and built up a hill. As we turned and headed back I told the 206 pilot, "It's all yours." I was drained from the concentration of the session.

I turned back to Adrian and Hugh. "Damn good job, Rock. Spot on," Adrian said, both of them giving me a big thumbs up. I smiled and returned the hand gesture. I eased back in the seat, relaxed, and enjoyed the scenery. My mind drifted to thoughts of my father. He never said much about my skydiving career— nothing about winning three first place medals at the Nationals or two first place medals at the World Meet. But I'm sure if he had been riding in the back of the 206 with Hugh and Adrian, I might have gotten a *Good job, Rocco*, out of him.

I met the rest of the team back at the motel. Adrian and Hugh went to their room to look at the film they just shot. I went down and got a late breakfast. I felt good. I liked getting the chance to fly. I could see that the skills I had developed during my flying career had paid off. We needed those shots, but not one pilot at that airport—at least none that Adrian knew—could deliver the goods. The time and effort I had put into my flying career had paid off in a big way.

I went for a walk that evening to have a little time for myself. Puerto Ayacucho was a small town. Most of the people ran small shops selling vegetables, fruits, fish, and meat. I remember seeing big fish hanging by their tails, flies buzzing and landing on the dried scales. I don't like fish, and yuck, this was another reason not to. The streets were made of red bricks formed from the red clay that the town was built on. As you walked down the street, you could feel how the ground was swollen in the heat. When the rain came, it would flow under the bricks and make voids. Then the bricks would then be squeezed down again from the weight of the cars, busses, and trucks that drove over them.

I felt lucky to be here and take in the ways of the local people. As I walked I came upon a small church. An iron fence surrounded it, and the stained glass told me for sure what it was. As I got close, I could see that the door was open. *Strange,* I thought, *but then again this wasn't home.* I opened the gate and walked up the step. Why? I guess I wanted to ask for help. I sat on the step a while, thinking. Thinking about the jump I was going to make. Thinking about the rest of my team. Wondering. Time went by—how much I couldn't tell you. I was thinking of what to ask the Lord. Not so much for me, but for the rest of my team.

I stood and walked into the church. In front of me was Jesus on the cross. Carved out of wood. The pews were empty. The place was all mine. This was my time. I walked down the aisle to the pulpit. I got down on my knees. I didn't hang my head but kept it raised looking at Jesus. Then I opened my mouth, and the words started to roll out. I asked God to give my team strength and courage and freedom from the fear that had come over them. I asked Him to keep them safe. And when I was finished, I thanked Him. I thanked Him for not taking me when I was horribly burned in a hot air balloon accident a few years earlier. Nothing else to say, I guess. I stood up, turned around, and walked out of the church. I went down the steps and back through the iron gate. Maybe it would help. Couldn't hurt.

That night I held a briefing and told the team what I saw on my flight over the top of Autana. I told them to stay away from the hill at the north end. The center looked like the place to be. I told them about our exit order—who was first, second, third, and so on. Mike, an expert British climber and skydiver, and Adrian were out first. At 500 feet they were to each drop an M-18 smoke grenade. This would show me, the spotter, what the wind was doing. Adrian had a camera and once he landed could start taking pictures. Mike would then scout for a good landing area for the rest of the team, mark it, and set up a wind sock. Next out would be Mitch and Hugh, then Gordon and me. The others would follow. Once we all landed, we'd form up and go from there.

We went our separate ways, most to their rooms. Mitch and I went to the bar. After we finished at the bar, I headed up to my room. On the way and I saw Hugh and Gordon doing some last minute packing.

I stuck my head in the room and said, "Gordon, can I come in?"

"Why sure, Rock" I walked in and sat down on the edge of the bed. I asked Hugh if he got any good footage from the flight we did earlier that day. He told me it was excellent.

"Good," I said.

Then I looked at Gordon. I said, "You know tomorrow is the big day. Are you ready?"

He answered, "As ready as I can be."

With a serious look, I said, "Look Gordon, we can land one

of two ways. We can come down and stand up like I've shown you, or we can bust our ass like that last practice jump we did. Now when I tell you to flare, you pull those damn toggles down to your ankles. You hear me?"

"Right'o, matey. I surely will!"

I stood, patted him on the back, and went to my room. The next morning I was up early. I took a good long shower knowing it was going to be two weeks before I would get another. I went over to double check all my emergency equipment in case I missed anything. I knew that I hadn't, but I owed it to Gordon just for his satisfaction. I didn't want to lie to him if he asked me if I checked it.

I locked my room and went downstairs for a good breakfast. This also would be the last for two weeks. Most everybody was at the table, all of them buzzing with anticipation. Personally, I thrive on this type of pressure, and I seem to perform better when I'm faced with it. After breakfast we all got our rigs loaded on the truck and went to the airport.

The sun was just coming up as we drove up to the DC-3. We checked our equipment, loaded the 3, and were soon in the air. There was a layer of clouds at 6,000 feet—it was solid enough to block the shine of the sun and leave a dreary gray. *Too low to jump, too thick to see through*, I said to myself. The tension was thick. Nobody said anything. Usually they'd all be talking back and forth, laughing and carrying on—but not this time. I even caught the Major—who usually acted macho and pretty cocky—having what seemed almost like an anxiety attack. His head was hanging low like a dog that had just been beaten. I could see his chest rise and lower as he sighed. I figured it was time to knock his ass back to reality.

"Major," I said, "you are chicken."

He puffed up like a toad and said, "No, no. Me no chicken, you chicken," pointing his finger at me. On the Major's side was a 9mm Beretta pistol. On the other, a big ass knife I would have liked to have. My comment broke the ice. The team started to laugh, all but Bill. I got over close to him and said, "Hey, man. You'd better stand his ass up when you land. Might just shoot your ass if you crack him." Bill didn't see the humor one bit as he sank back into his own thoughts.

I left the team to go back to the open door on the DC-3. I put my goggles on and stuck my head out the door. What a view—solid green below and the massive limestone formation shooting upward toward the sky. The pilot was heading straight towards Autana. The cloud layer disappeared about 10 miles to the north of the mountain. There it stood—the challenge of my life. It didn't intimidate me as much then as it did when I first saw it. Now I'd seen every inch of the towering rock. Even the top.

Adrian had provided me with a lot of information about Autana. He said Autana and other tepuis in South America were the remains of a large limestone plateau that had eroded over millions of years. Isolated limestone rock formations were all that was left of the plateau after the erosion occurred. The tepuis tended to form as isolated entities rather than in connected ranges, making them host to hundreds of unique native plant and animal species. In 1985 there had been more men on the moon than had ever been on top of Autana. The only other expedition before us was in 1970 when a team of explorers landed on the top by helicopter. Climbers then rappelled to the big cave below and mapped the tunnels inside. On top of Autana was a variety of plant and animal life like no other in the world. High above the jungle floor, protected from all of mankind's elements, its beauty and mystery had lasted. Our job was to explore these ancient mysteries and document them.

It was time, time to go into action. The first pass of the DC-3 over the top was to throw wind drifts. A wind drift is a 12 inch wide, 22 feet long bright yellow streamer. A weight is fastened to the end. It simulates a parachutist weighing 170 pounds under a 28-foot round canopy. I had three of them. Adrian and Mike stood in back of me. I called to the pilot for a correction. The DC-3 responded. I looked out. *The wingtip, is it level?* I asked myself. It was. Again my eyes went down to the jungle. I was watching the plane's flight path, and the mountain was directly in front of us. Good.

As we got closer to the top of the mountain, I could see the blue of the canopies where Mitch had dropped our cargo. The green on top of Autana blended in with the green of the jungle below. The canopies provided a good reference point for me to spot and determine when and where we would jump. The top, at 4,300 feet high, was not that big—300 meters by 500 meters. That was it.

As the plane crossed the top of the mountain, I threw the wind drifts. The bright yellow showed almost fluorescent as they fell. The pilot brought the DC-3 around in a low circle and started his climb to our exit altitude—9,000 feet above the top of the mountain. As the plane started to climb, I kept my eyes on the three wind drifts. I was waiting to see where they landed to determine the direction and speed of the wind. It was important to have a little wind because it helped you when you landed. The new square canopies we were using had a forward speed of 25 mph. You would flare the canopy right before landing, and that would start to slow your forward speed. If the wind was blowing towards you at 10 mph, your canopy would then slow from 25 mph to 15 mph, and landing would be easier. Ideally you wanted your canopy to be completely stopped when you were one foot above the ground.

As the DC-3 started to climb, I watched the wind drifts fall and land. I couldn't believe what I saw. All three of the wind drifts landed on top of the mountain. *Damn the luck*, I said to myself. I looked at Adrian and said, "Every single one landed on the top!" Then I yelled to the pilot, "Bring me on jump run!" I never got out of position from the door. Flat on my belly, I looked up and told Mike and Adrian to get ready to jump. Why hell, this would be easy—there was no wind on the top surface of the mountain. The pilot reached 9,000 feet and brought the DC-3 around for our first jump run. I called, "Cut!" The pilot then pulled back on the power to slow the plane and give us a good clean exit. *Whoosh*—the first two jumpers, Adrian and Mike, were out.

I yelled to the pilot, "Bring it around!" I stood up and saw

Mitch and Hugh hooked together. Mitch was smiling at me, and I smiled back.

I went back to the open door. Adrian's and Mike's parachutes were open. I watched as they dropped the M-18s. Good grief—the red smoke looked like two pieces of red angora string as they fell straight to the ground below them. And then I saw what I had hoped for—the two canopies came to rest atop Autana, right where we had discussed in the briefing.

I looked at Mitch and said, "The airplane is all yours. I'll see you on top." He said nothing but gave me that smile of his. I walked to the front of the plane to put on my rig. Gordon was waiting as I approached him to hook up. One last time I told him, "When I say flare, pull those toggles down to your ankles." I hooked him to me and checked the connections twice. I told him to move towards the door. I looked back at my team and told them that the spot was straight up over the top of the mountain. They knew. This pilot was good, no corrections needed. I looked out the door and thought, *Damn, what a nice airplane.* I jumped. I looked straight down at the top of the mountain. I had been waiting, prepping for this few seconds of sheer rush for three months. I could hear the wind start to rush by my ears. I felt good, real good. 20 seconds went by, and then I opened my canopy. Reaching up, I grabbed my steering toggles. I wanted control as soon as I could. I peeled my goggles off.

I yelled down to Gordon who hung a foot and a half lower. "Take your goggles off!"

He cocked his head sideways and yelled, "I never put 'em on. I forgot!"

I laughed out loud. Then it was all business. It seemed like whatever direction I faced, I was always flying off to the side of the mountain. I looked down. Mitch was just landing. I saw him slide on landing, but both he and Hugh got up. I decided to just stay over the side of the mountain until the final approach. At 500 feet I started to set up for my final approach. Our homemade windsock was doing its job. I could see I was set up to land facing into the wind. Exactly what I wanted. I said to

Gordon, "Get ready. Closer, closer, closer, okay, FLARE!"

We pulled together at the perfect moment. Gordon was doing his job. I let go of my toggles and reached back to the bare lines and grabbed again. I pulled again with all my power, and man, did it pay off. Plunk. I stood up perfectly. Gordon went to his knees for no reason except to collapse from the rush. It was perfect! I slapped Gordon on the head and unhooked him. I looked up to see Bill's open canopy. I looked back at Gordon. His smile was priceless. He started picking me up and hugging me, telling me how good I was.

"It wasn't me, it was you. You did perfect. You made my job easy!"

I looked back up. The DC-3 was coming over again, and the rest of the team was getting out. Bill was on final approach. Damn, he was moving fast and then landed fast. He and the Major slid for 50 feet. They stood up. Good. They're okay. The next time I looked up, I could see bodies in freefall. I looked for Mitch. He and Hugh were walking towards me. Adrian and Mike were standing by the windsock.

Don came next. At a high rate of speed, he flared too high and crashed to the ground. *Damn*, I thought, *that hurt.*

Next, Phil came in too close to the hill. Crash. He hit the ground, rolling as he landed. *Damn, that hurt.*

Bobby, a field surgeon in the British military and the team medic, was next. His flare was late and he slid on his butt but jumped up. *Good.*

Jean was last. She turned to make her final approach way too high. "Damn it. Damn it." I said out loud. She's going off the edge. And she almost did. I saw her left arm go down to make one last effort to stay on top. *Crash.* She hit the rocks.

"Fuck! Fuck!" I said. I looked to Mitch.

He said, "That hurt." And yes, I knew the same.

Mitch and I were putting our gear away when Mike came running over to us. Jean had broken her leg.

I said, "What?"

"She's broken her leg badly."

"How bad?"

"Compound through the skin."

"Fuck."

Bobby started to run to her. As he ran he yelled that his medical kit was in one of the cargo boxes. We found the box and got it to Bobby. Jean lay in pain. Her right shin was broken in half, the bone sticking through.

"Damn it. Damn it," I said to myself. Don and Phil crawling after their hard landing, Jean badly hurt. The adventure had now turned into a nightmare. As I had feared, a weak link in the chain had broken. The DC-3 was circling above, and I thought that they might see our dilemma. Adrian was on our handheld radio broadcasting the bad news. The Major was digging into the cargo boxes looking for our portable shortwave radio. Nothing we could do now. It was all up to Bobby to help Jean. We all pitched in and moved the cargo to base camp. Finally, an airliner passing overhead heard the transmission from Adrian's radio. The airliner passed on the information. Jean's leg was bad—the worst I've seen in my years of skydiving. The damn thing looked like she had been shot. I admired her strength as I never once saw a tear.

Six hours went by and still no help. Jean had lost a lot of blood, and Bobby shot her full of morphine. Her eyes sagged a little, and her words were slurred. Mitch and I got most of the tents set up. I crawled inside mine and got my personal stuff unpacked—sleeping bag, small gas stove, first aid kit, a few mountaineer packs of food, and some personal items. I crawled out. Mitch's tent was next to me. I saw his head come out. He looked at me and said, "Hey man. Check this out."

I glanced in his tent and, much to my surprise, two big fat lines of cocaine were stretched out on a signal mirror. He said a Venezuelan girl who had done a tandem jump with Mitch gave him the coke as a tip after her jump. Cocaine wasn't my drug of choice, but I liked the way it gave me a little energy boost. I crawled in the tent, picked up a piece of plastic straw, and inhaled the yellow powder. This was high grade stuff and some of the best coke I had ever done.

When I climbed out of Mitch's tent, I just stood and stared. What an incredible panoramic view surrounded me. This was the top of the world. Everywhere I looked, nothing but jungle. To the west I could even see the Orinoco River as it snaked its way through the dark green forest.

I started to hear an old familiar sound. I knew immediately what it was—a Bell UH-1H Huey military helicopter, the same helicopter I had jumped from during the 1975 World Skydiving Championships. I wasn't the only one—Adrian and Mitch knew exactly what it was, too. We couldn't see it yet as it was coming in from the north, and the 300-foot hill blocked the view. We knew it was coming to pick up Jean. Adrian said that he would direct him in.

"We'll get Jean," I told him.

We put together a homemade stretcher and carried it to Jean. She had lain there six hours not knowing her fate. My hat came off to her now as she never bitched a bit. Not one word. *What a tough girl*, I said to myself. My hat also was off to Bobby who had never left her side, not only taking care of her injury, but caring for her—the person—as only a professional would.

The Huey came over the top of the mountain so gracefully, Adrian waited with his hands up and directed the pilot with sign language only an aviator would understand. He popped an M-18 smoke grenade to mark the landing zone for the thumping Huey. He laid the helicopter down, and as I saw it there, rotors turning, I thought the damn thing looked almost like a giant bug that belonged here in the lost world.

Mitch, Hugh, Gordon, and I were waiting. The homemade stretcher laid alongside Jean. Bobby instructed us how to put her on the stretcher as he supported her mangled leg. She made no sound. Once she was positioned on the stretcher, we picked her up off the rocky ground where she had lain for six hours. Matching one another's steps in a smooth, coordinated walk, we carried her to the Huey. The sliding door was open and waiting to take her Puerto Ayacucho for medical care..

After Jean was in the helicopter, we said our good-byes, turned, and walked away—all except one person. One of our team members had decided he wanted to get the hell off Autana and back to civilization as soon as he could—and obviously with no concern about the impact his abrupt departure might have on the other team members or the success of the expedition. He started running as fast as he could back to the churning chopper.

"What the hell?" I said aloud.

We all stood and watched him throw his carry bag and then himself into the helicopter. My God. I couldn't believe my eyes. All of us just stood there and watched the selfishness and cowardice of this so-called man. I was ashamed—ashamed that I had chosen this person to be part of this team. As he disappeared into the chopper, the sliding door slammed closed. I still couldn't believe what I was seeing. The Huey started to churn up for takeoff, the rotor blade picking up speed. *My God, the perfect example of desertion*, I thought, *and good riddance.* All of a sudden the high pitch of the helicopter blades started to slow down. The door slid back open. The carry bag came flying out onto the ground.

"What the ..." I said. Then he came flying out—and let me tell you, he had help when he left the chopper. Head first and on his stomach. The door slammed closed and the chopper was off. Humiliated, he scrambled to his feet. Picking up his bag, he went back to our base camp.

That night after we got our equipment sorted, everybody cooked themselves some food, and we sat around and bullshitted about the jump. Don and Phil had no broken bones, but they were still in a lot of pain. Phil was the worst. He had bruised his feet and twisted his ankle but nothing more. That was good news to all of us.

When dark set in, it was really beautiful. No lights from town to spoil the true quality of the dark of night. The stars were so close and so big. The wind was subtle and steady. It was all so strange. You would be looking out over the edge and a cloud would come by and swallow you up. I was pretty tired that first night. I went back to my tent after we ate to spend my first night on the top of Autana.

When I awoke I fired up my little mountaineer stove to boil some water for coffee. I really liked that little stove. It was about the size of a Big Mac container and ran on gasoline. I was impressed with all the camping gear that had been brought for our expedition. My tent was perfect—lightweight, very portable, and sufficient for the purpose. The small emergency radios did their job, thank God. I wondered how Jean was doing. We had dropped a lot of water onto the mountain—100 gallons—because we thought there wasn't any there—at least none to drink or to cook with. We had been briefed about using it sparingly.

Waiting for my water to boil, I dug through my emergency kit to see what it contained. I noticed a packet of pills. I picked it up and behold—morphine sulfate—my old pain relief friend I had learned to love while recovering from the severe burns of my hot air balloon accident. "For extreme pain," the package said. I was done working for a while. Nothing for me to do but kick back. I opened the pack and rolled a couple into my hand. I mixed the water and instant coffee into the cup I had brought in my kit. I rolled the pills in my hand again and thought, *why not*? Hell, it's a good day for this. I put the pills in my mouth and washed them down with a gulp of coffee. I rolled over in my sleeping bag and ran yesterday's jump over and over in my mind.

My thoughts went to my childhood. I thought of the days as a kid camping out with my friend Tommy in his backyard. I could still smell the musty wet scent of the canvas, packed full of canned goods from his mom's cupboard, our comic books in a pile by our candle. BB guns laid by our blankets. Each of us had our own little pile of stuff that we thought we might need to get by during that scary night. We were ready for anything.

My thoughts were broken by my old friend morphine taking hold. She was knocking on my door telling me that things were good. I lay back again and closed my sagging eyes. My thoughts went back to the burn ward at the hospital after my hot air balloon accident and to my little friend there, Jimmy. I could hear his teeth scraping together as that Jamaican nurse tore his bandages off. Then my thoughts shot to Jean. My God— was her leg ever in bad shape. I felt her pain. I took a deep breath and let it back out.

*Death is a hard thing to deal with. It comes in many ways. It's probably one of life's hardest challenges. But the utter truth is that it will happen to us all. All who live and breathe. No living being can escape it. We, the living, can comfort one another as time takes its toll. As I write this book, my Uncle Harold has just died. I mention him because, like no headstone ever could, I hope this book will somehow keep his memory alive. My lesson is to live life to its fullest. Take that time to smell the roses. In the end, we are what we are.*

I looked out of my tent. Scarlet macaws were squawking, and every once in a while I would catch a glimpse of their beautiful colors. They would soar on the thermals that came up the edges of the mountain. I crawled out of my tent and walked over to the rest of my team. Hell, I was feeling great. My old friend was back and damn, this time it was on different terms.

"Good morning," I said.

"Good morning," they replied.

"What's for breakfast?"

"Take your pick," they said and pointed to the piles of mountaineer packets that lay in one of the cargo boxes we had packed a few nights before. I dug down in the box filled with plastic packs of food. Each one had three good meals in it.

Adrian and Hugh, along with Gordon, were out filming all the new flowers, toads, and every other kind of strange and different plant and animal they could find on top of Autana. Mitch, the Major, and I were sitting in the hot sun at our camp cooking our asses off. The day was hot, and we were trying to figure out some way to protect ourselves from the burning Venezuelan sun. We tried to use the cargo canopies to provide some shade from the bright sun. The sun was hot enough to warm up the canned food that came in the packets of food.

Don and Mike went out to look for the spot where the expedition in 1970 had chosen to climb down to the big cave.

We knew the climbers had used a climbing ladder to make their descent—a ladder made with ropes and wood. Not a very big ladder—the steps maybe eight inches across and twelve inches between each step. Don and Mike returned after about four hours of exploring. They were carrying some long steel bars.

"What the hell is that?" I said. Don said that it was rebar left from the first expedition. We then used them to make a shelter from the sun, and it was perfect. The Major was in charge and knew what he was doing. After he bent one piece of rebar in a big curve, he bent another the same way. He crossed the two and tied them together in the middle. We stuck the ends into the soft ground and then covered it with the cargo canopies. It worked perfect. We put the food, water, and the camera equipment under the canopies in the shade. I laid in one of the big cargo containers and kicked back. It was like a big hammock, and it was comfortable. It was great to have some shade. The following days went by slowly. Most of my time was spent lying in the box of food.

A couple of more days went by and still no clue to where the previous expedition climbed down over the edge of the mountain. Mitch and I told Mike and Don that we would help them look. We looked over the aerial photos with Adrian, and he showed us where he thought the location might be. We marked it on the photo and went out to look.

What a sight walking along the edge. The scarlet macaws continued to squawk and soar on the uplifting air that rushed up the sides of the cliffs. Yellow cone-shaped flowers were everywhere. Adrian told us that they were called bromeliads, and that they were carnivores. The top of Autana was the only place in the world that this species of bromeliad grew.

Mitch and I made our way down a small ravine where some small trees grew. The whole side was full of big rocks. Walking was tricky and careful foot placement a must. I heard Mitch say, "Rocky, come here and check this out." I stumbled down the ravine closer to the edge to where Mitch was standing. He pointed down, and there, partially covered with rocks, was the climbing ladder. The ladder was broken in places, and some of the wooden steps were rotten. We eased closer to the edge. The incline of the hill was pretty steep. Not vertical but damn close. We took turns throwing baseball size rocks off of the steep edge. Not a good launch site for our BASE jump but a good place to start a descent by rope to the cave. Mitch and I went back to camp and told Mike and Don. They followed us back to the place where we had located the ladder. We helped them set the first set of ropes for rappelling and then went back to camp to finish out the day.

I had a good supper—hamburger in tomato sauce, mac 'n cheese, and cinnamon apples. I sat and listened to the rest of the team talk about climbing the next day. All the team had climbing experience. Mike and Don would make the climb down the next day to set the other two 500-foot ropes needed for the two lower sections of the climb. No, I hadn't hired on to do any kind of climbing. That shit did scare me. Not the physical part because I was in pretty good shape. It was the ropes being cut by falling rocks that freaked me out. That night I was out quick, tired from all of the hard walking. The next morning I was up early and out of my tent. Adrian told me he wanted to use me in some of the film. I didn't really want to do it, but all in all it was fun.

When I was done, I went back to camp to get some food and came upon the Major. He motioned me to come with him. Now I really didn't know much about him except that his main purpose for being with us was to make sure that we weren't doing anything other than what Adrian had told the Venezuelan government. He kept telling me, with some urgency, "Come. Come. Come to me."

"Damn dude, I'm coming," I said. "Hold on." When I got to where he was standing, I saw he had a small shovel. He was saying something to me in broken English, and I was trying to make out what he was saying. Major was shoveling two trenches that ran down an incline and joined together in a V-shape at the bottom. There he had dug a small hole. I helped him dig the trenches. I still wasn't sure what he was doing. Then he started to pull leaves from the bromeliads. When the leaves were pulled out, they rolled up into small tubes. Perfect small tubes. He connected the tubes, putting one into the other. He laid one end of the connected tubes into the small hole that was now full of water that ran down the trenches from the marshy ground above. Before you knew it, there was water coming out of the other end of the connected tubes, similar to a long pipe or a hose. "Damn," I said, "that's hot shit, Major," and slapped him five. Then I went down the incline to take a shower from the water now running out the end of the connected bromeliad leaves—a shower I never dreamed I'd be taking atop Autana.

The talk around the table that night was mostly about the climb the next day. Adrian looked at me and asked, "What do you think about hauling some stuff down to the cave?"

"Hell no," I replied.

He got a big smile on his face and came back, "Now it's my turn."

I had no idea what he meant and said so in no uncertain terms. "What do you mean, 'it's my turn'?"

"I'll never forget when you taught me to jump. Now I'm gonna teach you how to climb."

*Oh shit*, I thought to myself. *There was no way out of this one.* I said, "Okay."

After supper Mitch said he had something for me in his tent. I went in and sniffed the shit up. Back outside, I started pouring out my concerns. "Damn, Mitch. I ain't no climber."

He laughed. "That's okay, Rock. It's not that hard. When you rappel down, just make sure that you lean back and keep your legs apart and on the wall. Keep the rope tight in the figure of eight. Control your descent with your left hand and wear a glove."

"Shit," I said, not even wanting to think about it. "Whatcha think of the Major's shower?"

Mitch said, "I'm gonna take one right now."

"Cool," I said and went for a walk to clear my head. This was one strange place. The rocks showed signs of erosion as

I had never seen. One rock looked like a stack of different size pancakes that were about 12 inches in diameter at the bottom and got smaller towards the top. The stack rose up about 15 inches from the ground.

I went back to the edge of the top, and this time I took binoculars. Along the Orinoco River below I spotted smoke rising, and about 20 miles away was another trail of smoke. I pulled the glasses to my eyes and focused in on a small round hut that was made of mud with a thatch roof. Adrian told me there were some tribes of Indians in the Amazon region that still practiced cannibalism.

I went back to my tent and laid down, still thinking about the climb I was about to do. The next morning I was up early again and went down to the shower the Major and I built. I got back to camp just as Adrian was getting ready to brief the climbers—Mike, the Major, and I. I had a big ass backpack full of food and a twelve-volt car battery. The Major was first, then me, and last was Mike. We used tugs on the ropes to let the other climber above know we were down and under cover, protected from any falling rocks. As we would descend, rocks the size of peas to the size of footballs would come traveling down, and if one were to hit you, it would probably kill you—or at least knock you off the side of the wall. So it was important to hide when a climber above would start their descent. I climbed down the first section of the cliff after the Major. Then he and I climbed under a ledge and gave the 500 foot rope a big tug to let Mike know to start his descent. It wasn't long before it started to rain rocks—rocks of all sizes—and that's when I started to wonder about the possibility of the rocks cutting the rope.

While we were waiting for Mike, I looked over at the Major who had his hands full. He had his 35mm camera in his hand with about two feet of exposed film he was trying to feed back into the camera. He was having one hell of a time and was saying, "oh shit, oh shit, no good, no good." I watched him for a little bit, and then I couldn't hold back. I started laughing my ass off. This was funny and let me tell you, he really thought he would be able get the film back in the camera. He got really pissed and looked at me like he had never done—not even when I called him a chicken in the plane.

Then he said to me, "I kill you. I kill you." I just kept on laughing, because to me his frustration made the situation even more comical. By that time Mike had reached us.

"Get your ass down this rock Major," Mike said, "we don't have all day." The Major grunted something in Spanish, tucked the tangled mess into his backpack, and scooted down the next section of the wall. Before long a big tug came up the rope. I put the rope through the figure of eight device and snapped the carabineer in place. The second and third legs down the mountain were a lot easier.

We followed Mike to the entrance of the cave,. *My God!* My first sight inside the cave was something that I can't describe. No words could do it justice. It made me realize how powerful nature really was. This massive cave ran clear through the mountain. I was humbled. To provide some perspective on the size of the cave, sometime after our expedition a couple of my associates went to Autana to make another documentary. They launched a motorized ultralight hang glider from the edge, and the pilot flew the hang glider directly through the cave. Erosion had carved the ceiling of the cave, and it looked like an ice cream cone—the kind that comes out of a machine with all the swirls. Very impressive.

I sat down on a big rock, shed my climbing harness, and removed the backpack I had carried 1,200 feet down the mountain with the food to keep my teammates alive and the battery to power the lights for filming this natural wonder. I took out my camera and started to take pictures. On the ground was a pile of polished rocks similar to the pea gravel target that I always tried to land in when I was skydiving. The rocks were polished pieces of the same pink rock that the mountain was made of, but perfectly round as if they were man-made. I grabbed a handful of rocks and put them in my pocket. Then I walked around a little as I was in no hurry to begin the 1,200 foot ascent back to the top. The Major was like a little boy, running in and out of the smaller tunnels that surrounded the large one. Mike started exploring the honeycomb tunnels that seemed to go in every direction.

The climb back to the top was a challenge. I used a mechanical device called a Petzl Jumar, a rope clamp that tied to the climbing harness, to ascend the mountain and get back to the top. Once back on top, I told myself that I was done with all the hard work until our jump off the side of Autana and into the rainforest. I went back to my tent and found my bag of morphine sulfate. I rolled out two and drank them down with my orange drink. I then went down to our shower and sat under the trickle of water. As I washed the day away, I felt good— good that I could do my part for the team. That night I could hear the Major and Adrian in a serious conversation, all in Spanish, with their voices raised. I didn't know what was being discussed, but it sounded pretty heated. I slept with my Bowie knife by my side.

The next couple of days were quiet. Most of the team was still down exploring and filming the caves. I relaxed on top with my old friend. It passed the time. The days ran together and before I knew it, it was almost time for our BASE jump off the edge of Autana. Phil, an experienced BASE jumper with more BASE jumps than anyone else in the world at that time, helped us choose and mark out our jump site. He had been severely banged up by his hard landing when we first arrived on top of Autana, but by this time he was getting around good. Within two days we would make the jump. The equipment would come off by helicopter. I had never done a BASE jump but was eager to get off this rock. We packed the rigs and were ready to go. Tomorrow was the day.

When I woke I heard the sound of a helicopter, and this was no Huey. It was a Bell Jet Ranger. Adrian directed him in. After the helicopter landed, I saw Adrian talking to two military guys. He came back to me and said that the Venezuelan government was kicking us off Autana before our BASE jump.

I wasn't about to complain. I was ready to go and really didn't want to jump off the edge of Autana—for no other reason than I knew someone else would probably get hurt. We organized our equipment and were flown off the mountain in the Bell helicopter. The Venezuelan government confiscated almost all our equipment when we landed back in Puerto Ayacucho. We reunited with Jean at our hotel and spent a couple days sorting our remaining equipment and saying our good-byes. I was feeling glad—glad our team had accomplished what we did.

The NOVA documentary was released in 1986. The name: *Skydive to the Rain Forest.* If you watch it, you will understand.

Safely down on Autana: skydivers
Rocky Evans, Mitch Decoteau, and Phil Smith.

Above, the door is open on the DC-3 as the skydivers and BBC crew prepare to jump onto Autana's table-top mountain. Below, scouting the mountain before the mission.

Above, left, Rocky's father in his police uniform; above right, the grandparents and farmhouse that anchored Rocky's childhood. Left, it was always sports for Rocky as a boy.

Chapter Two
## HUMBLE BEGINNINGS

Three Rivers, Michigan. I was a kid not quite out of high school. My friend Rick Johnson and I went to a movie called *The Gypsy Moths*—Burt Lancaster, Gene Hackman—about three skydivers traveling the country skydiving. When the movie was over, Rick said he'd been wanting to try skydiving for a long time. Hell yes, me, too. I worked part time as a janitor at a machine shop. One of the guys I worked with was a pilot and told me of a place close by in Portage, Michigan, where you could skydive. I looked in the yellow pages and found the phone number. I called and they said yes, they did skydiving instruction. I told Rick, and we went to check it out. A little air strip on Austin Lake. And I do mean on the lake. Hell, you could throw a rock to the water from the small shack they called the clubhouse. It was $25 for the lessons and one jump, but Rick and I were only 16, and we had to have a parent's consent. We got the release forms and said we'd be back.

On the way home we talked about the ragged little clubhouse that had three long packing tables in it, and how the people there seemed okay. Sally, Rick's mom, signed his consent form that day. However, my mom and dad were a different story. It took three days of bugging them to get them to sign it. I was still in high school, senior year; Rick was one grade behind. With our signed consent forms and $25.00 in hand, we headed back to Austin Lake. It was Saturday morning in May of

1970. I can recall like it was yesterday how it all started at that little airfield at Austin Lake.

Rick and I had our first jump training that day. It included basic body position, canopy control, equipment malfunctions, parachute landing falls (PLFs), and packing. It lasted all day. But we didn't get to jump—the automatic opener for the main parachute container was off getting fixed. The Parachute Club of America (PCA) required basic safety regulations (BSRs) to be followed, and that started on your first jump. No questions or exceptions—an automatic opener on your main container was a requirement.

So we were sent home. Rick and I were all worked up and laughed all the way home about our instructors, the equipment, the airplane, and all that was entailed in that first jump course. We were back the next day, Sunday, but still no jump. The next weekend, still no jump.

The next weekend after that, we hit pay dirt. Rick was up first, climbing into his gear. The sight of him gave me butterflies, but I'll tell you, he looked right out of the movie that had inspired us, *The Gypsy Moths*. He climbed into Bruce Dillon's Cessna 180. Bruce had some first rate aircraft—two C-180s and a D-18 Twin Beech. They took off. The 180 had a particular sound of power that I'd always remember. Grinding to altitude, Rick was first out. At 3,200 feet the engine pulled back, which let me know that it was show time for Rick. I could hear the jumpmaster scream, "Go!" and Rick was out immediately. I was wondering what was going through his mind.

I was standing on the ground by the pea gravel, Rick's landing target. For a jumper to be in the best position to land in or near the pea gravel target, the airplane will fly over the top of the gravel into the wind and release the parachutist upwind of the target. This was 1970, and we were using round canopies. They were not very maneuverable. As a matter of fact, if you were a little off the wind line, you couldn't get back on. Therefore, if you were off, you landed "out"—out being not on the airport grounds. Your ideal speed was 5-7 mph. That was a pretty narrow margin to work with. So this really meant that the most wind that you could jump in was 10 mph. Today was a perfect day for Rick's first jump—winds 5-7 mph.

The airplane was flying around for another drop. Three in the plane with one jumpmaster calling. You were trained to follow the arrow on the ground. The student parachutist gets guided in by another jumpmaster on the ground. The number of jumps until you are off student status depended on how quickly you learned. Rick was going to land at the airport, but was off target by about 200 yards—not bad for his first jump.

We walked out to find Rick. He was over by some small trees and half of his canopy was hung up in the trees. When we got closer we saw his reserve was out. It would have to be sent back for a repack. Well, that meant I couldn't jump today because that was the only automatic activation device (AAD) for the reserve they had. So now I had to wait for the next weekend.

Rick was really liking it, really excited about what he just experienced. As we drove home I picked his brain. I wanted my turn so bad I could taste it. I called the next weekend before going up to the lake, and they said the reserve was not ready. So I waited for the next weekend and that was too windy. It was almost too long. Another week and I had to be retrained.

Finally, it was my time. Rick and I rolled into the airport in the morning at nine o'clock. As I walked up to Dennis, the jumpmaster, he asked me, " Are you ready?"

I said, Yep!" He told me to go put on a jumpsuit. Hell, that was just an old pair of coveralls! Jumpsuit on, I started to put the rig on, which was a B-4 with a chest mounted reserve. The canopy was a 32-foot round with a t-cut modification. Gear on, we walked to the C-180 and climbed in. I would be second out, so I sat with my back to the pilot's seat. First out sat by the open door which was removed for jumping. Third out sat in the back.

Now this was my first time in an airplane, so I had no idea what the flight would be like. We taxied into position and then started to take off. The door was off and the noise was horrific. Dennis was on his knees, hand on the door sill. The C-180 went bouncing down the rough grassy strip. Damn, I wondered if this plane was ever going to take off. Finally, we bounced our way into the air.

People often ask me if I had butterflies on that first jump. I had enough for all three of us on that C-180. On the way to altitude I was thinking, *This flying is pretty cool.* Everything was getting smaller and smaller—the lake, the houses, the cars.

Dennis was talking to the student in the door. I didn't know what he was saying but as he pointed to the door, I leaned toward it and I got my first look at the airport. *Shit.* The damn lake was big, real big. The lake was how I could locate the airport. If it wasn't for the lake, the airport would blend into the rest of the terrain below.

I saw Dennis look at his altimeter. It was an old aircraft altimeter in some kind of homemade mount fastened to his reserve. It read 2,000 feet. He started to get the static line wound into his hand and check the equipment on the first student. I can remember looking at my old, sage green military B-4 rig and couldn't really figure out how it worked. I could see the pack opening bands went up and disappeared beneath the center flap, and I thought they went all the way across to the other side. It didn't matter then because I was all ready to go. I had paid my money and not jumping never entered my mind. Still, the old B-4 being held closed by the pack opening bands was a mystery and was on my mind all the way to climb out.

Another check of Dennis' altimeter showed 3,000 feet. The jump was at 3,200 feet. The C-180 started its approach to jump run. I looked to the front of the airplane where the first student sat. Static line running over her shoulder, her hands folded on top of her chest mounted reserve. The look on her face was not that of fear but of questions—the same as me. Then she was gone.

Dennis was spotting to make sure we got out of the airplane at the right place, upwind of the target. The sound of his jumpsuit flapping in the 80 mph wind told me that I had to hang on tight or I could be blown off the airplane before it was the right time. Dennis had a Pioneer twin-zippered jumpsuit—

the same one that Burt Lancaster and Gene Hackman wore in *The Gypsy Moths*. But Dennis had something that they didn't have. He had a patch that said "Certified Instructor", and that made me feel good.

When it was my turn to jump and I swung my feet out of the plane, they blew back behind the step. They were supposed to be in front but the damn wind was so strong, it blew them back. I pulled them onto the step. I looked over my shoulder. Dennis yelled, "Climb out!" I rolled out into position onto the strut. Left foot on the step and right leg trailing, I leaned over the strut and looked back at Dennis for the slap on the leg. He was looking down for the right spot. He looked up at me and screamed, "GO!" I let go and I could feel my balls go right up in my throat. I damn near pissed my pants.

I looked up and saw my canopy starting to open. When it opened all the way, I shouted, "YES! It's open! Cool!" I checked my pants. Dry. Great. I looked up to see the canopy and then I looked down. My feet dangled free, the ground small. I looked up for the toggles, the little pieces of wood like little dowels about two inches long. There they were. I reached up and grabbed them. I pulled right and after a few seconds, I started to turn right. I remember the horizon starting to turn. I let up, it stopped. Then I pulled to the left, left toggle down. The parachute started to the left. This time I pulled the toggle down all the way. It took all of six seconds to do a 360 degree turn. I noticed how quiet it was, a peace I'd never known. Complete silence. I looked back up to the canopy. Damn, the thing would get big, and then it would start to get small. Shit. I hope this goddamn thing doesn't decide to collapse!

Then I couldn't find the airport. Where's the airport? I don't want to land in the lake! I looked down. No airport, just trees, houses. Shit. Where is the damn airport? I looked farther out. Nothing. Where is it? I looked to the lake, there's the lake, follow the shoreline. There it is. There's the clubhouse, there's the pea gravel, there's the arrow, yes, yes. I took my instruction from the arrow—run, hold, run, hold. I had no idea how high I was. I only knew I was following the arrow. The next command, turn into the wind, feet and knees together. I was looking down. *Slam.* I hit the ground, the parachute falling on top of me. I stood up and breathed a big sigh. I did it! I did it!

Rick came running up. "Hey man, how'd you like it?"

I shouted out to him, "Cool!" I had landed about 50 feet from the pea gravel. I felt good about it. I landed closer than Rick. Yep. I collected the tangled mess, and Rick and I walked in together, me telling him about my experience. What a rush! Again I checked my pants to see if they were wet.

That day, Rick made another jump and did good. We got our logbooks signed and went home floating on air. It had scared the shit out of me but I didn't let on.

The next weekend came and we heading back to Austin Lake. Jump number two for me and number three for Rick. The progression to getting off student status was five static line jumps—three being dummy pulls with a ripcord handle. Then freefall—three clear and pulls, three five-second delays, then 10, 20, 30 second delays, then off of student status.

June 9th was high school graduation. I had five or six jumps then. I was dating a girl named Kateri. I took her out to Austin Lake one time to watch me jump and then to a movie. She didn't seem too excited about watching me jump. The movie was more exciting for her, and for sure the pizza after was her favorite. Damn, that girl could eat.

I was working as a janitor and saving money for college. Every weekend Rick and I went to Austin Lake. Sometime in July we got off of student status and were finally free to jump on our own. Summer went by fast. We started to meet new friends—guys who were older and more experienced than us— Ken Coleman, Sam Brown, Sandy Reid, and Don Carpenter. Sam and Sandy were fresh out of the Army and Marine Corps—Sam had been stationed in Germany, and Sandy, a highly decorated soldier, spent most of his military career in Viet Nam. Ken had been a military cop, also in Nam. Don was in the reserves. Everybody was really cool, and Rick and I began to see beyond our western Michigan roots.

In the fall I started attending a college in Michigan called

Ferris State. I knew right away I didn't want to be there. Two weeks after orientation, there I was in a dorm with six others. I hated it. I tried out for their football team but really didn't want to do that. That whole school year seemed to take forever. Nothing to do but go to class and back to the dorm. I met a guy named Dennis from New York. He turned me on to smoking pot. That was pretty cool. We went at night to his room because everybody there did it.

While I was at Ferris State, I read about a skydiving club being formed at the school. Norm was a skydiver with 10 jumps. He started the club, and the first meeting was one Tuesday night. We all sat in the room filling out the paperwork. Norm asked how many people at the meeting had made a parachute jump. I and two others raised our hands. Norm was on 10-second delays. He asked one of the others who raised his hand how many jumps he had. He replied, "Two static lines." He asked the other, who said, "One." Then he asked me. I said, "73." The room was silent. The skydiving club got me by till the next summer when I went back home and hooked up with Rick again.

The summer of 1971 was good. Rick and I had just under 100 jumps by then. We went back at it every weekend. Rick and I moved quickly though the certifications. We got our A & C licenses. I picked up my jumpmaster rating. So did Rick. That fall we started to dispatch and teach skydiving, but that's as far as it went. I was supposed to go back to college, but I told people I didn't go back because I didn't want to waste my mom and dad's money. But I just flat-assed didn't want to go. I wanted to skydive. I wanted to travel and see the world. So I decided not to go back with no idea what lay ahead.

Then, out of the blue, Norm from the Ferris State skydiving club got back in touch with me and wanted to know if I was interested in teaching for the school. I asked Rick if he was interested, and he said sure. Then one day at work I asked my good friend, Smitty if he wanted to jump "for free."

"Hell yes," Smitty replied. So on the way up to Ferris State, as Rick drove, I gave Smitty his first jump course in the car. I couldn't teach him PLFs but I covered most everything else. When we arrived, I learned we had a good sized class of 17 students. Rick and I divided them up, and we started. We got paid $20 a person, and by 1 pm they were ready to jump. Everyone was finished by 6 pm, and then it was Smitty's turn to make his first jump.

Rick was in the plane with Smitty. As the airplane came across the target on the ground, I saw Smitty starting to climb out, and then he had instructions to turn and hold into the wind. He didn't. He went with the wind out and over a river. I was in the jump truck in a split second trying to chase him down. Now understand, Ferris State is in the middle of the Michigan, north of Grand Rapids a good hour, just off U.S. 131. It was in the boondocks, no doubt about that. I followed Smitty visually but then lost sight of him; he was going with the wind and over the river and then disappeared behind the trees. We finally found him, and he wasn't hurt so we laughed it up. Rick and I got paid, and we went home. Smitty bought the case of beer he promised for services rendered, and we drank it all up while feeling high over what we'd done. It had been a milestone day for us—teaching at a college and somewhere other than Austin Lake.

In some ways that was the beginning of my adult life and the end of a childhood that was a lot like most the guys in my small Michigan town, except that I liked to push the envelope a little more than most. If it wasn't for that, I'd probably be someone other than who I am today. Maybe a guy in a three-piece suit. Probably retired instead of teaching skydiving like I still am.

My first memories are of my mother and me standing in Lake Michigan sometime during the summer months. I remember lots of boats, a lot of people, and my mother pouring water over my head, my body, cold, so cold, the water. Starting to shiver and shake. My body naked to the world, no guilt, no shame, and Mom covering me with the dry warm towel.

I remember my mom, dad, and sister at a cabin up North in Michigan somewhere. I remember the white bark on the trees, something that I'd never seen before. It was there at that lake that I heard the sound of an engine so powerful I knew it couldn't come from any boat, and then got my first look at a real airplane and not only an airplane but a seaplane.

The seaplane had sounded like a small tornado, which struck fear in me. I remember my father and mother lifting my sister down into the wellpit when tornadoes threatened, Mom at the bottom, arms outstretched upwards as if praising The Lord, in a panic to grab my sister as it was a life and death situation, and it was. Me next, my dad picking me up as if I was weightless and passing me down into my mother's waiting arms and the smell of wet, musty and fresh apples and potatoes and cabbage that my Dad stored in the pit through the long cold winters. Finally, I remember my dad picking up the cover and putting it on in a quick but definite way. Our family would go to the wellpit whenever Dad would call the shot.

Family means a lot to me, and love—the kind of love I saw that my father had for my mother, a love that in some ways motivated me most of my life. When I was young I'd wait for him to come home from work and make a bee line for him as fast as I could. He would be talking to my mom about his day and this and that, looking at each other with total interest, and love and respect for each other. Day after day, through thick and thin, it was a love I would search for almost my whole life and finally after 59 years, it came to me as you will read as my life story continues.

My father was a policeman. When he wasn't working and could be home for dinner, Dad would sit at his place, at the head of the table, he would take off his hat, and of course my hands would reach for it. Dad would then put his hat on me, his son, and laugh because I would swim in the thing and it would fall from side to side, a hat with authority that no one else's dad had and a uniform like no one else's dad. My dad was special and I knew it from day one. Then there was his billy club, and the wide shiny patent leather belt holding keys, handcuffs, and extra bullets for his police revolver, a Smith and Wesson Model P. that I remember as so shiny, so big, so perfect. As I grew, my dad taught me all about guns. In some ways it was the same for most boys from my area of Michigan, but to me my dad always seemed a bit above all the others and pleasing him meant the world to me.

My father was in WWII in the United States Marine Corp. A sergeant in charge of soldiers. How many? I have no idea, but yes, in charge. He fought in battles such as Tarawa, Saipan, and Iwo Jima in the Pacific Campaign. And during his two-year service he was trained how to respect his weapon, as it was his savior, his only protection for him and his men. He never said a damn word about the war, as I am sure it was a terrible thing, but his Smith was clean, no pits, no rust, no scratches. When I was young I could only hold it and that was it—no cocking the hammer, no squeezing the trigger, no opening the cylinder—only to hold and that was good for now. I knew as I got older I would get my chance and so you will see later in my life this would play a big role.

As I was growing up, whenever I was afraid or felt doubt, my dad came into my mind and the feeling of pride I would get from his words of praise. Words that came now and then like when I caught a fly ball in little league with a diving shoestring catch. The praise, the big hand of my dad as he would rub it on the top of my head and move it back and forth and say, "Good job, Rocco!" The three words that set the structure of my life. The three words that no money could buy. Three words that you couldn't steal, three words, just three simple words. So meaningful, so important to me. They didn't come easy. They were not free by any means, so much hard work, so much. But those words were a reward such as no one could imagine. No one, only me, and they gave my whole life meaning. They didn't come from his mouth often. In fact, I probably heard them no more than five times in my life, but God did I try.

I remember many things about my childhood—fighting with my sister who was three years older, my grandpa and grandma Evans who lived on a 50-acre farm with a chicken coup, outhouse, a great big red barn, and a three story farmhouse where my dad and his brothers and sisters were born and raised,. . We grew apples mostly and asparagus, along with plums, cherries, strawberries, blueberries, etc. and had livestock like chickens and milk cows. I did lots of chores on that farm. I remember my Aunt Effie who lived in my grandmother's house with her son, Kent and taught Sunday School at a Lutheran Church in Three Rivers, which is why I went to Sunday School and Bible School for what that was worth. I did, at that time believe in God. And I remember when my little brother, Mike, who is 10 years younger, was born.

I remember my cousin Mokie giving me my first BB gun at age six. It wasn't that powerful but it worked. I spent a lot of time in woods with my BB gun and always felt close to God when I was out there . If any of my friends or family had a problem, I'd pray for them when I was out in the woods. One of my friends got sick and died when I was only seven, despite all my prayers. It was hard for me to believe in God after that.

As I started to move up in school I began to realize I had a gift for sports that would last through varsity sports in high school. My dad would play baseball with me every day he could when I was young and I just ate it up. This was one of the few times my father would tell me, "Good job, Rocco," so I would go all out to catch every ball, plus Dad would pitch to me and I would practice hitting. So baseball wasn't new to me when we picked up teams at school.

Dad also had a football in my hands at an early age. I learned how to throw a spiral and had good running skills. So when it came time to play sports, I had a good idea of how to play the games. When we went out for recess I would either be a captain, or be picked first or second so I was pretty popular with my team mates. I could hit the home runs and things that would get you looked at and could share this with the rest of the kids. It was very nice and made me feel special.

I could tell a million stories, but I'll just say I had a pretty normal childhood, the kind that most guys would envy. I was introduced to guns and hunting, which is something I shared with my dad. I had the thrill of being with him when he got his first buck. He let me finish off the deer with his .38 Special and gave me a "job well done, Rocco" when the buck stopped thrashing and lay motionless.

He also taught me how to fish and to hunt for pheasant, and along the line I got my own 12 gauge shotgun. And I finally got to shoot my dad's .357 Smith and Wesson revolver as a birthday present.

I had my share of accidents growing up, which was no surprise since I was always testing the limits. I made more than a few trips to the doctor or hospital to be stitched up. Sports were always a big deal for me all through high school, and then there were girls of course. The other big thing that comes to me when I think about growing up is trains.

I was around ten or twelve years old when my friend Tommy and I used to run along the tops of box cars sitting on the tracks, jumping from car to car. One of those times as I raced along the cat walk on top of the cars I suddenly realized the next car was uncoupled and a long way off. It was too late to stop so I leaped as far as I could and seemed to be almost flying. I made it to the other side where I crash landed, scraping up my hands and knees pretty good. When I looked at the distance I'd jumped and guessed it was over 20 feet I almost started believing in God again. One of my last adventures in high school before I became so focused on skydiving was when I jumped a moving train with two of my friends in freezing November weather for what we thought would be a short trip and ended up almost freezing to death as we hung on at 60 miles per hour. Something like two hours later we were forced to jump from the train when it slowed to 30 mph.

I knew loss in my young life. My grandmother died too early and in high school three of my best friends, including my best friend Tommy, were killed in a car crash when their Oldsmobile went airborne while speeding on a hilly road and crashed into a tree.

My first girlfriend was during the fourth grade. She was named Debbie, a little Italian girl. I can remember passing love notes to her—you know the ones: I love you. Do you love me? And then a yes or no to circle and pass back. And yes was the answer every time. When I passed puberty and learned to masturbate, girls were in my head all the time.

At Tommy's funeral, I noticed this beautiful young girl with Tommy's sister, Michelle. She was so tan, her hair brown with a ribbon on the back of her head, just starting to sprout. Head hung low, she followed Michelle out of the Catholic Church. After the service I asked Shelly who the girl was. She replied that Kateris was her name. Wow, that was a cool name. Once I saw her, I had to have her. Fate helped and when I ran into her by chance I asked her out. It took a while for her dad to say yes, but eventually he did. I ended up dating her all the way through high school and my one year away at college.

Rocky and his sister Dawn meet
over his bike—or is it hers?

Three Rivers. In southwestern Michigan, not far from Lake Michigan, it was a good place to grow up.

## Chapter Three
## THE NEXT STEP

November 15, 1971. In Three Rivers, Michigan, it was opening day of deer season, which was a big deal for locals like us. But my friend Rick and I had other commitments. We had loaded up Rick's car with our jump gear and were headed to Ferris State to jumpmaster some more students. As we were about to leave, Rick's stepdad Chuck and some other guys were packing Chuck's old army ambulance with the gear to go hunting.

Rick and I were north of Grand Rapids on our way to the college when all of a sudden, off to the side of the highway, we saw a buck deer running along the right of way fence. Rick drove up in front of the trotting buck, stopped his truck, pulled out his 20 gauge, and we both ran and jumped the fence. I saw him pull out his gun and *wham!* He shot the buck dead. We loaded it in the car, and a little farther down the road we pulled off, gutted the buck, and headed on to Ferris State. We trained and jumped the students, and when we got home asked Chuck if he did any good that day hunting. Chuck said, "Hell no!" Rick and I laughed and said, "Look at this," as we rolled the six-pointer out and onto the ground.

Fall passed and then winter. Not much skydiving went on in the winter in Michigan, so the rigs went in the closet and sat there until spring. In the spring Rick and I were back in the air. Rick and I both stepped up our gear to a Para-Commander (PC), a high performance round canopy. Ron, Rick's brother, also started to skydive. It didn't take long for him to complete his training, so now there were the three of us. I had probably 150 jumps by then.

I borrowed a B-4 container from a guy at our drop zone. It had a Capewell canopy release system, a new way to allow the main canopy to be disconnected from the harness. In the event of a malfunction, you would pull the Capewell covers down and cable rings were exposed. You would then put your thumbs in the rings and pull both down at the same time to cut away your main canopy. Then you went back into freefall and pulled your chest mounted reserve parachute.

On a jump with the borrowed rig, I did a 10-second delay. When the canopy opened, the harness stitching tore. The harness would have come apart except that the ends of the webbing were doubled over which prevented it from totally coming apart. My canopy started to spin, and I knew I couldn't land it safely. I reached for the Capewell release covers. The right one was two feet higher than the left because of the torn harness, but I could reach it. Covers down, rings out, thumbs in, a hard jerk downwards, and I was free from my main canopy.

I pulled the reserve handle and *whack*, the reserve was open. Back in those days reserve parachutes were not steerable, so you basically drifted with the wind. Now under my reserve canopy, feet and knees together, I slammed down onto the grass runway and nearly bit my tongue off. Damn, did that hurt. I held on to the handle because tradition had it that if you lost your ripcord, or experienced any other skydiving "firsts", you had to buy a case of beer. Plus you couldn't get your reserve packed if you didn't have a ripcord. My first reserve ride; I had to buy a case of beer.

Rick and I belonged to the United States Parachute Association (USPA), formerly the Parachute Club of America. We had to be a member to keep our jumpmaster ratings. The membership came with a magazine. On the cover of the March issue was a skydiver under a square canopy. This was the first time I had actually seen one. I read the article, and thought I would really like to jump one.

One day at the drop zone, a jumper we knew named Bruce came out and threw this new rig down and said that he had a square canopy. We all sat there dumbfounded. "Jump it, jump it!" we said. "How many jumps have you got on the square canopy?"

"Four or five," he said. "that's all."

"Come on, jump the damn thing, Bruce," we all said. He put the rig on and climbed into the plane and was off.

Rick, Ron, and I and a few of other skydivers were all out at the pea gravel as the plane came over the top. At 4,000 feet from the ground, you could see the plane pretty well. Bruce was on the strut. He fell for maybe two seconds and then pulled his ripcord. Immediately his pilot chute, bag, lines, and canopy deployed. Damn, did that thing open quick. And we could not believe the forward speed. One minute, here; next minute, there; next minute, way on the other side of the airport, then downwind, on his way to his final landing approach. Here he came and damn was he coming fast! All of 25 mph, just like the article said. At the last moment before hitting the ground Bruce pulled the toggles down and slid probably 15 feet after landing. Jumpsuit grass stained, he stood up with that smile only Bruce had. All of us just stood there amazed.

Bruce called out, "Who wants to jump it?"

Rick said, "Me!" and Bruce said, "Okay." Bruce packed the square canopy up and within 40 minutes, Rick was jumping it. When he landed, he did better than Bruce. He still slid a little but not much.

"I'm next!" I said after Rick landed. Bruce said, "Sure." I watched as Bruce packed the square. It was so different from our rounds. Bruce closed the container and gave me a little briefing. I put the rig on and strapped on my reserve. At that time I had a 23-foot Pioneer TriCon that was steerable in the reserve, so I felt confident that if I did have to cut away, it was a good reserve. Only going to 4,000 feet, you couldn't delay more than 10 seconds or the square canopy would rip your head off. I could tell from watching the other two jumps that the canopy opened hard.

I was at 4,000 feet coming on jump run, and in my mind I'm going through the briefing Bruce had given me. Once the canopy opened, you reached up and grabbed the toggles and pulled off the brakes. Then the canopy would go into full speed.

As I climbed out of the plane ready to jump, I was thinking about the opening. I wanted a good stable platform for deployment. I left the step, stability great, and pulled. I watched over my shoulder and saw the twin pilot chutes launch. About that time, *whack*, the canopy was out. *Damn*, I'd never seen anything like that.

The canopy must have been at least 15 feet from my Capewell release system. I was racing across the sky faster than I ever had before. Even on windy days, I had never reached that kind of speed. I reached up and grabbed the lines dangling from the big plastic toggles. As instructed, I pulled them sideways to take the brakes off. When I did that the canopy lunged forward, and the wind started to hum through the lines. *Shit, I was cookin' all of 25 mph.* I still couldn't believe the forward speed. I couldn't believe the wind. I'm looking down and using my feet to reference my speed and direction. I had traveled out to the lake and down to the other side of the airport.

Now I was at 1,500 feet. Bruce said at 1,000 feet, go with the wind; at 700 to 500 feet, turn toward base; no lower than 300 feet, start your final approach. I'm at 500 feet and on final, straight into the wind. Racing into the wind was an experience like I have never had. *Whoosh*—over the top of the pea gravel and as I'm just about to land, I pull the toggles down further and further until I couldn't pull any further. I was close to the ground and still moving forward. I hit the ground and started to slide. I skidded to a stop. The black and red canopy fell in front of me. What a ride.

I stand up. Everybody ran over to me. "What did ya think of that?" they asked. I said "Wow!" The canopy was a Paraplane made by Para-Flite. The first Ram-Air canopy that was out for public sale. Really, I was glad go back to jumping my PC. It wasn't as radical.

## Chapter Four
## RELATIVE WORK AND A DEATH IN THE FAMILY

At Austin Lake Bruce Dillon had a Twin Beech D-18 that could carry 10 people at a time and would take us to 12,000 feet, high enough for a 60-second delay. I had made a handful of jumps out of this airplane. You didn't have to climb out on the strut—all you did was run out the door and dive. All the regulars at Austin Lake were practicing relative work.

One day we were practicing an 8-way star formation. We were up in the Twin Beech grinding to 12,500 feet. Bruce was first in the door, Ken second for the pin. Then me, Rick, Don, Sam, Sandy, Ron. "Cut!" Ken screamed to the pilot. The noise from 450 Pratt engines fell off, and we heard the count— "Ready, set, go!" Out the little hole we dove. Bruce was base; Ken could get to him by 11,000 feet. I dove down, set up, and tracked into them in third place; Rick on the other side was in fourth place by 9,000 feet. Don was closing in fifth. Sam was circling, picking a slot in the formation. Sandy came in next. Ron was still outside the formation. At 4,000 feet we broke off. We were trying to get our Star Crest Recipient (SCR), an award given out to each individual who successfully completed an 8-way star formation.

We all broke off from the 8-way, tracked, and pulled. We landed, and all the people on the ground came rushing up and said someone had bounced—the unfortunate term used in skydiving for a skydiver with no pull who hit the ground dead.

We collected at the clubhouse and did a head count. Everybody was there except Ron, Rick's brother, one of my very best friends. My body went numb. Rick was in shock. The ambulance rushed over to the spot where Ron's crushed body lay. Then they were off to the hospital. Rick and I were right behind them in my '66 Buick Special. I was doing 90 mph down Portage Road right behind the ambulance with Rick screaming, "Faster!" The poor car had never run that hard in its whole life.

Hospital in sight, I pulled in close behind the ambulance, let Rick out, and parked my car. Rick ran into the hospital right behind the EMT people. I stood in the parking lot a few moments, still in shock and trying to get my bearings. Hell, I was only 19 years old and Ron a year older.

I went inside, and the nurses took me to the waiting room. I kept running the jump over and over in my mind trying to figure out what happened. The last time I saw Ron was at 6,000 feet. He was trying to close on the star. What happened? No one knew at that time. Hell, they still don't. Rick walked up to me, head hung low, and told me he saw Ron laying on the bed, his eyes black from his head being crushed on impact. Rick said, "Let's go," and that's what we did.

I started to drive; not a word was said all the way back to Three Rivers. I dropped Rick off and went back to my house. Mom and Dad were in the kitchen. I told them. They were shocked. I didn't sleep much that night. I ran that jump again and again through my head all night. I couldn't stop it. What was strange to me was that I didn't cry—for some reason I couldn't. It wasn't that I didn't care, I just didn't cry. What the hell.

The next day I drove Rick to Austin Lake to pick up Ron's car. The people there were all buzzed up with "what ifs". Bruce had a cutaway on that jump, and everybody said Ron collided with his parachute. That was a good explanation, but knowing what I know today, I don't think so. I've seen canopies that suffered collisions, and they were totally destroyed—broken lines, torn nylon, and other damage.

We buried Ron a few days later. I remember the funeral; I

was a pallbearer. While the priest was speaking, my mind went back and replayed the days that Ron and I shared. Good days. School days. Playing football, running track, pole vaulting, double dating, hunting together, going to school dances together. I was going to miss him. He was like a brother. But still no tears.

Rick and I continued to jump, and before that fall was over we had earned our SCR.

Rocky's first 16-way skydiving formation
in Zephyrhills, Florida

## Chapter Five
## OUT TO BEAT THE BEST

It was the spring of 1973. Ken told us about a boogie that was going on in Richmond, Indiana. There would be a Douglas DC-3 to jump from. It held 40 people. Damn, that was huge. My skydiving skills were getting honed. Just before we left, I got my Star Crest Soloist (SCS) award for participation in a freefall formation with eight or more skydivers. My number was 447 in the world. We caravanned to Richmond—Rick, me, Sam, Sandy in one van; Ken, Bruce, Don, Ray, and Johnny in another. I remember pulling into the airport in Richmond. There the DC-3 stood in all her glory—the airplane that made its mark in World War II. It carried our boys into D-Day, plus it pulled gliders, two at a time. What an airplane!

We registered and started to mingle. Ken and Sam were out trying to find enough experienced people to do a 16-way star formation. In 1973 that was a chore. We got 17 skydivers up and tried a couple of jumps. 13 on one, 14 on another. But no 16. The next day we came out fresh. Ken knew some other people who might be able to do the job. We then had 18 experienced skydivers and filled the rest of the plane with stragglers. The DC-3 had a door you could get out of quickly, and that's what it took to build this formation. Bruce, base; Ken, pin. The base was solid every time. They were a team. Johnny, solid third. Tom, who we met there in Richmond, came from Missoula, Montana. He was hot. There it was—a solid 14-

way. I started to close in. As I made my approach, I started to fall lower than the star. Damn it. Damn it. All I could do was look up at this perfectly round 16-way—and I wasn't part of it. We tried one more time, but I had no success. I was so mad at myself. All the other guys got in except me. Hell, it was a year and a half later before I got my 16-way SCR in Zephyrhills, Florida.

We formed a 10-way team we called the *Beechnuts* during the summer, picking up people from the Detroit area. They came to Austin Lake because we had a Beech airplane. 10 guys from Michigan. We got pretty damn good. When we weren't practicing a 10-way formation, Ken, Sam, Don, and I formed a 4-way team called the *Rainbow Flyers*. We practiced the new 4-way competition format that had just been introduced into the U.S. Nationals the year before. The competition rules said the team had to go out and build a 4-way star, then do a back loop and then reform into a different formation that was picked randomly just prior to the competition. Six different formations were possible—snowflake, Murphy star, Canadian T, caterpillar, star, bipole. We practiced these formations for the remaining part of the year.

Our 10-way team was getting pretty darn good. In addition to the guys I'd been jumping with at Austin Lake, three others—John, Jimmy, and Gary—filled up the other slots that made up our 10-way team. In the fall Ken told us of a big skydiving meet in Zephyrhills, Florida. We all responded without a second thought, "Let's go!"

So on Thanksgiving Day in 1973, we all drove down to Florida. This was my first time in Florida, and the weather was perfect. We arrived and were wowed by what we saw. There were at least six DC-3s, a Lockheed Loadstar, and a Lockheed 10E—the same plane that Amelia Earhart flew when she got lost over the Pacific. I was amazed. Teams from all over the East Coast were there from places I had never heard of. There were 25 or more teams including the kings of relative work—Jerry Bird's *All Stars*, Florida's *Ten High Bunch*, a team from Massachusetts called *Pieces of Eight,* and *The James*

*Gang* from Illinois—the best teams in the world. This was like the Woodstock of skydiving. Four days of competition were planned. I was in my element.

Smoking pot was popular during the boogie, and good pot was there in abundance. I had a feeling the planes I saw there might have had something to do with that. And smoking was a social thing there—it wasn't about just getting high. At night after jumping, Rick and I went out to meet all the new people. RVs were everywhere. The scent of pot filled the air. Plenty of beer, pot, and this new thing, LSD. We knew LSD was off limits for the duration of this meet. We had orders to stay away from it until competition was done.

Two days into the competition our 10-man team was tied for second place. When the meet was over, we placed second overall. We were as surprised as anyone—10 guys from Michigan had beat the big teams. The long ride back to Michigan was a good one. We laughed and bullshitted about the meet and felt good about our second place win.

That winter we tried to keep jumping to keep current, but the weather wasn't very jumper friendly. We made a few jumps but not that many. We were still looking for those low numbers for another SCR award—there was one more we wanted. This one was called the NSCR—Night Star Crest Recipient. We all got together one night in February and decided it was time. Bruce Dillon said he would fly his Twin Beech from Austin Lake to Kalamazoo and take us up from there. It was 10 o'clock at night when our 10-man team walked into the airport lobby in Kalamazoo with our parachutes hanging over our shoulders. Flashlights were duct taped onto our helmets, and we wore layers of warm clothes under our jumpsuits. It was dark, as dark as could be, no moon. All 10 of us were gearing up in the lobby, and all eyes were glued on us. Someone asked what we were doing, but most of them could figure it out.

Walking to the plane I had butterflies—not as bad as my first jump, but they were there. This was my first night jump. Most everybody had made one or two. My only worry was being able to see the base of the star when I jumped. I figured the closer I was to the base, the better. We took off in the D-18 and started the climb over the top of the drop zone. At 12,500 feet, like so many times before, Ken would spot. We had a piece of cardboard we leaned on to keep the wind off of us while the plane climbed. It was cold. On jump run, Ken took the cardboard off and passed it up to the front, and we belted it down so it wouldn't fly out. Ken was in the door, making corrections. It was time. "Cut. Let's go!" We heard the count and were out the door.

I could just see the base. I saw Rick in place and Sam closing. I made my approach, smooth and level. *In the slot. Don't reach. Get closer. There it is. Grab it!* As I took a firm grip, I shook their arms, the signal to open the grip. Now fly the star. In between altitude checks, I could see the others closing. At 4,000 feet we broke, tracked, and pulled. I landed in the pea gravel. *Good spot, Ken.* All 10 got out of the plane—but there were only nine of us on the ground. Where was Don? He wasn't there. My mind went back to Ron. Damn it, I wasn't ready for that. 10 minutes went by, still no Don. People started to freak. All of a sudden we heard someone yell, "Hey, hey!" We looked up at the lone canopy floating down. It was Don. When he landed, he told us that on exiting the plane, his parachute had a premature opening. Relieved, we laughed. We got our night 8-way. I got my number. NSCR 126. Yes! Now we were starting to get there!

One of the very first Strato Star canopies.

# Chapter Six
## NATIONAL GLORY

I t was 1974. I was working construction. Good money to support my habit—skydiving. During the winter I bought myself a new rig—the smallest and lightest parachute assembly in the world at the time. 28 pounds. That spring our 10-way team was feeling hungry. We started to train really hard for the U.S. Nationals in July in Tahlequah, Oklahoma. By now I was going out tenth in our 10-way formation, Rick ninth, and we were starting to get good. We had around 500 jumps by then. Every weekend it was practice, practice, practice. We were getting times in the high 20 seconds. Pretty damn good for a bunch of Michigan boys. The summer went by quickly.

Ken started a new drop zone in a small town right down the road from Austin Lake in Athens, Michigan—just 20 minutes from Three Rivers on M-60. A small private strip of grass in the middle of nowhere—it was the perfect location. At the Nationals the 10-way competition was going to be held out of Twin Beech D-18s, so we chartered one from Jackson, Michigan, for practice. We had a couple different teams that came from Indiana and Michigan to practice with us, so on the weekends there were 30 or so people at Ken's drop zone.

Our 4-way team went to the USPA Conference Meet, a regional event, along with our 10-way team. You had to place first in a regional competition to qualify for the Nationals—we won first place in both events. Our team kept practicing right up until it was time for the Nationals.

John Sherman at the Jump Shack, a harness and container manufacturer in Novi, Michigan, was developing a small piggyback rig—with both canopies located on your back—and he had the first prototype almost ready to go. But they had no main canopy small enough to fit in the main container. *Ah ha!* My little round canopy on my new rig would work. I told John I would put my Piglet canopy in his prototype if he would let me make the first jump on his new design. He said the reserve still needed to be tested. So I went up in the Beech and did a hop n' pop to test the new reserve. The rig design and harness fit were perfect.

So I had the first SST harness and container system. In today's sport it's known as the Racer.

This was an exciting and changing time in skydiving. New equipment and techniques were coming out—big strides everywhere in the sport. Rick and I were taking it up a notch, too, and found ourselves right in the middle of all the change. We went to Zephyrhills, Florida, for the winter that year. We lived in an old abandoned DC-3 and collected unemployment. It was great. Every morning we'd get up, shower, and skydive. I picked up my 16- and 20-way SCR awards that winter.

Tony, a skydiver from the *Ten High Bunch* team, organized the first skydiving formation other than a star. One formation we did was a 16-way butterfly—completed by 6,000 feet. We hummed it straight down right over the drop zone. Tony was a cool dude and way ahead of his time. Unfortunately he was killed while skydiving in 1975 when he was helping design the throw-out pilot chute. That hit home with me. Any death in the sport got your attention—and hurt a lot more when it was someone you knew.

Para-Flite had just developed the first relative work (RW) canopies called the Strato Star. Strato Star canopies were 5-cell Ram-Airs that flew real fast but weren't real good for accuracy jumping. But they packed up small. The canopy had 15 feet of bridle cord and was reefed with rings and ropes before the slider. It wasn't the greatest reefing system, but these were prototype canopies. They took five to seven seconds to fully inflate.

The Jump Shack built 10 red and white SSTs for our *Rainbow Flyers* team, and Ted Strong gave us 10 red and white jumpsuits. Damn, did we look good! We had the canopies for about a month before the Nationals. Sometimes the long reefing line would tie up, preventing the canopy from opening all the way. I had two reserve rides on this canopy. But with that said, it was a pretty cool canopy. We introduced the skydiving community to the SST and the Strato Star.

Rick bought a new van in Florida at the end of that winter. We drove it to Oklahoma for the Nationals where we met the rest of our team. Rick was our alternate back then for the 4-way team, and he was perfect for the slot. He moved quickly which was essential. I think of the 4-way as the 100-yard dash of skydiving.

We found ourselves surrounded by some of the best skydiving teams in the U.S. I wouldn't say we were intimidated. Not at all, because we knew we were ready, but I couldn't have predicted how it would all turn out. A bunch of 10-way speed star teams were on hand along with over 15 4-way teams.

Gary Dupuis was the chief pilot for the Nationals and gave the competitors' briefing. Damn, was he funny. A cracker from DeLand, Florida, he ran his own drop zone, the DeLand Sport Parachute Center, with a DC-3 that he owned, which later became known as "Mr. Douglas". The meet started out pretty well for us with our 10-way team scoring high enough that by round three we were in second place. Our 4-way team was also clicking along in second place.

The second day of competition was gruesome. Three rounds of 10-way and four of 4-way. We took first place in the 4-way. We had only a handful of practice jumps in the 4-way, but that was enough to earn us the gold. We were shocked and very happy. Our primary reason for doing 4-way was to stay active in competition. We didn't want to sit on the ground in between 10-way jumps. Now we were the champions!

The next day, the 10-way competition was finished. Our

*Beechnuts* team placed sixth, not very good for all the practice we had put in. We might have placed a lot higher, but John, one of the team's base people, was injured. He had a malfunction. His reefing line tied up on his Strato Star canopy. He rode it into the ground and broke his back. We were forced to bring in our alternate—not a good time for a personnel change.

After the competition Rick and I hauled John home with us in Rick's new van. We built him a bed in the van out of Coors beer cases. We had 36 of them. Those old enough to remember know that at that time no Coors was sold east of the Mississippi. We drank a few, and laughed all the way home while admiring our gold medal.

Rocky and his Rainbow Flyers teammates on their first national champion 4-way team.

## Chapter Seven
## WORLD CHAMPIONSHIP CHALLENGE

It was the summer of 1974, and Rick and I were back to work trying to make a barebones living. Now that the Nationals were over, Rick and I took a break from our skydiving. I'd been back to work for a couple weeks when I was bit by a brown recluse spider and hospitalized. My hand was very swollen, and I was sick with nausea, vomiting, and a fever. After a couple of days, my teammate and captain of our 4-way team, Sam, came to see me. He asked, "How long are you going to be in the hospital?"

I said I wasn't sure, and asked why he wanted to know. He said our 4-way team was going to Pretoria, South Africa, for the 1974 World Cup of Relative Work—all expenses paid.

Damn, man, I was on the U.S. Team. But here I was in the hospital. Again he said, "When can you get out?"

"Why hell, Sam, I have no idea," I told him again. Sam said I needed to get a passport, but I had no idea how to do that. So he did all the paperwork, and I had my passport photo done in the hospital. A few more days went by and I was hungry for real food. Rick climbed the wall of the hospital and brought me some fried chicken. That's a damn good friend. Not too many people would do that for you.

Our team had to leave a few days after that. I told the doc, "Doc, I got a chance to jump in the World Championships and come on, let me out of here." He rolled his eyes and told me that the infection could spread and I could lose my hand. Like most people, when you talk about skydiving, they think that you land like so much dead weight—like the soldiers raining down in World War II movies. Hell, this was 1974. We were jumping square canopies. We stand when we land. No understanding at all from the public.

"Damn it, Doc. Let me out!" He did. *Yes! Yes! Yes!* I was sprung. I'd been in that hospital 10 days and I was feeling pretty weak.

We were going to Africa, home of Tarzan. I knew it would be nice and warm. No more practice. Sam searched out a little info on some of the other countries in the competition that were ranked high in the ratings. He said the French were sending their military 4-way team. They would be the ones to watch out for. It turned out they were, but I knew from high school sports not to worry until the day you play.

This was the World Cup of Relative Work. A year earlier, in 1973, the first of the World Championships was held at Fort Bragg, jumping out of Chinooks, the military's twin rotor troop carrier. This year the competition one was in Pretoria, South Africa—the only place on earth that still had official segregation. I didn't realize what that meant until I got there.

On the day we were flying out, Rick and I each ate a peanut butter and jelly sandwich loaded with red bud pot as we drove to Kalamazoo. It was grade A Colombian pot that none of us had tried before. By the time we got to the airport, I was flying high as an eagle. So was Rick. We got on the plane and soon fell asleep. We flew from there to Detroit, then New York, and then on to Pretoria, South Africa. We were on a Boeing 747 which at that time was fairly new in the airline industry, and the plane was huge. We flew for about 24 hours and arrived the next day. I thought about our upcoming accommodations in Pretoria. I knew Rick and I were staying in one room and probably Sam, also. Cool. Rick was 21 and I was 22—and we were flying halfway around the world to the southern tip of Africa.

The meet director picked us up and drove us to a 5-star hotel. Once we were all settled in and had our gear sorted, he took us to the airport where the meet was being held. The dirt at the airport was red and hard as bricks. I could see at least 15 DC-3s—the South Africans called them Dakotas—and at least nine C-185s.

After checking out the drop zone and the airplanes, we went back to the hotel and over dinner we talked about what we were going to do the next day. The dining room was huge with lots of tables, and all the waiters were black. It seemed like a scene I imagined from the old south playing out in the present. The toilets were labeled separately for whites and blacks. The segregation continued to surprise me throughout our stay in South Africa.

It was kind of hard to go to sleep that night. I took a shower and watched the water go down the drain—in a counterclockwise spiral—the opposite direction from the northern hemisphere. The next day was sunny and a little cold. We went to the drop zone and filled out paperwork for our photo IDs used to manifest. On the back of the card was a space to for contact information—in case we got arrested. I sure didn't think that would happen, but this was a different country, and I definitely didn't know what to expect. It was hard for me to get used to being in Africa. You might think that only a real dumbass would believe Tarzan was going to come swinging down from the trees on his vine, jump on a lion, and stab him with his big knife. But that was me—kind of keeping an eye out just in case.

A total of 18 teams from all over the world were competing in the 4-way. But we were confident of our team's success—even if maybe we shouldn't have been. Because of that spider bite, I hadn't jumped in a month. But my jumps were current prior to that, and I was going out 10th in the 10-way team event because my reflex skills were quick. A month off wasn't about to change that. Hell, we won the Nationals with seven practice jumps and had probably 13 total jumps when we got to Pretoria—a far cry fewer than the French 4-way military team with over 700 jumps.

Of course, the French team didn't have to pay. They got all their equipment for free and all the aircraft support they needed. So these soldier boys might be a problem.

Sam manifested us, and we geared up. When we pulled out our equipment and the rest of the competitors saw our gear, they were all stunned. Here they were—five SSTs. The canopies were not aired out, and they all asked, "What kind of main canopy?" We told them that they were square. They couldn't believe it. As I said, we had the very first Strato Stars. The Strato Star packed up small and fit perfect in the new SST container. With our five sets of equipment lined up for all to see, every one of them red and white, we knew we had a special edge.

When we got our gear on, all the other teams gathered around us checking it out. I knew they wanted to watch us land our square canopies. We waited for military trucks to pick us up. When we finished manifesting we were taken to the airplanes to load. We went up in a C-185, all silver with a springbok logo on the side. The air support came from the South African Air Force. At the U.S. Nationals, we jumped from a C-182, not a C-185. So Ken, the first guy out, had to climb out onto the wheel, not a step like on the C-182. The airfield elevation was at 4,000 feet, and we knew landing would be a little more difficult because the air was thinner than we were used to in Michigan.

We went up for our first practice jump. With no door on the side of the C-185, it was cold with temperatures hanging in the low 60s in the morning. Climbing to altitude we saw the countryside spread out below. The ground was a red color. The city of Pretoria was similar in size to Indianapolis and spread out over quite a distance.

We got to our jump altitude—9,000 feet. We climbed out—Ken on the wheel, Don on the step, Sam on the strut, and me in the door. We jumped and then were free flying headed into our 4-way star. We got into our star formation quickly and set up for the back loop. At that time we hadn't learned how to consistently do a good 4-way back loop. We knew the basics and the things to avoid—don't throw your head back, stay tucked until you finished the back loop, and keep your eyes open so you could see everyone else in their back loop. In practice we usually came up short on at least one of these basics. We also saw that often when three of us were level, one person would be either high or low.

We broke, did the back loop, and came back to the star. We held the star for five seconds. The practice jump went okay, but our moves were slower than in the past. They were in the five-second range for sure, but we hadn't jumped together for a month. I tracked off and deployed my Strato Star which opened as designed. All four of us landed in the pea gravel and you would have thought Elvis had just landed. Everybody came running out, acting like they couldn't believe what they saw. Damn dude! We just stood there answering questions, a lot of them in languages we couldn't understand. I couldn't believe the big deal, but I understood a little better after looking at the equipment from the different countries. It was completely different from one country to the next. Some of the stuff was for sure out of World War II.

I learned that Jerry Bird's team, *Wings Of Orange*, was supposed to arrive that day. They were coming from Czechoslovakia and Hungary after doing some demo jumps. We were excited at the prospect of having some more Americans here. And old Chet Poland was here to support the U.S. team. We made another jump and went for lunch. Bird's team showed up later that day. These guys were great entertainers, showing their skills from juggling to acrobatics. BJ Worth was one of the young dudes on Bird's team, with about 220 jumps, if that— punk kids right out of high school.

It was good to see Bird. I hadn't seen him since the Nationals, and then he and his team hung out with the other California teams. We were just four unknown skydivers from Michigan, but we were good skydivers with big hearts and a lot of desire. Bird brought down a great big chunk of Moroccan hashish and gave us some. I had come to Pretoria thinking we would have nothing to smoke, but that turned out to be wrong. In two days, Rick scored a half pound of weed. It was nice at night to smoke a little weed at the end of a busy day. Plus it knocked the edge off so the competition doesn't get you so uptight.

It didn't seem to be an issue. We would build our 4-way after we exited the airplane. Back then we never launched the 4-way; we used our skydiving skills to build the 4-way in the air. It was good practice.

That night, they had a big party for all the competitors. Bird's team was at their best entertaining the crowd as they had done so many times before. We went to bed early. Competition would start the next day. I was ready! I felt good physically, considering I was in the hospital less than a week earlier. And our team felt good about our three practice jumps that day.

Before we went to bed, we had a smoke. Rick, Sam, and I smoked pot pretty much every day. Don didn't smoke at all, Ken sometimes. The USPA team leader, Paul Tag, of course not. Don't forget, it was 1974. Rick and I loaded the pipe and went over to Don and Ken's room. We shot gunned through the keyhole and filled the room with smoke. We didn't worry about trouble from the USPA. Tag knew that all of Bird's team smoked, and I would think by this time he knew that the three of us did, also.

The next day was the first day of competition so with the pot buzz, we slept pretty well. We got out of bed, showered, and got ready mentally to compete. Damn it was cold; the temperature was down in the 50s. I dressed as warm as I could, and then the shuttle delivered us to the airport. Sam went to the competitors' briefing at 8 a.m. where the rules were explained and the rounds drawn. This competition was six rounds just like our Nationals. All those rounds didn't trouble me or the rest of the team because we really liked to jump. The more the merrier.

About halfway through the meet the French protested to the judges and said we were pulling too low—below 2,000 feet. The protest came on our third jump. Our team was neck and neck with the French at that point. We knew we were pulling at 3,000 feet, but because our canopies were reefed with a 10-foot reefing line that ran across the top of the canopy through rings that were attached to the pilot chute, it took almost 1,000 feet for the canopy to open. The judges turned to their video to settle the issue. They could clearly see that it was taking about five seconds for the canopy to fully deploy. The French protest was denied.

During the next three rounds we edged the French team out by a couple of seconds each time, so by the end of the competition we were in first place. Bird's team won in the 10-way, hands down. Once again, the team in second place was the French. So the U.S. teams won the gold in 10-way speed star and in the 4-way event. The meet took three days.

That day our 4-way team put our rigs up for sale. Lots of people were interested. Rick and I sold ours for $1,500 each. We got our money and felt pretty rich. Back then $1,500 was a lot. The next day a "big way", a large star formation, world record attempt was planned. But Rick and I decided to ride the train to Johannesburg, where we could buy ivory to take home. We had been told that if we left the city of Pretoria we might risk getting arrested—even though we had a "get out of jail free" ID card. We didn't care. After breakfast the next day, Rick and I told the rest of our team we were going to hang back and stay at the hotel. When they left for the drop zone, Rick and I got into a cab and went to the train station.

Like everything else in South Africa, there were separate trains designated for white passengers and black passengers. Rick and I had no idea about what to do. It didn't feel exactly right to participate in the segregated system, but we did like most other passengers and boarded the train designated for whites. We found our seats. As we rolled through the countryside Rick and I smoked some pot. We had our "get out of jail for free" cards, so we felt pretty safe. Looking back, I'm glad we didn't have to test how powerful that ID card really was. We had the train pretty much to ourselves, so we walked up to the dining car, got a beer, and bullshitted about the competition. After about an hour and a half, we pulled into a large train station. We had no idea where we were, except that we were somewhere in Johannesburg.

We set off walking. Every once in a while I would think about Sam, Don, and Ken back in Pretoria jumping with others at the competition and attempting to set different star formation records, and I kind of wished I was there. But I also wanted to see more of South Africa. I had read about Johannesburg, and I wanted to see it and say I'd been there. As we walked the city streets we came upon a jewelry store. Rick and I went in and looked around. The store clerk came up and asked how he could help us. We asked to look at jewelry carved from ivory. He showed us a few pieces, but we didn't buy anything.

By now it was about 1 p.m. We had a couple of hours before we had start back to Pretoria, so we went to a few more stores. In one store Rick bought some unusual stones. I bought a beautiful ivory necklace for my girlfriend and some other knick knacks for my mom and dad and little brother. Then it was back on the train to Pretoria. We arrived back at the hotel, went to our room and had another smoke, laughing it up the whole time. No one on our team was any wiser about how we had spent our day. Later that day Sam asked us what we had done all day. We told him that we just hung out in Pretoria checking out the sights.

The awards banquet was that night. I remember standing on the podium listening to the band play the Star Spangled Banner and watching the American flag being raised. It's no surprise that at that moment I thought, *Well, Dad, let's see if you can beat this one.* I remember bending down as the official hung the gold medal around my neck. When the National Anthem quit playing, and everybody had their medal, I picked mine up and looked at it. This was real gold and damn, was it nice. The real deal.

When we got back to the U.S., we paid for the rigs we had sold, bought brand new ones, and had money left.

## Chapter Eight
## BACK IN MICHIGAN

After returning from winning gold in Pretoria, I spent the rest of that fall and winter working and saving money for the next season. I was dating a girl from Saginaw. Joyce and I were married that October, and I moved to Saginaw with her.

That winter I drove to work in Novi, Michigan, northwest of Detroit, where the Jump Shack was based. My 10-way team member, John Sherman, owned it and gave me a job. I wasn't a rigger then, so I learned how to sew and started to build subparts for the new SST. We used templates and would mark them out on a big rollout piece of colored nylon Para Pack. After they were marked, I would use the hot knife to cut out the pieces. The pieces would first go to a binder who would then bind them together. They would be bound with binding tape, inspected, and sent to final assembly. I learned how to sew on a single needle, a double needle, a double throw zigzag, and the big harness machine. I liked the job, but it was a two-hour drive from Saginaw and, after an eight-hour workday, two more hours home. It was a little too much.

I was laid off from my job around Christmas and collected unemployment for a while. It was after Christmas when I got a job driving an auto parts delivery truck. I worked that job up to the next season of skydiving. Then every weekend I went down to Ken's drop zone in Athens, which was about two-thirds of the way across the state. Joyce didn't like it. Well, that was too bad for Joyce, because nothing, absolutely nothing was going to stop me from this season.

Our 10-way team disbanded so that gave us time to concentrate on our 4-way *Rainbow Flyers* team. We made almost 100 practice jumps preparing for the 1975 season. We learned how to do good back loops. The 4-way and style competitions were the only skydiving competitions that required a back loop. The back loop was the hardest maneuver of the skydiving competition. This was way before video cameras were available, so it was hard to analyze what you or the other three team members might be doing wrong, so there was no way to critique the maneuver afterward. Sometimes you could find a freefall photographer with a 16 mm camera to photograph you, but then you had to get it developed and put it on a projector to view.

That summer we were asked to be filmed as part of a documentary being made by a friend of Ken's. The freefall photographer was named Steve, and he jumped with a 16mm on his helmet and shot some pretty good footage. One day we were doing some freefall photography at Austin Lake. The five of us went up in a C-182 and exited. Our jump went down pretty good. After break off, I saw Ken with Steve in front of him filming his parachute opening. Ken waved off and pulled. Then Steve pulled.

I was just above the two of them and could see both of them perfectly. After Steve pulled, I saw his canopy deploy into a classic line over. His canopy looked like a perfect bowtie. He had a spin to the right going on, and this was not a landable canopy. I started screaming, "Cutaway! Cutaway!" No cutaway. Steve continued to ride the malfunctioned canopy. I thought he was going to go all the way into the ground, still spinning. I watched the main canopy go slack. I saw Steve tumble once, and then I saw the pilot chute from his reserve start to leave his container. Seconds later I heard the cracking of tree limbs. I was above him at least 1,000 feet on a Strato Star canopy. And then, nothing. He went directly into the woods across the street from the airport. I knew what it was like in those woods—I had landed my new T-10 parachute in there once and went clear through the tree branches before getting hung up about three feet off the ground.

When I looked down from my canopy, all I could see were people running to the woods in a panic. I knew Steve was dead. No one could be alive after falling through those trees. I landed close to the road that separated the woods from the road and climbed out of my gear.

I ran across the road and into the woods. I was close to the spot where I had landed with my T-10. As I got in farther, the EMTs were rushing out, carrying Steve. Sam, my teammate, was walking toward me. "What's up," I asked. "Is he dead?"

Sam replied, "I talked to him."

"What?"

"Yes, he was conscious," Sam said.

I said, "No way."

Sam told me to go deeper into the woods. "You won't believe this."

The woods were getting a little marshy. I could feel my feet starting to get sucked down. Making that "swoosh, swoosh" sound.

Sam pointed, "Look at that." There was a huge crater over a foot deep that formed in the marsh where Steve landed. Then Sam pointed up. "Look at that," he said, pointing to the broken limbs. They had helped break Steve's fall. "Damn," I said, and told Sam about hearing the limbs breaking from 1,000 feet up.

The next day we found out that Steve was still in the hospital. He had no broken bones. They were going to perform surgery to check for any internal injuries. The surgeon extracted a long sliver of wood that went up the side of Steve's neck. His neck was stiff where his helmet and camera were. When he went through the trees, a big limb at least an inch in diameter had jammed in his helmet and stuck into the Styrofoam. It was stuck in there so far that I couldn't pull it out. The helmet was still fastened when we found it in the woods.

A couple days later, Steve got out of the hospital and came out to the drop zone. We all wanted to hear the story. Steve told it to everybody, and I'm sure he got sick of it after a while. I know I would. But it was quite a story. Not many people have gone all the way in without even breaking a bone.

By this time our 4-way team had over 120 practice jumps. It was hard to believe that we had just won the World Championship the year before. In skydiving it's the same as winning an Olympic gold medal.

* * *

September and October were bow hunting months in Michigan, and I looked forward to it. It was a good way to relax between the '74 and '75 skydiving seasons.. I bought a new Browning compound bow and it was a good one. Browning was one of the first compound bows. It was rated at 60 pounds. Hell, after I went through the trees in '72 and crashed on the runway, my left arm had been damaged. I had a recurve bow then that was made by Fred Bear. I had a good sized buck come within 15 yards and I could not pull my bow back enough to make a good shot. I missed him twice.

I finally healed up enough to really shoot this new bow correctly. I really liked the speed from this Browning and I could shoot it pretty well. It felt good not to focus on my skydiving, to relax and really enjoy something else. I had been playing semi-pro football but that was over and I was excited to try out my new bow.

It really felt good to go out into the woods and be able to have a little peace and quiet. It's so cool to sit still and quiet and be accepted by nature into its environment. You can collect your thoughts and really get close to all the animals. That's when you know that you're doing it right.

There was a guy named Schultz on my crew at work whose dad had a big parcel of property west of our little town. He had a bow and the two of us would go bow hunting together after work. I had never killed a deer with a bow and had always wanted to. I was getting ready to go out to hunt like I had been doing for a couple of weeks. My mother told me that it would be good to take my little brother, Mike, with me. She said you need to take him because he has no father. I felt bad but told her that Mike doesn't own a bow and I was hunting on private property. I didn't want him or me to get caught. Mom went to the K-Mart and bought Mike a bow and some hunting arrows with the broadheads for killing deer along with a hunting license. I had him wear his camouflage pants and a shirt that I loaned him and away we went.

I took Mike out to my special place and put him in a tree where I had seen deer—a lot of them. Then I walked down the edge of the corn field that paralleled a hedge row. Perfect for white tails. I sat in a big oak tree on a corner where the woods and the corn field and hedge row met. I had in mind to smoke a fat joint while I waited.

A good old friend that I knew from high school grew this killer sensimilla pot. The plant grew big in Michigan. I've seen pictures of plants sixteen and seventeen feet high. It was grown in town on one of the three rivers that the little town was named for. Now this was a very high quality marijuana and the taste was like a strong hashish taste. I wouldn't say it was as good as some I had smoked that came from Central America but it was certainly close. There is nothing better than a good joint rolled out of Michigan sensimilla. The high you get is pretty strong. As I smoked I became more aware of the beautiful Michigan autumn scene surrounding me. Everything was perfect. I had a big-ass oak tree to sit in—and dude, it was big. It was a hard tree to get into but someone before me had nailed up some boards that I'm sure they also used them to get into the tree. So there I was, high, happy, and with a perfect spot to shoot from.

As the sun began its final descent in the western sky, I could feel the change in temperature. I had fired up my joint not only to get a little bit of a high going but also to see what the wind was doing as far as strength and direction. After a couple of good puffs I put it out. I was really starting to enjoy my hunt. Probably an hour had gone by since I left Mike in the tree. All of a sudden, I heard a scream. This was no ordinary scream. It was one of anticipation followed by my name. It took me a couple of seconds to figure out who it was, but I still didn't know why he was screaming. Well, that got answered quickly as I saw my brother, Mike, bow in hand and screaming. Looked like a crazed Indian. The next thing that came to mind was he had fallen on one of his arrows. I climbed down way faster than the climb up. I started to run to him, thinking *what the hell?* One could only guess. When we met, Mike started to blather. "I got him! I got him! Hurry, he's gonna get away!" I finally slowed him down and got his story straight.

Apparently some deer had come in and Mike had shot all three of his arrows and had missed. He got out of the tree and was lucky enough to find all of his arrows. He climbed back up and waited.

I knew how he felt because I have been there more than once. I can still see it in my mind's eye: There it stood, in all God's glory, a pure white tail. So smart, so good with hearing, eyesight, and smell that it was almost impossible to get close enough for a shot with my bow. If you can get close enough for a bow shot, you're either extremely lucky or you're a good hunter. I shot. I missed. I shot. I missed. I shot. I missed. That was it. I usually take only thee arrows. I figure if you miss three times then the deer deserves to go free.

After his three misses Mike climbed back into the tree. He told me that they had come back and that he drew back his bow again, taking aim for a broadside shot. He let the arrow fly and *whack*, the arrow found its mark, but not in the side. Just when Mike let go, the deer had turned, and the arrow hit him smack right between the eyes. The broadhead sank deep, clear to where it screws into the shaft. The deer started to flop just like anything else that gets shot in the head.

Well, Mike pulled off the shot. He was lucky and that's all it was. Then he jumped down and shot the deer two more times. When I finally got there, I couldn't believe my eyes. There it lay, a perfect specimen. One arrow was buried clean between the eyes. One of the next two went through the leg and into the buck's other side, while the other entered through a front leg and through the back. The poor thing looked like a pin cushion.

It was after all this had happened that Mike came

screaming my name, running to the edge of the corn field where my oak tree stood. When I got to him, piss was running down his leg. He kept screaming, "Hurry! Hurry! He's gonna get away!" At that point I had no idea what he was saying. He was totally spent. Then he told the story.

Now the hard work. I gutted the deer and we started to drag it down the hedge row, being careful not to be seen. I had a Dodge pickup and we threw it in the back. It was a little button buck, antlers just barely showing. Weight gutted, about 140 pounds, a respectable deer with a bow. Well, Mike got his picture taken for the local paper. What a picture. Mike's chest was all pumped up and pushed out. My God, that boy can sure pose. He had his *Cat* hat on and with his curly hair—I mean tight curly hair kind of like a fro—well, it was a damn good picture.

Schultz and I went back to his father's woods and I built a ground blind on the side of a hardwood and covered it up good. It bordered an alfalfa field that was perfect for white tail deer. Deer sign was everywhere. Big ass tracks, scrapes, and some buck rubs that were just starting. The next couple of nights, we hunted and on the third night, I was sitting in my blind. It was one of those still evenings. The scent of sassafras was coming from the woods. Then the wind would shift and the sweet smell of cut hay would fill your nose. So pungent, the hay smell, but just as quickly it would give way again to the smell of root beer. Sassafras is all over the woods in Michigan and root beer is made from its roots.

I had fired up a big fat Michigan joint and drew on it hard. You ask any connoisseur of pot and they will tell you the same—the odor is strong and it carries. When I blew the smoke out I would watch it and see exactly where the wind was coming from. The deer are so sensitive when it comes to smell.. The smoke seemed to take its own direction this evening as it rolled out of my mouth just to linger motionless to the wind. I thought, *not good*. While you are on the ground, your scent travels through the woods. The animals that are scent protected can pick it up from a half mile away. When you're in a tree, it's a lot better—the higher the better. I had no tree stand so here I am on the ground. Well, I thought it's a pretty evening to be out in the woods, no matter what. After a couple more hits and smoke watching, I put the joint out. Forty-five minutes passed. The setting sun was just on the tree line. Deer like to come out starting now, clear into the night.

I started to get ready. There's a certain time in the birth of the night, from evening into dark that comes and goes in the flash of an instant. One moment there's light and then it's dark. I would think only a real hunter would know about this, or anyone who has spent a lot of time in nature. I had experienced it many times. You kind of blink your eyes for an instant to get them adjusted. It's weird and it really does happen. It happens fast. Like I said, it happens just as the sun slides past the horizon.

The sun was still at the tree line as I watched a big fat woodchuck scrounging out in the hay field. Then I looked up and saw a doe half in and half out of the woods. Deer are very smart. Here she was, looking, smelling, listening for anything that would tell her to duck back in—don't let your guard down, wait until you're sure.

My head was the only thing moving on me. The wind was in my face, I could feel it. *Don't change. Be still*, I told myself. *Keep facing that direction. Just stay there.* The little doe popped out, too small to shoot. I waited again. A deer stuck its head out. This one had horns. A 4-pointer. Again, my heart jumped a couple beats higher. This was the one. Motionless we both stood, waiting for one to move. I had his ass. He didn't know I was there. And I knew he was. I only wanted him to look away or drop his head.

Then it happened. He dropped his head—for what I didn't care. Motion for motion, as his head dropped, I drew. I stopped and settled once, my bow string was back, feather in the corner of my mouth. I take my point of aim. This was a close shot. I only had his neck but I had all of it. I focused on the base, his head still down. I figured this was the moment. I could feel the string slide down the pads of my fingers, so smooth I knew that my arrow would fly true. It had a good start. Sixty pounds of force is a lot. The arrow screamed toward the small buck. *Whack!* The arrow found its mark. In an instant, the little buck shot back into the woods. It was over. So quick, so sudden. I looked again. Nothing but the same landscape I had looked at for the past three nights.

Now the hunt was on. I'd been bow hunting for a long time with no luck. I take my brother out and in one night, he bags a deer. Not only did he shoot one with his bow but shot it in the head. And his deer ran nowhere. It just dropped. This one damn sure ran. The little doe was gone as well. It's well known you don't immediately chase after a deer that you've wounded with a bowshot. You wait for them to lie down and bleed out. If you hit the deer in a good spot, they will all do this. So I figured this was a good time to fire up that joint. As I fired it up, I thought things couldn't be more perfect. The blind was in a good spot. The wind was good. I waited for the right deer. The shot was clean. Now to wait. And I did., for about 45 minutes. The joint was burnt down to a roach. Out of my pocket came my empty 35 mm film canister. I put the roach in it and put it back in my pocket.

I put my arrow back in the quiver and left my bow in the blind. This was my first hit on a deer with a bow and I was waiting to see what had happened. I walked to the place where the arrow struck my deer.

I was amazed. The blood was in the trees, on the ground, everywhere. The blood trail was very clear. As I followed the blood trail I heard a sound like only an arrow makes when you kick it. I looked down and there it was—my broken arrow, blood soaked, feathers soaked. I stood up and looked ahead. There it was, not more than twenty yards from the hit. As I walked to the little buck, I could see he was lifeless with a big strawberry on the base of its neck. I rolled him over and spotted another one on the other side. For the first time I understood how deadly a bow and arrow could be. Since then I've killed probably eight to ten whitetails and one 250-pound black bear.

Chapter Nine
## THE DRIVE TO REPEAT

We had over 120 practice jumps before the 1975 U.S. Nationals in Tahlequah, Oklahoma. We didn't have to compete at the Conference Meet in 1975 because we had won the U.S. Nationals the year before. Plus we also won the first World Cup of Relative Work in 1974. In South Africa the world meet was called the World Cup, but in 1975 it was changed to the World Championships. I don't know why except that was how the FAI did it. So this year it was the World Championships and I wanted it really bad. Still married, my wife would ask me how much longer would I do this and I said I didn't know. That was the truth because I didn't. How could I answer that question? All I knew was, I wanted this.

I would deliver auto parts during the week and on weekends travel down to Athens—about a three hour drive one way. I'd practice Saturday and Sunday and then drive back. I did this all summer until July.

The Nationals were held in Tahlequah and went on for a week. We were at our prime. Our skydiving skills were honed to a fine edge and we expected to win. We drove out to Oklahoma and got set up in the dorms, registered and made a couple of practice jumps. There were quite a few 4-way teams and, rumor had it, a top grade team from Florida and the Golden Knights, along with a couple of other hot teams. This year we didn't have to bother with the 10-way event. That was great. We wouldn't be distracted.

We had made all the practice jumps we needed and like I said, we knew we were ready. Green County, Ohio was another good team we'd need to beat. They were third in 1974 and had made a lot of practice jumps. Of course, everybody knew we were back and ready to kick ass. We had posted really good times in our practice jumps, so we intimidated a lot of them. We were having fun.

The next day, the officials held the competition briefing in the morning and then drew the rounds. I can't remember what the order was but we started out in the lead and hell, we were in first after every round but one. We jumped from C-182s and that's what we practiced out of before the meet. Not to brag, but we weren't surprised when we captured our second straight National Championship.

There was a pretty good fight for first in the speed 10-way. *Captain Hook's Sky Pirates* from California ended up winning. So everything was set for the U.S. in the world meet.

Now this was what was called the "on year." From then forward the World Championships would be held every other year. The World Cup would happen during the "off year". Our whole trip was paid for including luggage, clothing, jumpsuits, and helmets—all with the USPA insignia. We didn't change a thing because we had our fall rate down and all the other things that come with staying in sync while doing the back loop and coming out on heading and altitude.

We would get to keep all of the goodies, but the best part was that we were given enough money to make 80 practice jumps. We used every dime, plus we had access to a video ground-to-air camera on a gun turret. This was the new state of the art judging machine and a big, big learning tool. You could mark on the monitor after the 4-way was built and see who was out of place after the back loop. This was a cool way to tell. Up until then, all we had was our own debriefing.

We did make all 80 jumps and our team was as tight as tight could be. We were coming off three big wins: 1974 Nationals, 1974 World Cup, and 1975 Nationals, and now here we were heading to the 1975 World Championships of

Skydiving in Warendorf, Germany, to be held out of Bell UH-1H Huey helicopters. Damn, this was going to be fun! We were going to take our wives to Germany with us, which was a little bit of a distraction. They would meet us in Warendorf. We were traveling on a military flight for families of military personnel there and back. The wives flew commercial.

Before departing for Germany, the USPA decided to send us to Lakehurst, New Jersey for a week of practice out of Huey helicopters. Now for 4-way, the change to Hueys didn't really matter but in 10-way, it was a big deal because it was a no show exit and you needed good forward speed of the aircraft. That's what they used for the relative wind. Also, the exit was out of the right side door and all our practice was from a left side door. Everything was a little bit backwards. All the 4-way team had to do was freefly our 4-way together and then set up for the back loop. The meet was from an altitude of 10,500 feet, so that was a piece of cake for us.

When we got to the Lakehurst Naval Air Station, the site of the Hindenburg tragedy, we were under the supervision of our team leader from the USPA. I was excited to make our practice jumps from the helicopter—that was an aircraft I had always wanted to jump. We picked up an alternate when we were at the Nationals—a guy from Spokane, Washington, Craig Fronk. Craig had been part of a very competitive 4-man team called *Bunkey-Rocky-Herman-Fronk*. Earlier in 1975 the team's plane crashed on the side of a mountain killing two of the team members. Another was paralyzed, and Craig had been hospitalized for a month. I knew Fronk from the competition the year before when their team finished second behind us. Well, after winning in 1975 Nationals, we didn't have an alternate so the four of us chose Fronk because we'd seen how good he was in the 4-way event.

At Lakehurst all five of us participated in the practice jumps. We would ride to altitude, and the alternate would follow us out, dock 5th and then drop out. We would back loop and then go into our next maneuver. Basically this was just a bunch of 4-way fun jumps. We would climb out on the skid, back loop off it, and then into the hookup to the 5-way. When we landed, we would go over to the packing area to pack.

The base had a skydiving club and a few of the club members were hanging out and watching us. One of the members, a girl, caught my eye. She was just plain beautiful—blonde hair, blue eyes, and beautiful body features. I started a conversation with her and found out she was from Colorado. After we made a couple more jumps I chatted with her some more, and then we parted ways. The next morning we were back at it. When we landed, there she was. I laid my parachute down and we started to talk, and then she asked if she could help me pack my parachute. "Of course," I said. I asked her if she would like to go out for a walk in the evening, and she said yes. Well, I was married, but I said to myself, *Self, we're just going out to chat and that's okay.*

*Captain Hook's Sky Pirates* team was having one hell of a time at Lakehurst trying to get their exit down. That's the tricky part in speed 10-way. That base has to go out stable and on a heading so everything can be slot perfect. No. 1 problem was getting the air speed. The chopper could only get them 70 mph; they liked 90. Plus the other thing giving them a fit was going out the right side. This was part of the exit problem. Make 500 or 600 jumps going out of the left side and then change to the right, and your perspective is 180 degrees out of whack. And these two things were getting the best of them—to a point where they were starting to argue and point the finger at each other. We remarked to each other about how the 10-way team was starting to fall apart. We didn't like it because we were all on the same team—the U.S. Team. Meanwhile everything was running smooth with our 4-way. Choppers are easy to spot from. When you look down, you can really look down; it's a very clear view. I think we did 15 practice jumps out of the Huey.

We all had matching suits and U.S. team luggage, and we looked good. I was hoping that this flight would be shorter than the South Africa flight and, of course, it was. Before we took off, Craig gave me a 10 mg valium so I could sleep. I slept all the way to Frankfurt. We transferred in Frankfurt from the C-141 that carried us from the U.S. and boarded a Sikorsky S-64 Skycrane helicopter with a troop carrier box. Once all were on board, I was sitting next to Al Krueger. He was captain of the *Captain Hook's Sky Pirates* 10-way team and had an artificial arm—his very personal contribution to the war in Vietnam. Cool guy. I fell asleep on his shoulder like a little boy leaning on his daddy.

We landed in Warendorf, the location of the World Championships. We walked out of the tailgate, and all eyes were on us. Our hosts had set up the competition area as a half moon of tents, and as we started toward the American tent, I looked around and saw all the tents flying their country's flag. I was shocked. There were twice as many teams as the year before in Pretoria. Twenty-eight countries. Yes. Good competition. The same French team was here. I wanted to kick their ass—just like my teammates Sam, Don, and Ken. We still hadn't forgotten their protest against us.

Everything was now in place. It had been a long two weeks of traveling and training but now was the time. Bell UH-1H Hueys lined the perimeter. Emblems of the German army and air force were marked on their sides. It reminded me of the days when my dad and I sat in front of our TV and watched *Twelve o'clock High* with Robert Stack and *Combat* with Vic Morrow. Pretty damn cool to be in the country that my dad and his brothers fought against in World War II. This was one more thing that drove my competitive spirit to the level that it would take to win this championship.

After greeting our wives, we took our gear to our U.S. tent and I'll be damned if Chet Poland, the old jumper in the van from back home wasn't there. This old guy was a relic and was at just about every parachute meet—Z-hills Turkey Meet, the U.S. Nationals, the Freak Brothers Convention. At all of these events, he was there with his big Dodge Maxi selling souvenirs—pins, patches, magazines, and jewelry. He was about 75 or so and looking more frail. When I saw him in Germany, he was down to about 110 pounds. His hair was white as snow and he always wore a bandana. His body was loaded with parachute tattoos. I never knew what he had done in his life, but I could tell that he had a few jumps under his belt. We put our gear in the tent and didn't have to worry about it—Chet was watching it.

We were told all the dorms were full, and Joyce and I were going to stay at a guesthouse—a pretty common type of lodging in Germany. This was way better because it was in town, and I would have a chance to see a little of how the German people lived. I was 23 at the time. This was my second time overseas, so I felt a little more comfortable traveling abroad than the first time when Rick and I went to Pretoria. We left the drop zone and met the owner of the guesthouse who showed us our room. The bed was great. The headboard was solid wood and handmade. The mattress was perfect—not too hard and not too soft. On top of the bed was a down comforter that was at least 10 inches thick. The pillows were the same. I felt like I was sleeping on a cloud.

When I woke the next morning I was well rested and hungry. I looked forward to eating a huge plate of ham and eggs and hash browns. My jaw dropped when the only food I saw on the breakfast table in the dining was slices of cheese, salami, ham, and other food I couldn't even identify. A basket of hard rolls was there, also. I was pissed. How was I expected to exist on this crap? I made a ham and cheese sandwich, drank some orange juice, and that was it. Out the door and waiting to get picked up, I bitched to my poor wife. I learned later that this was a traditional German breakfast. Now, I'm not saying the food in Germany was all bad. At the meet there were vendors that sold brats and pommes frites—french fries. Damn, they were good, and I ate little else while I was there. Heck—I was just a farm boy from Michigan!

The van picked us up, and I saw that Sam and Don also had their wives with them. I said, "How are we gonna exist on this crap they are feeding us?" They said to quit bitching and shut up. I did. We went out to the drop zone and started to mingle with the competitors—the English, the Australians, the Swedes, even the French. The French had made one replacement. I figured that was a good thing for us in that it would break up the camaraderie of their team. I turned out to be right.

We got to make a couple of practice jumps. In 1974, our times were in the 5-7 second range. This year we were consistently in the 4-5 second range. This was going to be our meet and we knew it. We started out good and kept up a good pace. This was a 10-round meet and we were ahead after every round. I think there was only one round that we scored below the high score. We dominated and led everybody else, including the French, by four seconds. Four seconds was nuts. Then it rained for two days and nobody jumped. We were now in the final day of competition.

*Captain Hook's Sky Pirates* team was having their ups and downs, still trying to get their 10-way exit down. At one point, they were arguing amongst themselves so bad that it was tearing the inner core of the team apart. Our team told them to concentrate on their problem at hand, and that was the base. Even though the base was having problems, the divers could still get down into position so when the base did form, the divers were in place. They took our advice and from round six closed the gap on the leaders. They squeaked ahead in round 10 and won their event on the final day.

We still had to do round 10 of the 4-way. Like I said, it had rained two days. On the second day at three in the afternoon, we got the call that the competition would resume. "First call for U.S.A. 4-way." We were all there but Ken. Where was Ken? Second call for U.S. 4-way team—still no Ken.

Sam told Craig, "Get your rig and get ready." Third and final call for the U.S.A. 4-way team. No Ken. Fronk started to gear up when Ken came running. No one said shit to him. We all walked to the loading area. We bent down to simulate our 4-way position before the back loop. Sam said, "Let's set a world record." All four of us smiled, slapped five and climbed in the chopper. The ride to altitude was quick, as it had been for the first nine rounds. The exit was smooth—smoother than any before. I recall sitting in the 4-way, smiling as Sam gave the count. The release and my back loop were so smooth, and the other three must have been the same, because we came back together so perfect it was as if we never let go. Smooth. We always said smooth makes fast, and it did. We got down and waited for the time. It came in at 3.2. Damn, that was a world record! Never had anyone turned in that kind of time. We won the gold. Gold overall and a new world record. It couldn't have been better.

I'll always remember the awards ceremony. Three sets of podiums for first, second, and third places were set up with three flag poles behind each for the national flags of the medal winners. We all wore our team suit coats and we stood on that podium so tall, so proud. We were called up twice to get the gold. Both times the national anthem played. I remember bending down to receive my medal with a million things racing through my mind, most of all how all our hard work had paid off in more than one way. I thought to myself, *we are one hell of a bad ass team. We are the best there is. We are the WORLD CHAMPIONS OF THE 4-WAY EVENT!* Then we stood next to *Captain Hook's Sky Pirates* team as we were awarded the medals for the overall champions. The National Anthem rang out again as we bent forward to receive the overall gold. Yes, the U.S. had the best relative work skydivers in the world. No one could dispute it.

Cliff and John, skydiver friends who were part of our *Beechnuts* 10-way team in 1974, had come to Germany to watch the meet and hang out with us. With the meet over and our championship secured, we all planned to meet in Locarno, Switzerland, in the Swiss Alps to jump at the Locarno drop zone. We—John, Cliff, my wife and I—were going to travel by train. We all had rail passes. This meant we could ride any train anywhere in Europe. I had never seen mountains and was eager to see the Swiss Alps. Not only to see them, but to be able to freefall next to them was just plain awesome.

Departure day came and we hauled all our stuff to the train. We had a lot of baggage so it took a good team effort to load and unload. We rode the train to somewhere in southern Germany. The train stopped; we unloaded and got off as the train rolled down the tracks, and we waited for our connecting train to Switzerland.

I heard Cliff say to John, "You got our bag with our rail passes and traveler's checks and passports?" John said, "No, I thought you had it."

Well, neither one of them had the bag. It was still on the train, never to be seen again. Cliff and John then had to head to Berlin to the U.S. Embassy to get new passports. They also had to get their travelers' checks and rail passes replaced. After they realized that their documents and checks were gone, we parted ways. Joyce and I rode the train on to Locarno. The scenery was spectacular. Absolutely breathtaking.

When we arrived in Locarno we took a taxi to the drop zone. It was the first time I had seen a Pilatus PC-6 Porter plane. What a jump plane. All turbine and one badass airframe. Air America used this airplane in Laos and Cambodia during the early 1960s. It looked like a Cessna 180 but bigger. The whole 4-way team was there, and the drop zone manager, Urs Frischknecht, took us to jump. Urs gave us a ride through the mountains like no other—flying straight at sheer cliffs and pulling up at the last instant, almost straight up into a stall before turning the airplane sideways to recover over a steep valley. Hell, the flight was way better than the jump.

At the end of the day Urs took us to a restaurant up on the side of the mountain that faced the drop zone. The restaurant was famous to the locals as they could watch the jumpers in freefall drop past the restaurant. Too cool. We spent a couple of days there. Eventually John and Cliff got their problems solved and also made it down to Locarno. I was glad that it all worked out for them.

Joyce and I left Locarno and headed to Barcelona, Spain. Another long train ride. Barcelona was really dirty and the people were all poor, or at least that's what I saw. There were probably better parts but getting off the train you really have to know where you want to go, and we didn't. We spent a short time there and headed back to Luxembourg, where we met up with Sam and his wife to get ready to fly out for home early the next day. We wanted one more night to remember our championship trip to Europe, so we sent our wives off to catch their commercial flight back to the U.S., and Sam and I went downtown to a local topless bar. We had about eight hours to kill before our departure to the U.S. on a military flight.

We left the bar and made it to the military base, reeking of alcohol. We got on our flight to head home. The C-141 had no insulation, and the damn thing was cold. I was sick and hung over all the way home. It sucked. So then we were back home with two gold medals but no money. This was a good thing, but it had taken a lot of time and effort. And now it was done.

I went back to work in Saginaw driving the auto parts delivery truck and doing the married thing, but it just wasn't me. Joyce and I weren't getting along and decided to split. I grabbed my rig and some clothes and went to the bus station. It was about 9 p.m. I called my friend Rick to pick me up at the bus station in Three Rivers. The bus arrived about 1 a.m., and he took me to my mom and dad's house. They weren't real happy, but they left me alone.

Chapter Ten

## DC, REDSKINS, AND
## FAREWELL TO MY HERO

I suppose it's no surprise that it was a woman who led me to live somewhere other than Michigan for the first time. With my marriage over, my mind started wandering back to Marcia, the blonde I'd met at the Lakehurst Naval Air Station during the fall of 1975 while training for the World Championships. She was a very pretty girl—tall, blonde, blue eyes, great figure. Marcia was still in the Navy and stationed in Suitland, Maryland. I knew how to get in touch with her, and I did. It didn't take long for me to decide to go to Washington, DC. I had never been to DC before, and Marcia had an apartment close by in Forestville, Maryland, so it seemed like a fun new adventure. I decided to just go and see what happened.

Well, I didn't have any money, and I needed to get some. I took a job on a garbage truck, hanging on the back and running out to get the trash, then bringing it back to dump it in the compactor, and then running the can back. What a stinking job. Anyway, it was money. After two weeks, I had saved enough money to get a flight to DC. I booked it and left. Marcia picked me up at the airport and away we went.

I spent a week or so looking for work. I remember having only a nickel in my pocket during that week, and that was it. I finally got a part time job at a furniture store as a janitor four days before Christmas. The owners were Kenny and his partner, Art. They were old friends from school. Both of them were real cool, young—only a couple of years older than me. I remember Kenny driving me in his car somewhere, and I could smell pot as soon as I got in. Then I glanced in his ash tray and it was full of roaches. After a while he and I even started smoking pot together.

Marcia had to work on Christmas Eve, so there I was stuck in our little apartment by myself. I had a portable radio, a pint of rotgut vodka, and some orange pop wondering how the hell a world champion had ended up in a situation like this. But it had been my choice, so I sat there and focused my thoughts on the things I was going to do in the future. I also thought about the young couple next door, recently married, the wife ready to have a baby—thinking that for them a baby was a heck of a good Christmas present. I got up Christmas day, and Marcia was just getting in from work. She was talking to me about how screwed up everything was and how being broke was a bitch. She went to bed while I stayed up that day working on restoring an old antique dresser she had.

A few days after Christmas we met the couple with their new baby coming out of their apartment. We stopped to chat with them, and I said, "Let me see the little thing." They pulled the blanket off of her face—she was so tiny. She brought her little hands to her mouth and that's when I saw—her one hand was deformed. Missing several fingers. My heart sank. I had to walk away while Marcia continued to talk with the couple. I thought about God and how he was supposed to be so all-powerful. But then if he was, why would he do this to such an innocent and beautiful little girl? I thought about how this would affect her future. When she was old enough to date boys, what would they think about her hand?

Over the years when I thought of how cruel life could be, and how bad I thought my life was at times, the picture of that beautiful little baby often came back to me. But as bad as I sometimes felt, still no tears came to my eyes. I often wondered what was wrong with me because I could never cry.

After New Year's I got a second job at a 7-11 near our

apartment. Yes. Now I had two jobs—9 a.m. to 3 p.m. at the furniture store; 3 p.m. to 11 p.m. at 7-11. I started to bank a little money.

I went out and bought a real NFL football and would go out next to the furniture store to practice punting when I needed to get out of our small apartment. I knew that I still had a gift, and sometimes when I kicked it good, the ball would spiral so clean, so true, so far, so high. I started to time the kicks, and on the good ones I could get at least five seconds hang time and a distance of 60 yards. That was at least as good as the professional kickers and better than many. I thought I might have what it took—I just needed a chance. As luck would have it, George Allen was head coach for the Washington Redskins, and during the spring of 1976 he announced the team was holding a free agent tryout camp. I was excited at the possibility, but the camp was still a ways off, which gave me time to deal with my personal issues.

My mom told me on the phone that my dad was sick, and they really didn't know what was wrong. I made arrangements with my boss at the furniture store to take time off. Kenny said to go back home and spend time with my dad. Marcia was driving out to Colorado to see her family, and so on the way out she dropped me off in Michigan. She met mom and dad and my younger brother Mike, and then headed out on her own to Colorado. Dad was starting to get more sick. The doctors thought that he might have cancer.

As always, skydiving was never far out of my mind. The *Rainbow Flyers* were going to the Nationals again this year. We had won the 1974 and 1975 Nationals and the 1974 and 1975 World Championships. Now our 4-man team was planning to compete in our third Nationals. Ken's drop zone in Athens was just down the road from Three Rivers, 25 minutes away, and that made it easy to get to practice. We were so polished and confident. This was going to be our meet and all four of us knew it.

During this time Dad started going for chemotherapy. His hair fell out and he was real sick from the treatments. I had to push him around in a wheelchair. Sometimes I would pick him up in my arms to carry him from his wheelchair to my truck. So many times he had picked me up as a child—so many times, and now it was me picking him up in my arms. This was a moment in my life I wish I could erase. The thought of my father—so strong, so smart, the man who set the standards in my life—seeing him deteriorate day after day. I was there without question to be his legs, his life—what was left?

One day during that period my friend Chimp and I were sitting under the apple tree with my old man—the tree that so many times produced the sucker limbs that the old man would tear off in anger to switch me, my sister, and little brother. On this day, the tree was full of apples and shaded us from the afternoon sun. It was quiet. We sat and bullshitted about the old days when Chimp used to work in our asparagus patch as a young boy. My dad looked at Chimp and said, "Chimp, you got any of that pot?"

Our jaws dropped as far as they could. Chimp said, "Yeah, Bungy. I got some. Why?"

"Well, roll one of those marijuana cigarettes. I want to try it before I die!"

Chimp rolled up a big fat joint and fired it up. He took a big pull and passed it to me, and I did the same. I passed it to Dad, and it seemed like he knew what to do without instruction. He inhaled and pulled a big hit into his lungs. And as quick as it went in, it came out. Coughing and coughing, he said, "Goddamn, this shit is terrible. How in the world can you kids smoke this shit?"

We told him to relax and that it would get easier. Dad hit the joint again and coughed again and said, "What the hell." Chimp and I coughed and laughed. Pop said, "Forget that shit."

Throughout my life I always knew my dad was one hell of a dad. He was the best there was, none better. I loved my dad like nobody else. He stood so tall, so strong, so real. I felt good that I was his son. At that moment I finally realized he really did recognize all the things that I had accomplished, and that I had always gone above and beyond for his approval. I also knew that he knew what he meant to me and how hard I worked to be the best I could for him. And I felt at peace—a peace that no one else could understand, a father and son thing that you can't explain. I felt like I had the heaviest of loads off my chest. Finally, I knew. Thank God.

Dad died a couple of weeks later and I was ready, as ready as one can be when they lose their dad. He was only 51 years old. The funeral was like no other. When the services were done, the funeral procession was full of cop cars—more than I or anyone else had ever seen from local to county to state. It was amazing. I still did not cry! What was wrong? Why couldn't I cry?

I was ready, as ready as one could be for the Nationals that year. Our team didn't have nearly as many practice jumps as the previous year, but we had enough. Enough so that when we got to Nationals, we knew this competition would be fun.

We started strong. The Golden Knights, the U.S. Army's parachute team, were trying to beat us—like so many teams— but they had a long way to go. They didn't have two National Championships and two World Championships under their belts. So we—the *Rainbow Flyers*—had an edge. And again we won. Again we walked away National Champions, and again we walked away broke! In any other sport, there would have money to be made.

After that I went back to DC, and Marcia and I separated. I moved into an apartment with my boss Kenny on the 18th floor off of Kenilworth Ave near the 495 beltway that circled DC. I was now the warehouse manager and making good money. I told Kenny and Art that I was going to the free agent tryouts for the Redskins up at Dulles airport. I think that they thought I was nuts. But this was for my dad. I made a vow at his grave that I would try one last time to go to the pros. He knew. He knew better than I.

I got the information about when and where for the tryouts, and I went. Damn, what an experience. When I went to the field house, it was like making a parachute jump—all the paperwork. Many free agents flew in to DC for the tryouts.

We all sat together while George Allen gave a speech. Then it was show time, and that's what I was waiting for. A couple of punters were in front of me. My turn. The first one was good, maybe 50 or so yards. The rest started to rock. It just got better. At one point I was punting the ball over the fence.

The coaches all took notice—enough that I got invited to come back in a month and a half. I drove home thinking about my old man and how good he would have felt about my performance—I know I did.

I went back to work and told Kenny and Art, but I really don't think they believed me. It didn't matter to me. I felt good. I remember the special team coach kept telling me—kick another one. Here, kick this one. When I was done, the coach asked me where I went to college. I told him Ferris State in Michigan. He said he had never heard of it. Not many people had outside of Michigan.

I worked with Kenny in DC for about six more months, and then I went back to Michigan to help my mom out. I did go back to tryouts at Redskin Park, but my performance wasn't that strong. If you're going to be in the pros, they're looking for consistency and after leaving it for so long, I lacked that. I played semi-pro football for a couple of years in Michigan, and that was fun—a lot of fun. Kalamazoo All Stars. I played the 1977 and 1978 seasons. We won the championship in 1977 playing teams from Detroit, Grand Rapids, Indianapolis, and Racine, Wisconsin—pretty good teams. But we played in the summers, and it got in the way of skydiving.

## Chapter Eleven
## THE BIRTH OF ACCELERATED FREEFALL

Well, I was still skydiving in the 4-way but this year's rules changed. They took out the back loop and made the event sequential. You had a set round with five formations. Time started on exit. You had 45 seconds of working time. We went to the Nationals and only placed 6th or 7th, and that was it for me. I put my rig in the closet and quit for a couple of years. I was burned out.

One day I was out at Austin Lake drop zone hanging out. I wanted to jump so I asked Van my friend Van if I could borrow his rig. Borrowed gear is a "no no", and here is why. I put on Van's rig and went up on a jump. We did a 4-way sequential and after we broke off, I tracked off. When it came time to open—Van's rig was an old hand deploy with the belly band—I reached in to pull the pilot chute and found it hard to pull out. I tugged at it a couple of times and then reached in with both hands and tried again. I got it out and when I threw it, it wrapped around my wrist. *Fuck no!* I had a pilot chute around my wrist. The pilot chute was inflated and I was trying to get the damned thing off of my wrist. I messed with it and messed with it. I lost track of time. I knew that I was chewing up the altitude but was engrossed trying to get the damned thing off. I looked down and the ground was rushing up like I had never seen before. I knew I was low. How low? *Lower than I had ever been.*

Back in the old days at Z-hills, we would freefall to 1500 feet, to 1200 feet, even to 1000 feet looking for that thing that you had heard from other jumpers called "ground rush." Well, here it was. Ground rush like I had never experienced. I thought, *Damn, I wonder if this is going to hurt.* But I didn't give up. I knew I had about five feet of bridal above me, and if I pulled my reserve it had a good chance of tangling up, so I reached up and grabbed a handful of bridal and pulled it down. I tipped down head first and grabbed my reserve ripcord. I didn't have to look for it. I came across with the same hand that had my bridal twisted around it. I could feel the steel. I grabbed it and pulled it out and down. *Whack!* My round reserve found the clean air and opened. The reserve oscillated twice and I landed. I knew that I must have been at 300 feet or so. I landed no more than three seconds after opening. I remember after the canopy opened, I looked out and saw the sun shining over the lake all big and orange. *That is low!* Did my life flash before my eyes? None of that; I just wondered if it was going to hurt when I hit the ground. I got back up to the drop zone quickly. Everybody came running out to see what had happened. I still had that damn pilot chute wrapped around my arm. On the ground it took probably 20 seconds to get it off my wrist. Scared? No time to be scared, only to act.

In 1979 Sam called me and said that Ken had talked to him about a brand new student program that he was developing. He said that instead of the old static line training method, the instructor would take a student to 10,500 feet, hang on to them, and then launch a three piece off the step. Then the instructor would have the student do three practice pulls and at 3,500 feet, the student would actually pull the ripcord. I thought this was a cool way to teach. I had over 3,000 jumps at this time, and at least 2,700 were relative work jumps.

Sam got the seven-level training outline from Ken, and he and I started to train students using what is now known as Accelerated Freefall (AFF) in May 1979. Our first two students were Pat Hagen and Pete Meyer. Sam and I trained them just like Ken described in his new program. The first student was Pat. This guy was a natural skydiver. When you had been in the sport as long as I had, you could tell. I knew Pat would be a good one. We started his Level 1 AFF training out of a C-182 at Austin Lake. We had the gear Ken suggested. We bought a Strong Enterprises student tandem harness, a PC for the main, and a 26-foot Navy conical for the reserve. We had a Sentinel auto opener on the reserve. For its time, it was the state of the art.

We got Pat geared up, and Bruce Dillon (still around after all these years) took us up to 10,500 feet. Pat got it all. Sam was the primary instructor and I was the secondary. Sam gave Pat an introduction to spotting and Pat was eating it up. That day the wind was light and variable. He called the cut straight up and told Pat to put his feet out after me. Sam climbed out. Pat did as he was instructed and swung his feet into position. After Pat got into place, his feet on the step, his hands on the lower part of the strut, I picked up a grip on the top of his rig and on the corner of his harness down on the right side bottom of his container. He checked in and said it just like Ken wrote. I said, "Climb out." His right hand came up and over Sam's left. When he made the motion to go out, Sam reached in and picked up a leg strap grip. Pat got out and into his position. His chin up and over the leading edge of the strut. Left foot on the step and trailing the right. He then checked in saying it verbally, "Check in." I said "Okay." He then looked to Sam and said, "Check out." Sam said, "Okay."

At that moment he looked straight ahead and said verbally, "Up, down, arch!" and as he stepped off, as he was taught, he went off at a 45 degree angle from the aircraft so he didn't tear off the inside jumpmaster. Pat did a "circle of awareness" (COA)—looking at the ground below, his altimeter, his secondary instructor, me, and then at his primary instructor, Sam, for certain hand signals. Then Pat started his practice pulls as he was trained—*Look - Reach - Pull - Relax*; *Look - Reach - Pull - Relax*; *Look - Reach - Pull - Relax*. After the last practice pull, Pat checked the ground again, his altimeter, the ground, his altimeter, and repeating that until he reached 5,500 feet and gave a flash of his hands, opening and closing them twice to indicate that he had altitude awareness. He focused on his altimeter until 4,000 feet, and then, *Look - Reach - Pull* and count one thousand, two thousand, three thousand, and so on until line stretch.

When the student would pull, the secondary instructor released and the primary instructor rode out the pull. Back in 1979, Sam and I didn't have any radios so we used the arrow to guide in our student. Pat landed pretty close to the pea gravel. All in all, it was a perfect jump. We gave him a good debrief and passed him to his AFF Level 2.

Well, Sam and I were ready to take Pete up for his training. We got him suited up and took him for his AFF Level 1. We took off and climbed to altitude. Sam and I did exactly what we did with Pat. The only thing difference was that Pete didn't get up and over the strut and when we left the plane, he got behind us and rolled us around. Sam and I didn't have much experience getting out of this situation, so we rode it and rode it and finally got stable—but we were so low that poor Pete never had time to do anything. All he had time to do was pull. His canopy control was not as good as Pat's, but he still landed on the airport grounds. Sam and I ran through the jump in debriefing but we still had no idea why this happened. I do know now. After thousands of AFF jumps, I learned what to expect.

After Pete rolled Sam and I around on exit, we started to think that Ken's new program could seriously get out of hand. The next time we jumped with Pete and Pat, we decided to land in some big fields out south of Austin Lake. We didn't have a big ground crew, and Sam and I didn't want our students in the lake. At this time, AFF Level 2 was leg awareness. After the three dummy ripcord pulls, the student would extend their legs, out and then in, and would notice the pitch change, and then, *look, reach, pull.* This is the way it was done.

Pat put on his jumpsuit and got a briefing on spotting along with the new dive flow. We climbed in Bruce's C-182 and away we went. Pat sat with his back to the panel. At 6,000 feet, Sam ran him through the dive; at 9,000 feet helmet and goggles. At the time, we were throwing wind drift indicators. Sam had already thrown the WDI and he and Pat watched it together and picked out the opening point. Now in spotting, you have two different points. You have the exit point and the opening point. The two are completely different. I've sat in on recent AFF jumps and noticed that this very important part of skydiving was not being taught. The GPS, and red and green lights have taken its place.

When you teach spotting correctly to the student, the student will have an understanding of the wind, and wind line. Just look and see how many skydivers kill themselves under a good solid canopy. This is directly related to a misunderstanding of what the wind is doing. With square canopies getting smaller, faster and more maneuverable, many people assume that's the main reason tragedies occur. But too often, it's not the canopy; it's the person under it that is the real reason.

Back to Pat and his Level 2 jump.. Sam has him all set. He is in the door; they are on jump run. Pat's head is out and Sam is spotting. With the first two levels, the student just observes his JM spotting the aircraft. He doesn't do anything but watch, although he does understand what's taking place. Sam gives Bruce the corrections and cries out, "Cut!" He then looks to Pat, "Put your feet out after me." Pat swings his feet out and places them in front of the gear leg and puts his left hand on the strut and his right hand in the corner of the door. He checks in to me, and I say, "Climb out." I pass my grip to Sam and he picks Pat up on his harness. Pat gets into his position—chest on the strut forward, trailing the right leg. Check in to me verbally saying the words. I say, "Okay," and then check out to Sam. Sam says, "Okay." Looking straight ahead it's up, down and then arch. The count is verbal for a reason: It gets all three of us in sync.

Sam and I learned from the bad exit with Pete. We would keep the student forward as if we had an out of sync exit, and we still could see him beginning to leave and would go with the student. Pat had the exit down. After he jumped all three of us came off the step. Get off smooth, finish smooth. Pat had good awareness and would start his "circle of awareness", or COA—a term used in AFF training meaning to observe your heading, read your altimeter, and look to your jumpmaster for any hand signals. After that Pete's three dummy ripcord pulls were clean. He had plenty of time for his leg awareness. He noticed his pitch change, and his altitude check was right on the money. Then came a good clean pull with a good one thousand, two thousand, and so on counting to his parachute deployment. Sam released and tracked down, and I rode out the opening. Again Pat landed in the field we had marked with a white sheet. This landing area was a lot better because we didn't have to worry about the lake. Pat stood up and cried out, "Yahoo!" Sam and I felt good that we could take someone new like Pat up and watch him excel.

After his jump we showed him how to field pack his parachute and walk in. This also is important. I have talked to instructors who had their student break a foot or leg on the way back from their jump. That would suck. I always taught my students all the things they needed to make their jump safely.

Now it was Pete's turn. Sam and I ran him through the exit a lot of times so he had it down good. He didn't want an unstable exit and neither did we. This time Pete did a good job. He went through his Level 2, no problem.

Now Pat wanted to complete his Level 3. Sam had the outline form as Ken had written it. We were all new to this and each level became a little more complex. So we moved carefully, sticking exactly to what Ken had detailed. So while Pat got the briefing from Sam, reading it from Ken's outline, I was getting it for the first time, too. I was as new to this game as everybody involved. As Sam was looking at instructing this new training, I was looking into what Level 3 was all about and saw that this was a cool thing.

Now the way Level 3 went was exit, check, slow circle, one dummy ripcord pull, swing to a three-way, and the student again practices legs out and legs in. At 4,000 feet the instructor moves into position for the pull and everything else is the same. Don't forget this is 1979, and Level 3 has changed since.

Pat did great. This time on the ride to altitude he participated in the spotting. Pat was actually telling Sam the corrections, and Sam would tell Bruce, the pilot. The time came for the cut, and Sam told him to cut. Again Sam said, "Put your feet out after me." Pat swung into the door, left hand on the strut and right hand in the corner of the door. Check in to me, climb out, put right arm over Sam's, and Sam picks up the grip. Pat over the leading edge trailing his right leg. Up, down, arch. Exit was good and clean. Circle good. One dummy ripcord pull. Sam and I moved to the three-way. Legs out. Short circle, actually. Pat could see us good out front. Legs out, okay, legs in, okay, neutral, altimeter, heading, altimeter, heading, 5,500 feet flash, 4,000 feet, look, reach, pull, count, perfect, just perfect. Pat's canopy control was great. Pete was gone that day so I took Pat up on his Level 4. Again, Sam and I were taking this step-by-step from Ken's outline.

This was the very first accelerated freefall training ever done outside of Florida—I think Ken had trained less than five students—and so the training method was very new. All the jumps that we made were shared with Ken as research for the development of the AFF program.

Ken, like I said, had trained four or five students down in DeLand, Florida. Ken worked for Ted Strong at Strong Enterprises in Orlando as his shop foreman. Ken hooked up with longtime owner/operator of the drop zone—the DeLand Sport Parachute Center—in DeLand, Florida, Gary Dupuis. Gary had owned "Mr. Douglas," a well-known DC-3 that at that time everybody in skydiving knew. After Gary had tired of the airplane, he sold out his share but kept the drop zone. He was the one who inspired Ken to come up with this new concept of AFF.

In the 1960s static line progression training was the training method. If a student was stuck on 10 second delays, the instructor would go out with a hand hold and let the student go once they got to terminal. And they did take note of one thing—once the student was at terminal, they had way more control. Once they did that for a couple of jumps, they had no more problems. So Ken and Gary really are the ones who came up with the concept. Gary let Ken do it at his drop zone. I'm sure that Ken wrote the scenario of the seven levels, but I'm also sure that Gary gave him a lot of input. Ken also worked with others who gave him input. In May of 1979, like I said, he sent Sam the lesson plan, and that's where I'm at now in the story.

Now Pat was on Level 4 and so was Pete. We would work with them separately. Sam took Pat, and I took Pete. By now, these guys could spot a little so we let them go on their own. We took them to a drop zone in Michigan. Sam got down with Pat and gave me a thumbs up. I knew Pat would smoke it. Now Pete and I had our turn on a Level 4. This was his fourth jump. I had him check his gear and gear up under my supervision. Once we got our gear on, we did a practice scenario and then got on the plane. At 6,000 feet I checked his gear again. At 9,000 feet we went through the jump; at 10,500 feet the door came open, and Pete started to spot. He called the cut, and I told him to put his feet out. He swung his feet out and put them on the step. Then he said, "Check in." I told him to climb out. Again, I kept him over that leading edge because I didn't want him to roll me around. I said, "Okay." He looked forward and gave a good up, down and arch.

After the exit he did a short circle—ground, altimeter, secondary. After this I would grip switch to a front position. I gave him the relax signal and let him go. Now this is the one thing that I wonder about. I knew that as long as I had a grip on the student, I was okay—I was in control. It was at the point of release that I didn't really know what to expect. Well, now I was going to find out. When I let Pete go, he started to wobble and turn involuntarily—not fast but definitely out of control.

I flew up and grabbed him. When you grab a student like Pete you can feel the tension in both of you. And this being my first Level 4, I really didn't know this. I learned that from the thousands of AFF jumps that I did after those early days. I stopped Pete. Checked altitude. So did he. I gave him the relax signal. We were at about 7,000 feet. I released him, and again he started to spin. I flew up and grabbed him. He checked his altitude and *look, reach, and pull.*

I tipped up on my head and practiced my straight down

dive position because I knew if I was going to start doing this, I needed that skill. Tight and straight and head down, I ate up the altitude. I fell upside down until I started to get a little ground rush and pulled. Hell, I hardly even slowed down for the pull. When my canopy was fully open, I checked my altitude—somewhere around 1,600 feet. I liked getting down quickly so I could watch Pete's canopy control. Pete was better than Pat under the canopy, but Pat was definitely better in freefall. I met Pete in the packing area as he put his rig down and got it ready to pack. And that was another thing we taught our students—how to pack. It builds confidence in the student when they know how to pack, and it also gives them a better understanding of their equipment.

I talked to Sam about Pete's jump. We decided to do the jump again. Now understand this, a lot of what a student learns is the feedback that he gets from the instructor. The student doesn't know what really goes on. They are pretty much loaded up with fear and adrenaline. You replace the fear with knowledge. I really had no idea what to tell him at that moment; I did know he was scared. If it was today, I would tell him that there's only four things that it takes to skydive. I'm talking here about freefall, not parachuting. Parachuting is when you are under your canopy. Pete did do the jump again, successfully, and needless to say, Pat and Pete both graduated. It took Pete nine jumps to get off student status and Pat six. I was amazed. Both bought gear, and Pete is still jumping.

The four areas, or primary objectives, begin with altitude awareness and pulling the ripcords in the right order—these first two will save your life. The other two primary objectives are to have stability (three-dimensional) and directional heading control—APSD. This is all it takes to actually freefall in control and save your life. Through so many years of instruction starting with Pete and Pat and thousands of other AFF students, I have refined and simplified the art of freefall skydiving to just these four areas.

Just to highlight this—if you have an AFF student who fails a level, then I guarantee you will find that the area they failed will be one of these four. When you simplify what you are teaching, it gives the student more space to concentrate on the primary goals.

Out of all the four areas in skydiving, the most difficult is directional heading control. This and stability are the tools that a student needs to maintain control. And as they go forward into their skydiving career, these four things will not change. As a professional skydiver, I still need these four tools. This is all it is in freefall skydiving. This is the part of AFF that no one really knows. God knows how I've tried to spread my blood-soaked knowledge that one gains only from hands-on work—actually doing it. It's so sad to work in such a tiny world of arrogance—more so in DeLand, the drop zone that I helped to become what it is. The home plate of AFF. Yes, maybe the geological center spot. No one there was at the real birth of the AFF program, but they like to take the credit. A lot like the USPA. Just stating the facts, and so sad.

I lost one of the best friends anyone could know when Ken passed. He was a one-of-a-kind petrson. He always told me—and made a big point of it—don't sell yourself cheap. Yeah, I agree. After his death Ken's wife gave the rights to the Accelerated Freefall training program to the USPA and to this day, they control the program. Ken might have come up with the original idea but it was put into action and refined with Gary's help, along with mine. Sam, Hoot, TK, Charlie, John, and a couple other people also made significant contributions to the development of the AFF training program. So it wasn't totally Ken. Far from it. Gary was a big part as it was his drop zone, and a lot of the scenarios and the seven levels came about with help from Gary's input. What I'm saying is building the basic structure was a team effort.

Now the actual AFF jumps made in DeLand came down to Hoot and myself. We trained all the new AFF students who came to DeLand in this new way of instruction. Hoot was doing the most. He was a quiet guy who never said much, and didn't like to instruct—but then neither did I. Still, I liked what I was doing well enough, and not too many people could make a living doing skydiving . So I taught as primary, and Hoot would be the secondary. Now Hoot was good, real good. I knew if I had a problem child as I called it, I could count on Hoot to be there. You get a student spinning so fast that they flip upside down and start to tumble and spin at the same time, you don't have much time to catch them and then get them into a controllable situation. You'd better be damned fast and very aware of your surroundings like altitude and your landing spot.

Soon after I moved down to DeLand, when Gary owned the drop zone, I started to work for Ken. He was starting to have some success with getting the AFF program out, not only in the U.S. but also in Europe. We had a guy named Stan working with us in Europe. I don't really know what country he was from, but I think he was German. It really doesn't matter—the fact is, I really couldn't get Ken to do too much as far as the actual jumps; he was too busy trying to get the program out there into the public.

So the actual training of new students fell to me and others I've mentioned. Once I had this guy on a Level 4 jump. As soon as I let him go, he started to spin, and I mean spin rapidly like a ceiling fan on high. I had to get to him before his spin became too out of control. Well, I waited too long. He went into a violent spin so fast that his center of gravity changed, and then he went on his back. When he did that, he started to eat up altitude.

I was head down going straight towards him. I was almost there to his main ripcord. I would have taken the reserve ripcord, it didn't matter. I was so close but yet so far. Every time I would reach to get his ripcord, I would start to float. Well, I was so into it and all I could see from him was a facial expression that said nothing—absolutely nothing. I watched as both his hands came in but didn't grab a thing. Each time they came back out with nothing. Still falling, I made one more attempt. I never thought about my altitude. My goal was to catch him, but I never did. Thankfully his automatic activation device (AAD) fired. I saw his pilot chute release and then I looked at the ground. *It was so close!* I pulled and was open at about 600 feet.

Another time, after Pete and Pat completed all levels, a friend of Pat's started AFF training. He did well on Levels 1 and 2. On Level 3, we thought we'd see if he could hold a heading. We took him out like any other Level 3 student and transitioned to a three-way. He did his pitch control, and then Sam and I let him go. He started to backslide and went on his back. He recovered and got stable, but then again brought his legs up and went on his back again. I chased and chased him. I was so damn close—but not close enough. Again his AAD fired.

When I look back, I'm amazed and proud. We finished training Pat in six jumps, and he was damn good. Six jumps and now he could skydive. I'm talking spotting and all of the tools I described. It was so cool. Now, most people are not like Pat. As a matter of fact, for most people it takes at least eight or nine jumps. It depends on both the instructor and student.

The USPA had no idea what was going on. They might have heard rumors of what we were doing, but when they learned about it in 1981, the organization said that this type of training was going to kill people and would be bad for the sport.

When I lived in Washington, DC, I hooked up with the USPA Executive Director, Bill Ottley. Bill and I were good buddies. We went waterskiing, skydiving, and flying in his Bonanza N-001WW. Bill was a good man to hang out with. We would spend hours sitting in his two million dollar townhouse talking about skydiving, flying, the 1974, 1975, and 1976 Nationals and, of course, the World Meets. When I left DC, Bill still headed up the USPA. Once in a while I would call up the old dude and chat with him. The topic of AFF would come up, and Ottley would tell me that the AFF program would never work and how I needed to STOP doing it. He really and truly thought, as did so many people at that time, that we were going to kill all these students and that AFF would never fly with the USPA. *Well, now look where it's at, Otts* (as he liked to be called by his fraternity buddies at Yale University).

## Chapter Twelve
### DANGER WALKS BESIDE ME

I need to back up to 1978 when I was in a pretty serious car crash. I was going out on opening day of duck season with my skydiving friend John, our baseman from the days of the *Beechnuts*. John was driving, and we went out to a place I knew east of Three Rivers, my hometown in western Michigan. When we reached the spot, we got out our shotguns and then realized that John had brought the wrong shells. That was it. Well, we put our guns back in his car and headed back to his house to get another gun.

When we started to drive down the road, it was raining so John and I took a short cut down Fisher Lake Road. It had an S curve where an old steel girder bridge was. John and I were headed right for this, and I noticed he was going a little fast. Now it's 1978 before seatbelts were and he had a steel dashboard in his car. I yelled, "Slow down, John!" Too late. We slammed into the side of the bridge, and his car just stopped. I flew into the windshield and smashed my face on the dashboard. I pulled my head back out of the windshield. Damn! I looked at John and reached to feel my nose. When I grabbed it, it made a crunching noise. I looked at John and said, "Hey man, is my face all screwed up?" John said, "Not bad, but you got a bloody nose."

Then I took John's rearview mirror and pulled it around and checked out my face. My right eye stuck out, and I could see that something was broken on the right side of my face. The whole right side of my lower eye socket was broken. John took me to my mother's work. She worked for Dr. Porter, the doc who took care of me in the hospital when I had hepatitis.

Mom came to the door and screamed. She cried out for Dr. Porter. When he saw me he said, "You have to go to Kalamazoo to get fixed."

Away I went. After a few hours on the operating table I was back out and recovering in a hospital room. *Here we go again*, I thought. You have never seen a black eye like mine. This was the shiner of shiners—damn, this one was a whopper. And the blood and debris that came out of my nose—terrible.

After about a month I got the stitches out, but my face was still messed up. The doc scheduled me in for another surgery to reconstruct my face. He brought me in as an outpatient, and this time I was awake for the procedure. I got all checked in and they put me on a portable bed before pushing me into the operating room. They had me lay down on the bed on my stomach.

The nurse said, "Okay, I'm going to put this needle in your right butt cheek." She stuck it into the right cheek at the bottom where it rounds down to the thigh. After that, they waited. When it was good and numb, they cut through the skin and took out some small slices. Then the doc stitched it back up. Now they rolled me over on my back. I heard the two nurses talking about mixing up some cocaine sulfate. I watched as the nurse poured the pinkish white powder into a little bowl. I asked her what it was for, and she said she was going to stick it up my nose and then re-break it. I thought, *Damn, what is up with this?* They started to jam gauze up my nose. I thought, *Damn dude, this is going to really hurt.* Not only did it hurt, it went clean up into my throat.

Then they froze my right eye and the doc started to cut on the edge of my eyelid. He peeled my skin back and flapped open about two inches below my eyelid. The pieces of skin from my butt were placed inside of the eyelid. Then they sewed my eyelid back and pulled out that big piece of gauze. It felt like it came down and out from the middle of my head—coming out, coming out and out and out, and when the end came out it felt like my eyes were being sucked into my head like a vacuum. Once it was out, I felt so good. I could finally breathe out of my right side. Now here comes the closer: The doc got up inside and re-broke my nose and repositioned it so as the nostril holes were lined up and that was that. Totally amazing.

* * *

Now I want to go back to Pat's AFF Level 4 jump again, mainly to elaborate more on the levels. During his briefing we told him that on this jump he would have only one instructor on the reserve side—normally the student's secondary. Pat would be in the spotting position, and he would then take charge and spot the airplane. When the airplane was in position, he would tell the secondary, Sam. Sam told the pilot to cut. Sam then told Pat, "Put your feet out." Pat got into his pre-exit position. "Check in," he said aloud to Sam. Sam responded with "Climb out." Again Pat climbed out into his exit position—hands a little wider than shoulder width, trailing the right leg with his chest and chin up over the leading edge of the strut. He took a good look at Sam and did a verbal, "Check in." Sam responded, "Okay," with Pat looking straight ahead. Up, Down, Arch.

Sam waited for Pat's COA and then hand walked to the front. Then when it felt good, the release. Pat stayed on heading to lock in control. Then Sam gave Pat the turn sign. Pat did a 90 degree right turn and stopped. Check altitude. Above 6,000 feet, turn back. Another circle. Above 6,000 feet, Sam signaled Pat to turn left 90 degrees. Check altitude. Above 6,000 feet, turn back.

Pat now was in freefall. He would fall until he got to 5,000 feet—5,500 feet flash, relax till 4,000 feet. Look, reach, pull. Count one thousand, two thousand, three thousand, and so on. Line stretch. Sam would stay close and would be there just in case.

This is the moment right there when you better not drop your guard. This is when it can get out of control quick. Pat did really well. He smoked it. His canopy control was excellent. I believe when you teach spotting and the student understands the concept, it gives them a better understanding of what's going on with the wind direction and speed.

Ken's outline had Level 5 exactly the same as 4 except the student did 360 degree right and left turns, and that was the only difference between the two.

Now Level 6 is my favorite. I really like to chase and stay with the student. It is a big challenge. On Level 6 the student is challenged to show that he or she can meet the four objectives that it takes to be able to skydive. Four and five are directional heading control, six and seven are out-of-control to in-control situations. This is the big test of stability—the student's worst nightmare. By this point, Pat had a pretty good knowledge of his equipment, which included being able to arm his AAD.

Pat got the Level 6 briefing and away we went. Now all these jumps were out of a Cessna C-182. Again Sam and Pat in the aircraft. At 8,000 feet, Sam did the gear check and talked Pat through the jump. At 10,500 feet, Pat would get in the spotting position. Pat would make his own corrections to the pilot with Sam overseeing him. Once the cut was made, Pat would get in the door in a diving position towards the tail of the airplane: Right hand on the rear door post, right foot on the lower front of the door frame, left foot on the step, left hand back on the wing strut. Pat then checked in verbally and Sam said, "Okay." Then Pat would get a good heading down and out at a 45 degree angle and then, verbally, up, down, arch.

Once out of the aircraft, Pat started to arch. He did not flip over and maintained a strong arch. Now this is no linked exit. The student does a solo diving exit. Once they are out, the arch is what gives them stability. And that, my friend, is the scariest part of learning to skydive.

After they get stable, they have to pick a point on the ground and maintain their direction. Here we go! This is the point I always try to make. Skydiving is probably one of the simplest sports that you can do. It's so easy. It's 90 percent psychological and 10 percent skill. All you do is jump out; the earth sucks and all you do is fall. Period. There is no actual physical work. The hardest, most physical part is the walk to the airplane and the walk back when you land.

Pat never went unstable after he dove out. Sam was in front of him. All we taught students was to check their altitude. Above 6,000 feet, back loop, stabilize; still above 6,000 feet, another back loop, stabilize, check altitude. Hold heading until 5,500 feet, and then look, reach and pull. Pat again smoked it. It was so nice when you had students like him. And you do, but not often.

Finally Level 7—Ken called it the graduation jump. This was done according to the outline Ken had written, which Sam and I followed. I'll mention again that Pat was Sam and my first AFF student.

Pat again went through his gear check. Then Sam briefed him on his Level 7. Now Pat was on his own. Let's not forget, he was jumping a PC and had a Strong student tandem. At the time, this was the newest and the best in student gear. He told the pilot what he wanted as a jump run for his wind drift run. Then he and Sam got into the airplane, climbed to 2,000 feet, and came in on jump run for the wind drift indicator at 2,000 feet. The pilot flew into the wind. Pat called for the corrections to be made and directly over the pea gravel, Pat threw the wind drift indicator. The pilot then circled to the right so Pat could see it at all times. Once it landed, he and Sam talked about where the opening point would be.

Now Pat sat back down and waited for the remaining climb to altitude. It took maybe 20 minutes for the climb. At 9,000 feet, Pat gave himself a gear check and rehearsed the Level 7 with Sam. At 10,500 feet the airplane came onto jump run. Pat was spotting on his own, making his corrections. Pat told the pilot to cut. The pilot reduced the power, and Pat got into his solo exit position just like his Level 6.

Check in with Sam.

Sam gave the okay.

Pat pushed off into a front loop, stabilized, checked altitude; above 6,000 feet, back loop, stabilized, check altitude; above 6,000 feet, back loop, stabilize, check altitude; still above 6,000 feet, right turn 360 degrees, check altitude; above 6,000 feet, left turn 360 degrees, stop on heading; above 6,000 feet. Now he started to track—a new skill introduced on his Level 7.

Then at 4,000 feet, look, reach, pull. Count and once open, canopy check. Then he started his canopy control. And again, Pat had no problem with his canopy control. Pat was a natural. He could have graduated in six jumps but Sam and I decided that we wanted him to do a Level 7 just to see how a student would do.

On each jump we would fill out the student's log book. This is the only record of a student's performance, and it's up to the instructor to provide a good description of their jump. What I have just explained is the outline of Ken Coleman's Accelerated Freefall Course as it was in 1979. It really hasn't changed that much, except that the student wasn't taught how to pack, and I didn't see any spotting being taught at the big drop zones— DeLand, Z-hills, Perris Valley, Skydive Dallas, and others. It was really too bad because that training really gives the student a much better understanding of wind direction and speed.

The new USPA 2011 AFF teaching scenario was not nearly as complete as Ken's. It shows. Look at how many people die under a good canopy—at least half. I believe that yes, the square canopies of today are a lot more responsive and smaller. I also know that when you teach spotting and skydiving fundamentals and do a good job at it, the student retains this for the rest of their skydiving career.

Sam and I trained a couple more students and really the only thing that is worth writing about is a guy named Ron, a friend of my student Pat.

I already told you a little bit about this but I am going to tell the story again. Ron was on a Level 3. His first and second levels were really good so Sam and I figured that his Level 3 would follow suit. We were jumping at Austin Lake and again the landing area is small so we were landing at the big fields to the south of the drop zone. We had learned from Pete about being rolled on exit so we kept him forward and we had a good exit—nice and flat. He did his dummy pull and transitioned to the 3-way. Then, legs out and legs in, followed by a good COA and again legs out and legs in. When he brought his legs in, he went too far and flipped on his back. At that point Sam and I lost our grips. He was now on his own. I caught him and got him stable, and then again he brought his legs in. Again he tore free. At this point, he started to tumble and then he would arch over, but his legs were so tucked that the tumbling would start all over again.

I'm standing on my head now and I'm two feet from grabbing him. So close but yet so far. Now I'm closing in to within inches. All of a sudden, I see a pilot chute appear. I looked down and the ground was *right there*. I pulled right then. I had enough time for a couple of turns and then landed. Ron landed his round reserve and did a good job.

When he got back, Sam and I did a debrief with Ron, and we asked him why he didn't pull. He told us that he didn't think his parachute would open if he was unstable. Well, I can't blame Ron. If the student has failed to learn, it is because the instructor has failed to teach. This is a truth I picked up after many years this experience. And at that moment, it was so true. We never brought that up in Ron's training. This is a very important part of a student instruction. Plus Sam and I didn't like the fact that going into our 3-way, as instructors, we gave up the control grips on the student. This is a good example of an instructor so engrossed with a student that if the AAD hadn't fired we both would have been killed. AADs save lives. Pete said he could see my fingers in freefall. How about that?

This is not for everybody—AFF instruction. I lost a real good friend to AFF. He did the same thing that I was doing except both student and instructor got killed—an instructor chased a student clear into the ground.

* * *

Ken was holding an AFF seminar in Florida, and he asked me if I would help. So I did. I had a 1975 VW van and it was all done up to camp in—just what I needed. It was a good time of year to get out of Michigan—January 1980. Ken had a good turnout at the DeLand drop zone for his seminar. He had approached the USPA about a waiver so the course could be recognized by them. They turned him down. They said AFF was dangerous and that if we kept it up, we were going to kill people.

Well, that didn't fly with Gary Dupuis, owner/operator at the DeLand drop zone. Gary had been Chief Pilot at the Nationals when I competed, and Chief Pilot at the Z-hills meets in 1973, 1974, 1975—the real big ones. He told the USPA to take a leap (in so many words), and we kept on. The seminar was cool, and I learned a whole lot. I went back up for a couple of months to Michigan before heading to Florida to live permanently.

I liked this skydiving for a living. When I got down to Florida, Ken was living in Kissimmee, Florida, and still working for Strong Enterprises. Now as the AFF program got bigger, Ken would book students in, but I did most of the training and jumping. Hoot was around for Levels 1, 2, and 3.

I had a new student in from Holland named Stan. Now back then it was a strange thing for a foreigner to come to the U.S., but the new *non-certified* AFF program was on a roll. The word had reached Europe. Stan didn't speak English well and brought a friend to interpret. This was a big problem, along with Stan being over 54 years old—not in bad shape, but he looked like he was 54.

Well, Hoot and I did his Levels 1, 2, and 3 and then it was all me. I helped him suit up, and we got into Ken's C-182, 1776Y, with its cool paint job in red, white and blue. We climbed to

10,500 feet and then we were out on a Level 4 jump. I swung around as he did his COA. I let him go even though I felt tension. I'll be damned—this guy started to spin so fast, I couldn't get a grip. As soon as I would grab him, the force from his involuntary spin would just tear my grip from him. This happened several times. I could always get them if they were turning. But when they flipped over on their back they became so hard to stabilize. This is what old Stan did—he flipped over on his back and there he laid like a turtle. I'll never ever forget the look on his face. I can see it now as I'm writing this book. He is on his back, reversed arch and falling like a rock. Both hands are coming into his chest as if to grab a ripcord. Then they would go back out with nothing in them. Christ, why doesn't he grab the handle? Even if he did grab the reserve on this particular rig, it would cut the main away and pull the reserve pin at the same time. *Pull something!*

I stood on my head. I was closing fast as I made this last effort. I caught him. I grabbed his main and let him fall away. His main started to deploy. Again I looked down—just like the last time I chased down a student—and the ground was SO close. I was open below 800 feet. And again when I landed, I swore to myself this was the last time I was going to chase these goddamn students—no more. That was it. I'm not going to do it again. That was the last. And I never did it again. If you're reading this book and you are an AFF instructor, please, please pay attention. You cannot do any good if you are dead! And if you chase enough of these out of control students, you will bounce!

I want to tell you about a particular student named Adrian Warren. He was a BBC producer and in 1985 was the leader of BBC Expedition to Cerro Autana, Venezuela. I was a part of that expedition—told in Chapter One of this book—that parachuted on top of the giant table-top mountain. He came to me for training in 1981—the work Ken and I were doing had drawn international attention. I had logged over 700 AFF jumps before the balloon accident.

Adrian came to DeLand with another Brit named Don Whillans—a short, kind of stocky guy who said he weighed 13 stones. Now I don't know 13 stones from 13 rocks, but I did know that he was pushing 230 pounds and was no taller than 5'8". But the man appeared to be in good shape. Adrian was

5'10" and about 160 pounds. I ran both of them through the AFF course. Hoot and I jumped with Adrian first, and he did very well. Next was Don. Don did very well, but he fell like a very heavy bank safe.

That night we were in the airport bar and after a few drinks and talking, the truth came out—Don was a famous climber who had made several climbs on Everest and many of the other highest mountains in the world. He came with his wife who was a very nice lady. I really enjoyed their company and looked forward to jumping with him the next day.

The next day came and Hoot and I took Adrian on his AFF Level 2 jump. As I expected he did well. Now with Don, being the stocky guy that he was it was a different story. We took him up on his Level 2 and Don did okay, but he had a kickass fall rate and had a little problem with his 5,500 feet check. But he was still good enough to pass. His weight is what would mess him up. I thought that he might break his leg on landing so I suggested that he might want to focus more on his climbing career. I didn't want him to get hurt. So Don decided to go on holiday with his wife, and Adrian continued with his AFF training and completed the course.

The cover of Rocky Evans' first book, Truth

## Chapter Thirteen
## DEATH IS NO STRANGER

In the summer of 1981 I was getting a lot of students from all over Europe. I trained at least two or three students every couple of weeks. I was starting to get a little burned out as I was the only one doing the instruction and jumping. I was looking for a diversion when Ken told me he had a contract to go up to Illinois to teach a group of hot air balloon pilots how to skydive. This sounded good to me. I could take some time and see my mother and brother and take a bit of a vacation in Michigan. Everything fell in place. Gary was taking a C-182 up into Tennessee, and I got a ride with him to Knoxville and flew commercial from there to Michigan. This was a good way to get my mind off of the AFF gig for at least a couple of days.

Well, I made it up there and was enjoying my few days off. I think it was a week or so before I met up with Ken, and then we took off for Evanston, a suburb on the north side of Chicago.

During the ride Ken and I talked about the AFF program. He was adamant that he didn't want this new program going to the USPA, because we hadn't even discussed how we were going to rate the students or the criteria that would be used for someone to earn this rating. Ken wanted to set it up independent of the USPA. He wanted only that the USPA recognize his program, but he had no intention of the USPA having any rights to this new and elite way to train skydivers. We also discussed the dangers involved in expanding the program too quickly. Almost all the way to Evanston, this was the main topic.

Ken and I got to the Windy City Balloon Port at about 12 noon. We started our class at 1 p.m. Ken was doing the lecture, and I was assisting him. We were covering the basic instruction for the AFF course including equipment, emergencies, dive flow, and canopy control. We took a break at 4 p.m. and then finished up at 6 p.m.

It didn't get dark until about 8 p.m. and while Ken and I were hanging out with some of the pilots in the class, the guy who set up the whole contract with Ken asked Ken and me if we wanted to go on a balloon flight. Ken said sure he would. I guess he did it because he felt obligated and probably he did want to go—I knew he had several balloon flights under his belt.

He looked to me and said, "Come on, it's free."

I said, "That's okay. I'm tired from the drive and the classroom time."

Ken said, "Come on, let's go."

I told him I was tired. He came over and said to me under his breath, "These people are going out of their way to show us a good time, so let's go."

Well, I went. I didn't want to do anything but take a shower and kick back. Maybe smoke a joint. Needless to say, they had this large six-passenger basket, one of the biggest in the world. The launch site struck me as weird—like a big giant sink hole. I guess it was probably a really good place to launch a balloon because it was protected from wind.

Ken came and got me and the two of us followed Jamie, our pilot, and the guy who had set up the training contract with Ken. I watched as they used the burner to fill the balloon with hot air. This balloon was twice the size of the one I had jumped in the Florida Keys.

I was still a little tired from the trip and the little bit of instruction I did in Ken's class. So I just kind of kicked back and watched and did as I was told. When it came time to load the basket, I remember there were three other guys that got on with us. To this day, I never was told or heard their names.

It came time to load into the basket. I climbed in and then Ken. The rest followed and the pilot, Jamie, was last in. After we were all on board, the Jamie hit the burner and the balloon inflated full and round. The ground crew held tight to the ropes that kept us in place. The balloon shot up like it was full of helium. There it sat big and full, wanting to fly but held back by the tether lines—it reminded me of a stallion horse that had been lassoed and was trying with all its might to break free. I sat on the inside of the basket wondering where we were going. Little did I know, we would be flying to the power wires of death and destruction.

Once we were on board, I saw this guy come running, yelling, "Wait! Don't forget these." He had three bottles of champagne in his hands. He passed them to Jamie who stuck them down by the propane tanks. Now, these tanks weren't the little propane tanks that you see in a propane gas grill. These were half again as big. This was as big a hot air balloon as anywhere in the world. Most of the larger balloons took four people, this one took six.

I just sat and watched as I stayed in my little space inside the balloon basket. I don't recall any conversation with Ken at this time; I can only wonder what was going on in his mind. The tether lines were released up and out of the natural bowl that had protected the balloon.

I was already a little bit concerned. In the distance I noticed the black horizon associated with a thunderstorm. As in my first balloon ride, I noticed the silence of the ride only to be broken by the power of the burner. We were moving along at a pretty good pace—not like an airplane or helicopter, but definitely faster than a person walking. I would say at the end before we hit the wires, it was traveling as fast as a person can run. We never climbed any higher than about 400 feet.

I know that bad things happen in threes. The first bad decision that our pilot Jamie made was the choice to launch. The weather conditions were not favorable for flight, but he made the decision to launch the balloon. Now we were already up and flying. Off in the distance, I could see a thunderstorm starting to grow. It was pretty far off in the distance, so I really thought there wouldn't be an issue. I didn't say a thing, and here again I don't recall any conversation with Ken. The time from takeoff until the crash was no more than 20 minutes.

I remember looking down into people's yards. Dogs were barking at the big air monster. You could see the houses and yards very well as we drifted from house to house. Jamie, our pilot was keeping the ride no more than 100 to 200 feet in altitude. I do remember the gondola hitting an antenna of some kind and glancing off, the basket rocking slightly back and forth. That was the second mistake. Why in the hell didn't he climb to avoid the thing? I started to wonder about his skill level. *Didn't he see it? Why not?* Again, no one said a thing. I wondered about the paying customers and what they were thinking.

The balloon was picking up speed as we raced across the ground. I had one balloon ride previous to this, and I jumped out of that one too—but that was at 6,000 feet and I was wearing a parachute. As I thought back to my first balloon ride, I recalled the climb out of the basket was a little bit of a pain. There was nothing to really grab on to once you are outside the gondola. There are carrying handles made of wicker that hang from the bottom of the basket, but those were way down at the very base of the basket. I was already getting ready mentally for the crash landing, running this through my mind. I could feel in my bones that tragedy was dogging us. I knew if we hit the ground at this speed, the basket would start to roll. The last thing I wanted was to get slapped in the head with a propane tank or to get all tangled up with the three guys inside the basket.

Well, the first words I remember hearing from anyone came from our pilot, "I'm gonna land the balloon. The weather is looking bad, and I feel we need to land." I could sense a bit of panic in his voice. I looked directly into his face as he spoke the words. He looked panicked and unsure. I didn't like what I saw. *Damn it,* I thought, *why in hell did I go?* I knew I should have stayed on the ground. Too late.

Off in the distance was a big parking lot. Jamie pointed and said, "We're gonna land there."

*Shit*, I thought, *on the asphalt? That's gonna hurt.* Why in the hell he picked that point, I don't know. On the other side were power wires. Not little ones. These were the big ones with steel frame girders that looked like a big T. On the other side were big fields. Now Ken had told me that Jamie was some hot shot balloon pilot who had logged thousands of hours of flight. I had thought there's not much skill involved. All you really do is run the burner for lift and pull a tether line up to the top of the envelope. This line is hooked to one side of a big opening of the very apex of the balloon. When you pull down, it lets out hot air that collected at the top. When in flight, you pull down on the tether line to open the envelope, and once the apex is open, it releases the hot air and the balloon starts to descend. The longer the apex is open, the quicker you descend.

Also the longer it's open, the more time it takes for the balloon to respond.

At this point I'm really starting to get concerned. We were moving along at a pretty fast clip. The parking lot was coming closer and closer. We were not that high—maybe 50 feet. Jamie pulled the tether down, and down again to the basket floor. He was just a little too late. The basket came down. We were just about to hit the parking lot—maybe just six feet from the asphalt—when he let up the lanyard and hit the burner. He aborted the landing. My God, we were so close. All of us, all six of us could have climbed out of the gondola but he chose to abort. Why? Why? It made no sense. It still makes no sense.

The propane burner started to roar. Then there we sat— motionless. As if God himself had taken us in his almighty hand and grabbed us. Then time stood still. My mind raced, raced with different scenarios. Nothing sounded good. I looked down. We were definitely not moving. Forward, aft, up or down. Stuck. Stuck in what, by what? Were we hung up on another antenna or what? Then it hit me, power lines! The almighty power wires that were running perpendicular to the parking lot! These electrical lines were thick and heavy. I could tell by their support structure—34,000 volts per line. I was wearing a cool ass hat that Jerry Bird gave me, a cotton polyester t-shirt and Levi jeans, and tennis shoes. I knew enough to get down, way down into the corner of the basket.

I knew from my skydiving career that we were just plain screwed. I can still see the three passengers standing erect looking over the edge as if they were on an ocean liner looking at the sea below them. I never remember seeing Ken, let alone talking to him.

People have asked me why I didn't tell everyone to jump. That would have taken way too long. Each moment is like no other moment in one's life, and no one knows what a moment really is or how long that moment can last until you are there. No one knows how time can kill you or save you—until you are the person living the experience. Then you can explain.

Remember, I'm in the corner, the very corner of this gondola, and I know, I really know how screwed I am. Time again is our real enemy. How much time did we have from where the gondola came in contact with the wire? Now understand that as long as the basket was tangled in one wire, we were safe. Now what really happened is still seared in my brain. This is the largest hot air balloon in the world. It is massive. When the wind hits the balloon, it creates a lot of drag. Now again, imagine the gondola is stuck in the wires. Where exactly is the wire? It is just below the top lip where you climb in. So if you look over it, it would be a foot below you.

I'm sitting in the corner, looking past my arm, hands over my face, still in wonder. *Why am I here? What have I done in my life to be here? Have I been that bad a person?* I knew my answer was no. Since a child, I had believed in this thing called God. Then my mind went to all my friends who had died ... Steve, Tommy, Tom, Mary, Tony, and more. It wasn't a new place for me, not at all. I stared it in the face so many times. I guess I was used to it, the place where everyone eventually goes. I can honestly tell you that I knew we were doomed. I felt bad for the three passengers. They had no idea of what to expect. Like little babies. They hadn't had the training or the experience or the knowledge that comes with skydiving. I knew that when you came in contact with power wires, this was the very worst of all emergency landings. And they tell you, or at least I was told, to keep your hands over your face, and turn your head to the side.

The three passengers, last I saw, were looking over the edge of the basket. And I am sure that they had no idea of what to expect as I did. I knew for sure what the outcome was going to be—at least at that moment I knew. When the moment came, it came with more fire and more heat than anyone has ever experienced and lived to tell the story.

I'm down in the corner of the basket, hands on top of my head, forearm covering my face. Suddenly, a flash of blinding light was everywhere. So bright. The heat was so intense that it was unimaginable. When the two power cables came together, it was the sound that still stays locked in my brain. It wasn't like the sound of a welder as he strikes an arc with the rod, and it wasn't like the noise you hear when you have two 110 AC wires on an appliance come together. This sound was the sound of death. It roared with a noise that screamed extreme power. The time between when the flash, heat, and sound started until I jumped was no more than one or two seconds.

My last vision, the one I remember, was of those passengers looking over the side of the balloon. I can only imagine what happened to them when the two 34,000 volt power lines came together. I know what it did to me even though I was ready for the fire, the monster that was unleashed when the wires came in contact. I remember thinking, *God I'm burning. I'm really going to burn to death. This is finally it.* And again, my life never flashed before my eyes. For a moment I accepted it. Death. It almost felt like peace, finally peace. Maybe I thought this is where I will see the other side and you know, I had accepted it.

But the heat was so intense that I sprang up. My strong legs powered me up and out in one solid motion. I was now in freefall. I remember falling feet first, arms stretched out to my sides, swaying in slow circles using them as a balance point. Straight down, feet first, in perfect form. I never knew what the final destiny of the jump would bring. How could I? There was no time to look down and see where I was going to land. I really didn't care. I was out of the burning coffin, free in the wind. 65 feet up, one can get a good freefall.

I'm really not sure how long I was falling. It was damn sure long enough to focus on my body position. As I hit the ground, I instinctively went into a parachute landing fall. As soon as I started to roll, the roll just built up in speed to where I was tumbling head over heels, downhill, rolling faster and faster. I rolled into and then up and over a bush or small tree. I really don't know. I do know that I ran it right over. Once I was over it, I kept on rolling. Sand, dirt, grass, and leaves were being shoved in my mouth. My face disoriented, I couldn't believe it. Like a basketball rolling down this hill. Finally, I stopped. Finally. Still alive, wondering, *Did I break my legs?* I stood up. Fortunately, I did not break my legs. Yes, the skin on my arms was dangling in small clumps. My hands looked as if they were dipped in wax. My left hand was twisted upside down, obviously broken, with the back of my hand where the palm should have been. The smell was so pungent with the fragrance of burning hair and flesh. My t-shirt was burned away along my shoulders, the collar hanging there like a necklace. My hat that Jerry Bird gave me— gone. That too, I'm sure burnt. I was still smoking. Again the smell was sickening. Especially when I realized it was my own hair and flesh I was smelling.

The notion of time had deserted me. From the time I quit rolling down the hill until I stood up, I really don't know how much time had gone by. I do know after I stood up and saw that my legs were not broken, I ran, and I mean ran hard up the hill. My adrenaline was pumping. I was pretty burned up but also in shock. I know that once I made it to the top of the hill, it was only a few more yards until I was on a four-lane highway trying to flag down someone to get help for the people in the balloon.

When I reached the hill top, I saw the balloon and gondola. My God. The side of the actual basket was on fire. Flames were pouring from the top of the gondola. I remember flames, large ones pouring out the side of the gondola, reaching up 15 feet, licking at the side of the envelope of the balloon. The basket was producing the flames. The wicker was on fire. That was the part of the basket that made the first contact with the power wire after the envelope started to blow sideways because the gondola was tangled in the wires. Like a rabbit in a snare, lunging and jerking but no freedom, not yet at least.

To this day only one photo has surfaced of the balloon crash, shot right after the balloon broke from the wires. I had already jumped. But you can clearly see a second guy jumping out after the balloon broke free of the wires. He landed on a house roof and went clean through. He lived for a couple hours. I never went back to the actual crash site, but I do plan to go someday. Having survived a balloon crash so devastating, there are questions I still want answers to.

Only when the two wires burned through did the balloon continue on its skyward ascent. Like a bird shot in flight, wing broken, spiraling to the ground. I could only think, *My God, Ken.* I hope he got out. I knew, I just knew he was gone from that burning coffin. I watched it crash into the yard of somebody's house across the road from where I was standing. My mind racing, my body burning. The scent of burnt hair and flesh followed me. I stood motionless taking in the sight. The airship was as old as flight itself. The very first time man ever left the chains of gravity was in an envelope full of hot air. If you look in the history books about the introduction of manned flight, there it will be in its entirety—the conception of the hot air balloon.

Unlike the airplane, the power plant of the hot air balloon has not changed. Unlike the mechanics of the gasoline engine, hot air and its properties have not changed. Not only that, the fuel for hot air balloons has not changed either. That fuel is called FIRE. And as gravity pulled it down closer and closer to its destiny, with no power to resist, it crashed into the biggest ball of fire I have ever seen. One instant it was there, the next gone. As if some magician had waved his magic wand. Gone. A vision and memory I will never set free in my mind.

Then the question came—one I think anyone in my situation would ask. Is anyone alive? The vision, the memory would come back to me night after night in a dream, a nightmare—a dream of death and sorrow. One that I never wanted to see again. Like a skipping record, it would come back to haunt me over and over again. My dreams would always start with me in freefall and then my fall when I hit the hill. Rolling and rolling head over heels. I'm digging my fingers in the dirt, the smell of dirt pungent. My next image, the three passengers standing looking. Then they would turn to me telling me, "No. Don't jump. No." I would wake sweating, my heart racing, my bed a total mess, only to be glad when I realized it's the dream. The dream comes to me still, as it will forever. I'm scarred for life. It will never go away!

No one could survive that ball of fire. As I said, one second there and the next it was gone. There I stood, the details racing in my mind. A matter of seconds. One second, I was safe in the gondola free from gravity, the place I chose to be, the next, a slave to gravity. I stood in shock, looking at nothing, the fate of everyone with me in the basket ripping at me.

At that point the pain started to grab me. It was weird; I recall how a progression of the intense pain started. It didn't come on to me all at once. It was a gradual thing. An old couple stopped and came out of their car together. "Young man, come into the back seat and lie down. You're hurt."

I said, "No, no, I can't. My friend is in that balloon and I need to get him help."

"Please. Please," they pleaded with me. I responded with a definite "No!" The pain was intense. I knew it was over with. I could do nothing more. I looked again. Left hand upside down. Skin dripping off my arms, hand beyond description, t-shirt burned almost off. The sickening smell of burned hair and flesh. I surrendered to the shelter and comfort of the kind old couple.

Time had now stood still, like being in a bubble. Sirens were starting to scream, louder and louder they came. I lay in the comfort of the old couple's backseat. My God, I thought again about them—the old couple. The stain, the smell I knew would be left in their car. I told them how sorry I was to do that to their car. Their words were only of concern, kindness, and caring as I lay in their backseat wondering, *Where's Ken? Did he make it?* I didn't know. I made it, so maybe he did, too.

I don't know how long I laid there, long enough for the pain to finally pour out from the burns that were inflicted on my body. At first my broken hand was my only concern. The thought of the doctor resetting it. My God, the skin was dripping off the whole hand. Crawling up my arm, all the way up to my t-shirt sleeve still hanging by a thread. Then I looked to the right arm. It was worse, way worse. That I looked down to my legs. Those too were burned, but only a couple big spots. But again the skin was gone. My whole body shook like someone in a seizure. But my mind was solid as ever. I never really lost it, at least that's what I thought.

An ambulance stopped in front of the old couple's car. The EMTs were running to me, stretcher in hands. They tried to grab me, and I tore away. "No, don't grab me; I can climb on myself!" My God, their touch on my open wounds inflamed the pain. I climbed on the gurney. They put me inside the ambulance and then started their questions. I know there was a reason for all the questions, but I couldn't really focus on them. My wrist was starting to hurt. Funny how the two types of injuries—the burns and the break—felt different. The big relief was that they were pouring water all over me by the buckets. My God, the pain. I wanted something for it. Anything. The EMTs couldn't give me a thing.

It was getting dark by the time we reached the hospital. They scurried me into the hospital, then into a room where I lay. Now I was on a bed in the ER, and even though I hurt, I started to chuckle. *I made it. I hurt. Where's Ken? I hurt.* I wonder. I hurt. I wait. I hurt. *Come on, get me something for the pain!* I wait. At last a nurse comes in. She's got a needle and syringe. I get something. It hurts. Moaning. It hurts.

A nurse came in again but this time not for me. She grabbed a curtain and pulled it across the room separating it into two rooms. She told me that there was someone else in our party who had made it. *Ken. I knew he got out.*

A doctor showed up, finally. "You gonna set this wrist?" He came over to the table and picked up my arm. "Hmmm," he said. My hand still dripping—every finger was dripping skin. The smell was terrible. I couldn't touch a thing. And I didn't want anyone to touch me.

"Where's Ken?"

"Who?"

"Ken? He's my friend that was with me in the balloon. Is he dead?"

"I don't know," the doc said. "I'm gonna set this wrist. How's the pain?"

"Bad," I said. "Terrible."

He left. My mind went to the partition. I was going to see if that was Ken next to me. I couldn't get up off the bed. I hurt. The nurse again. Syringe in hand. Give me more. More. She stuck the needle in. Both times in my butt cheek. She leaves. I hurt. I hear voices through the curtain, more than two. That's got to be Ken. I know he made it. The doc is in my room again.

"How's the pain?"

"Better."

"I'm going to set this now. You ready?"

I've been ready. The smell of hell all over me—burning hair and flesh. I look down. My shoes were burnt. Full of dirt. Must have got that when I ran up the hill. My Levis—burnt. My arm is full of dirt sticking to my skinless arms. My hands were the worst. I can still see the loose and dangling pieces of skin hanging off. I'm wondering how bad are they? My shirt was the best—combo poly cotton, melted pieces of it sticking to the good pieces of my back, chest, and arms. My back and shoulders were burned pretty bad. My ears too, the right one the worst. The smell of my burned hair filled my nostrils. The doc had my arm in his hand. He says, "This is gonna hurt."

"I know. Do it!"

He's sitting in a chair facing me. He stands and grabs my hand. He starts to pull. I scream. He twists the hand. I'm still screaming. He lets go. The pulling is done, my hand is straight. "Yahoo!" I say. He looks at me and smiles. I look up at him and smile. "Thanks, Doc." He nods and leaves.

I hurt. Time is gone. There is no time, it doesn't exist. The bright lights beat down on me. Two nurses come into my room with stainless pans of warm water on stainless trays, scissors on the sides of the trays. I'm wondering, *Where's Ken?* One of the nurses says, "We are going to cut off your t-shirt." I say,

"Great." I don't hurt as bad. The morphine is starting to work.

"Can you sit up?" I say, "Sure." They start cutting. The smell is terrible. I ask, "Who's in the other bed?" One nurse responds, "We don't know." They cut. Pieces of my shirt are burnt and melted to my body. They're doing a good job. The pieces drop to the floor. My mind returns to the burning balloon fluttering down. I hurt. They put moist wet cloths on my back. It feels good. The burnt t-shirt is almost off. Patches of it are still stuck to my flesh. My pants come next. They're not so bad, no polyester. I think back to Ken. He was wearing polyester pants. I know how they must look.

The nurses are bathing my wounds. It feels good. Two men enter my room. "Harry Evans," they say.

"Yes."

"We have bad news. Ken is dead."

"Well, that's that," I say.

It surely wasn't a shock.

"He jumped after you, but he was too high."

I said, "Who's next door?"

"It was one of the other passengers." *My God*, I thought. I learned later that he had also jumped out of the balloon landed on top of a house and crashed through the roof. He died shortly after.

Chapter Fourteen
## THE LONG TRIP BACK

They transported me to another hospital with a burn unit. Things were not very clear to me at that point. I'm sure the morphine had taken hold. The next morning I awoke to a flock of nurses—one trying to stick me with an IV, another sticking a tube through my nose and into my stomach, and a third inserting a catheter in my penis. The IV was in my neck in my jugular vein. They were trying to make me sit up to change my bandages. *Good luck!* I was stuck to the sheets on my mattress. I remember not being able to get up from my bed. They soaked the bed with water. The scabs dissolved, and I was able to tear free. If that's what it takes just to get up off the sheets, what in God's name happens when they try and take the bandages off? Then they soaked me down with water and waited twenty minutes or so, and proceeded to pull my bandages off. *My God*, I thought. I was dazed. I floated in and out of the dreamy world of morphine. The morphine helped a lot, but the pain was still there.

It's 8 a.m. I see they have come to take me somewhere. *Please not there*, I think, but I know nothing. I listen. The nurses are talking about a debridement tank. It took three medical personnel—one to carry everything they had attached to me, one to keep me on the gurney, and one to push. Now what? I had no idea. They brought me into a room with a big whirlpool tank, or that's what it looked like. I recalled in high school when I tore my knee up playing football. Therapy on my knee included a whirlpool bath—that memory came flooding back when I saw the tank.

There was a ladder outside this tank and it was a good

thing. It was a bitch to get in being all burned up and on morphine. Plus I was dragging three sets of hoses. Once I got in, damn did it feel good. Real good. There were jets stirring up the water and making bubbles. I just relaxed, and then another nurse appeared.

"Hi Rocky," she said.

"Hi," I said.

She said, "I'm going to clean your burns." She had a stiff bristle brush in hand. *Uh oh*, I thought, *what is she gonna do with that?* My question was answered soon enough. She started on my raw back and scrubbed and scrubbed. My God, no one, no one has ever experienced this kind of pain. She scrubbed until the blood ran down my back. I screamed. I cried. I cursed—for nothing. She didn't stop until she covered every square inch of my wounds. Probably an hour and a half of scrubbing. Once in a while, she would stop to change her brush and clear my wounds of dead skin and plastic still burned into my flesh. I passed out momentarily.

When I came to, she said, "It's okay. A lot of my patients do that, and it's good because then you don't feel the terrible pain." Finally, she said the worst was over, you're done.

Two nurses coated me with Silvadene cream, bandaged me, and took me back to my room. "Damn, I'm sure glad that's done," I told them. They said the debridement was one of the most painful things you can experience in here. I said, "I hope that's true; I'm sure glad it's done."

The nurse said, "Yes, I bet, but you need to know that they are going to do this to you again at three this afternoon and again at eight this evening."

I said, "WHAT? For how long?"

"Every day until you leave." What could I do? Run away? I'm screwed. I'm just plain screwed.

Along with me in the room was a young boy, 10 years old. He got burned bad on his hands and face. His face and head were completely covered with a compression stocking—everything but his eyes and mouth. I was there six weeks and never saw his face. Such a good boy, Jimmy was. Some other kids threw gasoline on him and set him on fire. The kids who did it were twelve and thirteen. We became very good friends. His mom and dad came in every day to visit. They ended up being my mom and dad, also.

The burn center was in Evanston, Illinois, a Chicago suburb. I'm from Three Rivers, Michigan, just a little midwest town of farmers, factories and local businesses—a town divided into wards 1 through 4. Of course, you're going to have the so-called well-to-do, and then the comfortable, and so on. I came from 4th ward, Burrows School, the bottom of the list. I guess because 4 is the highest number, I looked at being from 4th ward as a good thing. How many dollars do you want? $1 or $4? Yeah, that's how I looked at it but that's not the way society always sees it. People seemed to determine your value based on your financial worth. The so-called upper class so often called the shots. Well, 4th ward and 2nd ward, we had our share of the black people and so did 2nd ward.

My best friend was Doochee. Many times, he stayed overnight with me. We slept in the same bed. We didn't care. Color never came to mind. Too small. Too innocent. It was a good time. No segregation. That came as we got older. We didn't care.

We were just what we were—little boys with nothing to get in our way. Just a simple way of life that we shared as friends. My mom and dad said nothing and neither did his mom and dad. Things were so simple back then. Friend? You couldn't ask for anyone better and in return I was one to him. We loved each other as only two young boys could. I have many really good black friends today, as I did then. But it's sad—society will always have its way and separate people by their money.

People with money tend to be very fake, plastic or unreal—just my experience speaking. There are a few that can be down to earth but few and far between. This is the way of the world, not only for us in our so-called free society having the right to vote for our leaders. The big problem with that is it takes money today to be noticed and put on the ballot.

Hell, when you really look at what we have to choose from, what do you expect? There really is nothing there. They're all fake. No one, no one is there for the people. I mean really—are there any financially challenged politicians?

My mind would drift in and out of these thoughts and dreams, instigated from the morphine. I wasn't really into this type of drug and what the effects were. I did dabble with a bit of cocaine and once or twice, heroin. Heroin only a couple of times. The first was best. I already told you of the euphoric feeling that it induced in me—one that you could never explain to anyone.

Now here I lay, not by choice but by circumstance. A victim of my love, my love of my sport. The sport of skydiving—my life. Hell, I knew that with AFF we were doing something that nobody else had ever done. Yeah, I bit it off and like Ken, chose to do it because I knew it was a good way to teach. Even if the USPA said we were going to kill students. We knew better. We did it because we knew. Now here I am, and my good friend was dead. Myself, almost dead. The immense physical pain— no one, no one, could tell it and make it understandable. I was in a place—a place that you never want to visit and with God's help, your children will never visit. The morphine pumped into me by the hour. I lay in bed like a zombie. Drool leaked from the corners of my mouth with no physical control. My mind drifted out and in.

The first week was like being shuttled between heaven and hell. One moment there I lay—so white and clean like one of Jesus' disciples. The next, stripped of my garments and then thrown onto a rolling bed, dragging tubes, going down to the hell that waited for me—the pain. I could tolerate it with help of morphine, my only friend. I couldn't tolerate the scrubbing without it. Without it, I pass out. What to do? Nothing I can do. I am a victim of my surroundings. I must get well. I decided this. This has got to happen. The days run together. I see no daylight. There are windows but no way to look out. They have them covered because if the sun comes in the UV rays will get in the way of the healing process. Either way, there is no day, no night.

Time went by. How much, I don't know. The morphine kept me in the world that it is meant to when someone is in this kind of pain. I remember that I would be talking to a nurse and then I would wake up—no nurse to be seen. I thought, *Where is she? Where did she go? What did she say? What time is it? Where in the hell is the clock?* Godammit, I hurt. I'm stuck in the bed. I can't turn. Blood and clear fluids are leaking through the bandages and then going into the bed. I can't move. I'm a victim of my own body leaking through the wounds then drying like glue, pinning me to the bed. My only relief is the nurses with spray bottles of water. When they squirt it directly on the wound where the blood and fluid have hardened, it makes it soft. How horrible. I'm selfish. I have no clue what that little boy of 10, Jimmy, who is burned way worse than I—one could only imagine how he feels.

One more treatment then I can be at peace through the night. I only know time from what the nurses say. I wake. It must be morning. The nurses are there with the usual stuff—cereal, milk, and juice.

All I really wanted was a cold glass of water—the kind that comes out of an old pump on Grandma's farm. It could be hot as hell and Dad and I would go down to the old pump house—an old shack made of barn wood and red as all barns. A concrete tank lay with a ¾ inch pipe coming out of the shack. Inside is where the old motor belt and pump were. Straw covered the bottom to keep it from freezing. Tattered old wires came up to a switch, one with a handle on it you could switch to OFF or ON. It looked to me at that time, like the one Dr. Frankenstein pulled down to throw the juice to the monster and bring life into its body. When the lever was pulled down it made contact with the electricity that powered the motor that drove the belt that turned the pump. I remember the old coffee can full of water. As a kid who had to work the asparagus fields, I remembered the old man bringing the crew of school kids up from the hot dusty fields to get that cold water that poured out of that pipe. Damn, there was no better. So cold. So cold it hurt your teeth. Frost would collect on the pipe. I'll never forget that taste, that smell, the pump house. Damn, those were good times.

Here I lay. Milk, cereal, some other stuff I don't like. How was I going to get better? I drank the juice and pushed the rest away. I thought about the days I lay in the hospital at Three Rivers with hepatitis and my friend, Rick, scaling the wall with fried chicken. I knew if I was back home he'd be there for me. He'd make sure. I cried. I'm lonely. I can tell that's what I'm feeling. I hadn't seen anybody I knew for a long time. How long? Too long.

I think it was day three in the morning when I woke up and someone was holding my hand—a hand I had known all of my life. One I knew well. So soft. So real. I looked up. My mom! Tears poured from her face as she said to me, "How are you, son?"

I said, "I'm okay, Mom. I just hurt." She said nothing, just stood there crying.

I looked again—my Aunt Ick moved to the bed as Mom stepped away. She stroked my forehead. "You okay?" "Yeah, I'm okay, Aunt Ick." "Good," she said. I asked her, "How's Mom?"

She said, "Not good. She's worried."

"I'm okay, Aunt Ick. I'll get better. Hell, I'm not dead, damn it." I told her how hungry I was and asked her to get me some food. She said okay and reached in her purse and gave me some candy. I knew my Aunt Ick would pull me through. Mom came back and took over stroking my forehead. Not much was said, at least that I remember.

The morphine was so strong that I kept going in and out of consciousness. I was happy to see Mom, although I was worried and felt bad. All I've done my whole life is bring misery to her. It seemed like I was always in some kind of predicament that left me hurting. No mother who loves her son wants to see him physically or mentally hurt. I couldn't say much. I was just glad to see them. I don't remember much. I was a physical mess. Mom crying. Aunt Ick hanging onto my hand. Me, laying there like a zombie, full of that life sucking, mind dulling morphine. I couldn't think straight. The nurse came to take me down to the tank. That meant that it was the afternoon.

Mom said, "I'm staying with Aunt Ick. I'll be back in the morning. I love you, son."

I felt bad for Mom. I said, "Okay, I love you. Bye Aunty Ick." "Bye, Rock."

The nurses stripped me clean of my bandages and hell yes, it hurt but now I had something to look forward to. My mother—the person who had poured water over my head and soaped me down when I was a baby, cleansed me. I knew her love had never changed from then till now. It felt good, comforting. Things were better now. Aunt Ick was my favorite. She looked back as she and Mom left and gave me a big wink. I looked. She knew.

They put me on the gurney to take me to hell. Well, before I left, guess what? More morphine. I didn't say no. I was getting used to it. Like an old friend. When it came on, it was comforting and protected me from the pain—emotional and physical. They carried me off. The sessions got worse. I dreaded them. At least now I could move in my bed. No more did I stick to the sheets.

The food sucked. Every meal was full of milk. They told me you need to drink this. It will help you get better. Good luck,

I told them. I knew that they were right but I just plain didn't like the taste of milk—plain and simple. No water. I could not have water. Water takes the protein out of the body. The clear fluid that came to the top of the wound is protein. This is the stuff that would leak through the bandages and stick to the sheets. All I wanted was something decent to eat. A good coke or a cold beer. No way. I couldn't use my hands. I had a phone but couldn't use it. A nurse would hold it when I talked. The news people were constantly trying to talk to me. I wouldn't talk to them. I just shut them down. No comment.

When I did get to use the phone, I can remember the blood that came off my ears. My right one burned, the top of my left one a little crispy but still intact. When I would talk, it was a dreamlike—I could hear the person but then I would slip away in the morphine state. I would hang up and look at the earpiece on the phone covered with blood. No wonder it hurt when I held it to my ear. I didn't use it much.

Day and night were hard to tell apart. As I told you, there were windows but you couldn't see out. I started to tell when the tub sessions were coming by the way the nurses would appear. The morphine injections were always in my hip, and the side of my ass was starting to ache. The same with blood—they came almost daily to draw it. Most of the nurses were pretty good at hitting the vein, but every once in a while, I'd get one that couldn't quite get it right. "Christ," I'd tell her, "give me the damn thing. I know I can hit it." I should have shut up. It just made them nervous and they would miss again. What a mess: An IV in my neck, a damn tube stuck up my nose and down into my gut, and a catheter in my penis.

My mind would take me back, back to the balloon. I could still see the poor bastards looking over the edge. I wondered about how bad they were burned. Their eyes boiling out of the sockets in their skull. Their faces melting as if they were made of wax. I shook the thoughts from my mind but they kept coming back and still do to this day. I would look at my burned up hands when the nurses would get me ready for my bath. In the tub, the nurse would cut the dead skin off. It was days before they got it all off. The nails on my hands turned black and fell off. I counted how long I was there by which nails would come off.

My morning nurse was young and pretty. I liked her. She

was gentle and caring. I would get an erection when she bathed me. I couldn't help it. I even told her. She laughed. I think she liked it, too. Sometimes she would touch it with the wash cloth. My God, I couldn't even masturbate, which was a good thing. I looked forward to our sessions together. Hell, I needed some relief.

Jimmy and I got to be pretty tight. He was on the other side of the curtain, but we could talk back and forth. They treated him like they did me. Just at different times. My God, the poor kid. I could hear his teeth grind together when they took his bandages off. Grind and scrape. I could only lay there and listen. We had a nurse on the afternoon shift who would come in and take our bandages off without wetting them down first. The scabs would stick to the bandages. All the other nurses used spray bottles of water and let them soak. Not this bitch. She was Jamaican and seemed to love seeing us in pain. She did Jimmy first—the poor kid was crying, teeth grinding as the bitch would rip the bandages off. Time had gone by and it must have been a couple of weeks with this bitch tearing the dried bandages off.

One day after our morning bath and re-bandaging, I said, "Hey Jimmy. Watch what's gonna happen when that bitch tears my bandages off this afternoon."

"What you gonna do?"

"You'll see."

They brought lunch and I'll be damned, no milk. Two juices. Cool. Toasted cheese, tomato soup. Yes, a real meal. After lunch, I fell into a deep sleep. It felt like the real thing—a long, restful sleep. I woke up to the nurse holding a syringe loaded with morphine.

"What side this time?"

I said, "Don't matter. They both hurt."

She stuck it in on my left side, and I could feel the liquid burn as she emptied it into my body.

"You're all set, Rocky." They all knew my name.

I was starting to look forward to the shots. I could feel it coming on like an old train rolling down the tracks. I could feel the morphine going through my body. My eyes starting to sag. The drool starting to seep from the corner of my mouth onto my pillow. I'm starting to dream.

I hear Jimmy say, "Here she comes." Right on time. She

always goes to Jimmy first. She starts to tear the bandages off dry as usual. I hear the poor boy starting to grind his teeth. That heartless bitch. I'm starting to come out of the morphine dream state. I see her pulling on the bandages and I start to feel Jimmy's pain. I hear him starting to cry. I look at the nurse bitch's face. She appears to be having fun. She tells Jimmy, "Lay still. Quit moving. Lay still." The words in broken English. She finishes with Jimmy and disposes of his crusty, bloody bandages.

I'm next. I am ready. I can see Jimmy's eyes through the stocking that covers his head. Bitch pushes the stainless tray to the side of my bed and stops by my side. The spray bottle full of water is next to a pan with water in it. She picks up my left arm—perfect, I thought, I'll need my right hand. My left hand is in a soft cast. She cuts the end free and starts unwinding the bandage. She's close now. I thought—here we go. She's starting to pull off the bandage which is loaded with the clear protein that comes to the top of my open wound. Damn, that bitch. I'm thinking, this is going to stop. I pull my arm back away. "Soak the goddamn bandages!"

She grabs my arm. "You stay still." She starts again.

I jerk back. "Look lady, soak the bandages."

She says, "I know my job. Don't tell me."

"Okay lady, do it again." She grabs my arm starting to pull off the bandages. Again I jerk back. "Fuck you," flies out of my mouth.

The bitch replies "You Americans have life too good," in a smart ass tone. Again she grabs my arm. It's time, now or never.

I came across with my right hand and grabbed her by her throat and squeezed it. I pulled her close to my face. Her eyes bugging out of her head. Slowly, I've got her. Now it was our turn. "Don't you ever, ever touch me or that boy again you bitch," and threw her to the ground. She ended up on the floor screaming at the top of her lungs. Several nurses came running—five, maybe six. They picked her up and took her out of the room. They asked, "What happened?"

I clam up. "Nothing."

They looked to Jimmy. "What?"

"I didn't see a thing," he says. They left and I looked to Jimmy. A smile came through the stocking covering that hid his scarred, burned face. It was a smile that I had never seen, but I hadn't smiled either—something that we shared.

I felt good as I said to him, "She won't touch us again. I promise."

The smile disappeared and a look of relief replaced it. "Thanks," he said.

"That's okay, Jimmy. It was time. Thanks for not telling on me." He said nothing. The smile came back. I knew I did good.

A new nurse came in and sprayed me down to soak. 15 minutes later, the bandages fell off. Once they came off, they were exposed to the open air. It burned, damn, did it burn. I really didn't know why but they sure did. I guess it was a warm up before the tank. Once out of the tank, the nurse would pat me down with a towel to dry off. Then they put this silver cream on the wound called Silvadene, followed by gauze pads. Then they would wrap you like a mummy. Damn, that felt good. The Silvadene was cool and refreshing, and it took away the pain. Back to the room and to the bed. No one said a word. Pretty quiet, no one said anything. Cool.

Well, after my morning session, a doctor came and started to talk to me in a gentle voice asking me how things were and how I felt. I had never seen this guy before. I asked who he was.

He said, "I'm a doctor."

I said, "Oh yeah. What's your specialty?"

He had some fancy ass word for himself. I knew what he was. He finally got around to asking me about the nurse ordeal. Why I attacked her. I told him she treated me and Jimmy like shit.

He said, "What do you mean?"

I told him, "She wouldn't soak our bandages."

He said, "Well, that's not a reason to do that to her."

I said, "Look, Doc, you're not in this bed like me and Jimmy. Have you ever been burned?"

He looked at me and said, "Sure."

"Well, why don't you let me burn you time after time and let's see how you're gonna do. I'm sure you'll pull back. I'm sure you'll try to stop me from doing it again. It hurts."

I pointed to Jimmy and said, "you see that boy?"

He said, "Yes."

"Well, you sit in this room every day and listen to him cry and grind his teeth when that bitch comes in the room to prep him to go to the bath. Oh yeah, by the way, Doc, stick around and you can go down and watch."

Then he said, "I'm wondering why you're not grieving your friend's death."

I said, "What do you mean?"

He said, "Well, you're telling everyone that when you get out of here, you're going to keep on skydiving."

"Why not?"

"What do you have, a death wish?"

I looked at this idiot and thought to myself, *I wonder how much this dick is going to charge me for this little session?*

I said, "Look Doc, I'm still here because I'm a skydiver with good training and I had the wits to get out of the basket while I could and didn't break a bone. I think that's pretty good. Death wish—where does that come into the picture?"

He replies, "Why, skydiving is very dangerous."

I told him, "Look, you have no clue about what you're saying. You have no knowledge of my sport. You don't know about the equipment, the training, the airplane. Nothing. Not one damn thing. Hell, you don't even know the fatality statistics that come into play when you rate a sport as dangerous. You come in here ignorant to everything that we just talked about. Listen, why don't you do your homework before you come back because I know you're a goddamn shrink, aren't you?"

"Yes," he said.

"They sent you 'cause I choked that nurse."

"Well, yeah."

I said, "Well pal, I can't be that crazy because me and that boy don't have to suffer anymore from her evil hands. Besides, she told me she hated Americans and I'm a proud American. I competed in two World Championships and carried the gold medals home to America. America, the country my father fought for. For the freedom to make choices. Choices like the choice I made yesterday for myself and my friend—it was the only choice that Jimmy and I had. Why don't you go now and kick our little conversation around and then you write your little report. Besides, you're the one who needs help. You are so shallow."

He turned and walked away. I laughed. *What an idiot*, I thought. Sad, so sad. They make way too much money.

Time went by. The morphine continued to take its toll. My body was healing. I could see new skin starting to grown. They took out the tubes. I could get out of bed and walk around. I could even wipe myself after a bowel movement. Mom and Aunt Ick came up to see me regularly. Aunt Ick would sneak me in food—Krystal hamburgers. Yes! And Coke—little ones. Mom was feeling better because I was getting better.

The doc would see me every couple of days to check my progress. He kept telling me that I would never have full mobility of my hand back to 100 percent. I thought to myself, *Don't tell me. We will just see, pal.* I had been in the hospital now for about four weeks and had started to heal up pretty good. My fingernails were gone and my hair was starting to grow back. I was still getting my baths three times a day. The food was better now that they knew what I wanted. I was going out for short walks and starting to get my strength back. Jimmy's mom and dad were there all of the time, so I had a little company. One day the doc came in and said maybe another week and I could go home. I told him it would be good to get out of there. I could use a cold beer.

He said, "Why wait? You can have beer now if you want it."

"What are you telling me?"

"Beer is high in protein. A couple a night would be good."

Now do you think I can run down to the 7-11 and get a 6-pack? Try again. I was laughing. I couldn't believe it. No water, but beer was okay. Go figure.

Jimmy's dad heard the conversation, and his folks liked me. They liked how I chocked that nurse. They had seen how she would tear the bandages off Jimmy's arms and legs. Well, the next time his dad showed up, he had a 12-pack of Bud. That evening after my last debridement session and when things got a little quiet, I strolled into the nurses' station and got me a cold Bud. I went back into my room, sat in bed, popped the top and pulled on the cold beer. Been a while. Sure tasted good. Thank you, Jimmy's dad.

Just before I got out, they put a cast on my arm and hand. I would have to have it on for a few weeks. It was damn tight and I thought the thing was too tight. My skin was just starting to come back on my left hand, and I really wasn't sure why they casted it. Why they would do that, I have no idea. How in hell do they think I can treat my burns? Made no sense.

I was feeling stronger and stronger every day. I finally told them, stop. Stop. No more of the morphine. I had enough of it. I couldn't wait. I wanted out. I wondered what happened to the AFF program. I talked to Gary a couple of times but not much was said about that, mostly about how I was doing. Well, I'm OK. What about my AFF program?

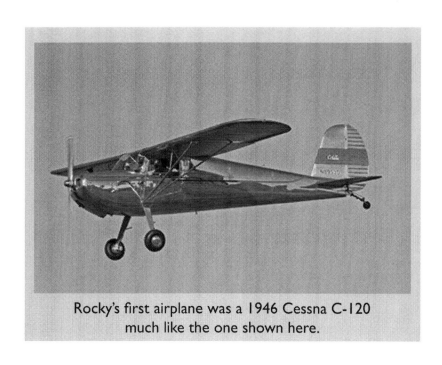

Rocky's first airplane was a 1946 Cessna C-120
much like the one shown here.

Chapter Fifteen

## LEARNING TO FLY WITH
## AFF STILL ON MY MIND

The days went by fast and I was ready when my release from the hospital after the balloon crash came. I was finally out—out under the open sky. I remember the sun, so bright. I felt like a mole stepping our into the light. The sun, so bright. I'm out. The smells came first—I could smell the grass, the dirt—yes! The clouds were so clear, so clean. I couldn't help but smile. But my mind was looking upward—I wanted to jump, I wanted to fly.

\* \* \*

I had started learning to fly before the balloon crash. At that point I think I had maybe six or seven towards my license. My good friend, Fog, was a pilot and a pretty good one. He made it through a couple of crashes, one of them just before I got back down to Florida. My friends and I, Hoot and Fog, flew in a Piper PA-11 that Liza Jones owned. We taught Liza and her two stepchildren, Eva and Edgar, how to skydive using the AFF program. Ken and Liza were working together to help the AFF program get started. What a nice lady. I trained her from her AFF Levels 4-7, transitioned her to a square canopy, and then worked one-on-one with her. Our goal was for her to get her 16-way before 20 jumps.

Liza had the PA-11 for years, and the three of us worked and to have the annual inspection completed. After that, all we had to do was to put fuel in it and fly it. Flying was something I'd always wanted to do but just never had the time or money. Sounds like everybody else I know. Before the balloon crash,

Fog was trying to teach me how to fly, and I was just plain terrible. Just terrible. Couldn't keep the damn thing straight. Couldn't flare at the right altitude. Fucking terrible.

I was staying with Gary Dupuis and my friend Hoot at Gary's house in DeLand. When we went home at night after jumping, Gary would talk to me about flying and what made the airplane do what it did. Night after night, he'd tell me about how the control surfaces worked. Lift. Drag. Thrust. Gravity. Different airplanes. Wing loading. Chord. Span. What to look at as far as airplane features before you climb in it. Then climb in and get familiar with the cockpit and the instruments. The whole layout.

One evening Gary had to fly over to Zephyrhills to deliver a Cessna 195, pick up a Citabria airplane for a client, and fly the Citabria back to DeLand. I went with him. Gary flew over and halfway back. Then he said, "You fly." This was the first time I had been in an airplane since flying with Fog. Stick and ball. Yes! The Citabria is a tail wheel airplane that is set up for basic aerobatics. Damn, it felt good. I made a couple of sharp turns to feel the airplane. The stick felt better than a wheel type yoke. I could feel the airplane better—360 degree access.

I had the DeLand airport in sight. The wind was nil to none. It was dusk. I set up and started my final. I sat up in the seat and shifted my rear around centering my body. I was on a pretty good glide slope and my speed was 70 mph. Perfect. I was coming across the airport property getting closer and closer to the threshold of runways. I crossed the edge of the asphalt. I looked down the side of the airplane. The Citabria was sitting stable in the air. No bumps. No thermals. Just smooth. *I'm close now. I can tell. Power back. I start to settle. I pull back on the stick ... not yet ... stick back more ... not yet ... stick back— rudders work to keep the old girl straight ... stick back ... back ... back ... chirp ... straight, straight, stick back, rudders going right and left, right and left.*

The airplane started to slow. I started to point my toes to apply the brakes. I remember Gary telling me if you felt yourself use them, you're abusing them. Ever so lightly, I pushed on the top of the rudder pedals. We stopped. I looked. I was right on the center line. I heard Gary say, "Good job, my airplane!" I let go of everything. Feet on the floor. I heard the engine start to rub up. I take a deep breath and released all that pressure that built up on the landing. *Yes! Yes! Yes! I did it! I got it! I can fly!*

We taxied in and Gary kicked the tail around. Perfect—right on the tie downs. We climbed out. I stretched. I heard Gary tie it down.

"I'm going to the office," he said.

I said, "Okay."

That was it. After that I never had a problem flying any airplane. C-150, C-172, C-182, Cubs, PA11, PA12, C-180, C-185, Beavers, single place Pitts Special. I just plain got it. That was just before the balloon crash and this was something that I was looking forward to when I got out.

* * *

When I left the hospital, the nurse gave me a jar of the Silvadene and a lot of gauze bandages. This is the funny part—I can't remember a prescription for pain. I'm sure I got one but I really don't remember taking anything for the pain. If there was pain, I couldn't tell. I had gone through the worst of the worst.

Before I left, the doctor told me what to do. Stay out of the sun was the big one. Exercise and stretch the skin. If not, I wouldn't get the full motion out of my arms and fingers. I was well shy of being able to make a fist. My right arm was tight. My right ear had the tip burnt and it was black. I had lost the tips on my fingers. Burnt off. My face itself made out pretty well. If I had not covered it with my hands and arms, I would have been like Jimmy. I felt bad for the boy. We got to be the best of friends in the hospital. I followed up on him that first year, but after that, I lost touch.

My mom and Aunt Ick drove me back to our house in Three Rivers. I was wondering about the AFF program. What would happen now? Damn, I had a lot of time in this program, and I didn't want the USPA to get it.

We arrived back in Three Rivers. Mom cooked me a solid meal. Damn, it tasted good with a cold Coke. Damn, life was good. It was almost hunting season which always lifted my spirits. After I ate, I walked through the cemetery visiting my friends and, of course, my dad. I said my peace to all of them and continued down to the St. Joe River. Damn, I was lucky not to break my legs when I jumped out of that balloon gondola—I felt really lucky for that. I walked back to the house and bullshitted with my brother Mike and his friend, Mark.

Aunt Ick had an attorney friend who pursued a lawsuit as a result of the balloon crash. I didn't have a dime, and I wanted to get back to Florida to continue with the AFF program. A good friend of mine named Dick just so happened to be in Michigan at a skydiving boogie. I think it was an annual Richmond, Indiana, boogie—the one where I went low on the 16-way on the first boogie there.

I got a hold of Dick and within two days, I was traveling south in Dick's big Dodge van. The ride home from Florida was long. I rode shotgun on the way down—left hand in a cast, right hand and arm wrapped in gauze. I had learned how to dress myself with the Silvadene and gauze. I had to be careful of the new skin because it would blister real easy. We stopped overnight in Atlanta and headed to DeLand the next day. The cast on my left hand started to rub a big red spot and the skin was gone. It started to stink—the nasty smell of rotten tissue. I knew that there was a problem but was going to wait before I chose to take the cast off.

I got to Gary's at about eight o'clock at night. Hoot was there but Gary was gone. Hoot said Gary was in Tennessee going to school for his airplane mechanic's license. Hoot and I hugged it up and as I looked him in the eye, I told him, "Man, is it good to be back home."

He smiled and said, "I bet!"

"You got some pot?" I said.

"Yep."

"Roll one up. I could use a joint."

Hooter smiled and got out the rolling tray. As he started to put one together, I asked him, "What's up with our AFF?"

Hoot said that the USPA was working with Ken's wife and had made her some kind of offer for the rights. I was shocked. I said, "What did Gary say?"

Hoot said, "Not much. Not much he can do."

I said, "Why hell, Hoot. The sons of bitches wanted nothing to do with it. What in the hell do they think they can do with it now? They have no idea how to do it."

He told me that in Ken's briefcase was all the paper work—the seven levels, the outline form, everything.

I said, "Who has the briefcase?"

"Ken's wife."

At that point, I started to see our program slipping through our fingers. The thieves from the USPA were laughing at us. They took advantage of Ken's death. They were dancing on his grave.

"You finished with that joint, Hoot?"

He said, "Yeah," and handed it to me. I fired it up and hit it a good couple times and then passed it back to Hoot. We smoked it down and he asked me, "How ya doing?"

"I'm okay. My left hand is in a cast as you can see. This thing is rubbing a hole in my hand. Smell it?"

Hoot took a sniff. "Smells rotten to me."

"What do you think I should do, Hoot?"

He said, "Take it off."

I said, "How?"

He told me that he had one on his ankle when he broke his foot on a jump. "Go upstairs and fill the tub with water and then sit in it and soak it."

"Then what?" I asked.

"Find the end and start to unwind it."

"Okay."

I went upstairs and did what he told me. I unwrapped it. He was right. The whole damn thing reeked of rotten meat. I sure could not have waited the full six weeks. Why hell, I hadn't had it on for a week.

Time went by. I stayed inside for another month, and then it started to cool down and I could get out. I was healing quickly. The tip of my right ear fell off but other than that, I was getting on pretty good. I still couldn't jump, but I could fly, and I did as much as I could.

We got the official word that the USPA had bought the AFF program from Ken's wife. I tried to get Gary to fight them but he gave up. Gary even decided to sell his drop zone. But before the sale, the USPA wanted Gary and myself and Hoot to help them run the very first AFF instructor course. They told Hoot and I that we couldn't have an AFF instructor rating because we were not static line rated. Of course, we told them to go get screwed and rightfully so. But we did take notice. We never sat in on the classroom, but I did pay attention to the practical part of it. I watched them as they tried to put together a series of six jumps and have the applicants be tested in the areas of expertise. Now who in the hell was going to score these applicants, and what areas are they going to be scored in?

After three days of disgust, I agreed to help. Two USPA instructors would be acting as my AFF instructors and practice taking me through the training program. Well, they treated me as if I was an AFF Level 3 student with a release. As they were suiting me up, I chose my own jumpsuit. It was a big, baggy suit, lots of drag. Why I chose it never occurred to them. Now these were USPA cream of the crop—the best of their best instructors. As they escorted me to the plane, my skin was still scabbed and my hand still messed up from the balloon accident. I should not have been jumping, but I had so much into the program—not only my time and all I had learned, but my good friend, Ken, was now dead. So I chose to jump to prove my point—my point being that the purpose of the program was not for everybody to get a rating. Hell, before his death Ken and I talked about only a handful in the entire U.S.

When we got to the plane, Mike and Don, the USPA instructors, helped me in and treated me as if I was a third jump student. I did nothing out of the ordinary in response— just went along with the scenario. We got to altitude. The door opened and they told me to get into the spotting position. Here's where the game began. Don pointed down and was giving me a full class in spotting. I kept saying, "What? What? I can't hear you. What are you saying?"

He started to get flustered and kept repeating himself to the point where I told him, "Let's go or we're not gonna make it back." Basically I took charge in that area of skill. I looked to the pilot and said, "Cut." Then I said, "Okay, Don. I'm now a student again. Take over."

He said, "Put your feet out after me." He climbed out and I swung my feet back on the step. My next move should have been to check back in with Mike, but I blew that off and started to climb out. Mike kept trying to get me back in, but there was no way. The spot was too long and for our own safety, I carried on with the dive. Check in to Mike. Check out to Don. Up, Down, Arch. I did COA, one dummy pull, and now it was going to get good. I saw one of them drop off and then the other. I sat stable keeping my fall rate with theirs. They were okay at relative work but these guys were no world champions. I started to spread out and as I did, I watched them start to go below me. I was laughing, laughing right in their faces. I kept them about five feet below me. They were screwed, and they knew it. *Why did you dumbasses let me put on that big suit?* I learned that very quickly in my earlier days of teaching AFF. And these guys are now teaching the class for the USPA.

Well, it wasn't a good enough lesson just to make them fall below. I needed to really make a point to these guys that they had no idea what they were doing. The way the student is evaluated is by testing works is the actual person who is judging the applicants plays the student in a make-believe scenario and puts them through the test on an actual jump and lets the applicants get judged for their air skills. Air skills are the part of AFF that keeps the student alive. These guys had no clue. Hell, they had no actual training time. They didn't have even one jump with a student. Hell, I had way over 700, more like 760 actual AFF jumps, and these idiots are going to refuse Hoot and I an instructor rating?

Well guys, let's just see what you got. They're low, still five feet below me as I passed through 7,000 feet. Hell, if this was real, how could they help me? They couldn't. They just laid there doing everything in their power to get to me. Well, I started to spin past 4,000 feet. They didn't even give me the pull signal—then past 3,000 feet, down to 2,500 feet. I'm still spinning. They have no choice but to pull their canopies. I'm still spinning down to 1,800 feet and then I pull mine.

Under my canopy, I could feel pain shooting through my left wrist as I turned base to final approach. I stood up at the large T. Mike and Don landed nearby. They immediately started back into instructor mode, helping me with my canopy and asking me about my jump. I looked at them with a smile and told them, "I am probably dead," and walked with them back to the drop zone. I made my point but elected not to give the USPA any more of my knowledge. I only wanted to make a point. And I did.

Now AFF training is known as a USPA program all over the world. And to this day I hate the USPA organization. I fought the organization for years and years with no one to help me. I even had to fight for Hoot and I to get our AFF instructor rating until finally we did. It might have been a long time ago, but they still owe me for my time, my expertise, my close calls, and Ken's death. Life's unfair, but I guess we all know that.

Above, Rocky's mother poses with his 1956 Cessna170B. Below, at Bob Lee's airstrip: (L to R) Dan Andrews, Jimmy the Geek, Gary Dupuis, Bob Lee, and Hoot. Rocky in front.

Chapter Sixteen

# HARD TIMES, GOOD TIMES

The next ten months were bad. Couldn't work. I had no money and nobody cared. Gary even fired me from his shop. My hand was still messed up; I really didn't feel safe training students. I lived on food stamps and pity—not a way that I would ever choose to live my life.

One day a letter came from Aunt Ick's lawyer. The lawsuit he had filed after the balloon crash had been settled. Two days later, I got a little money. Felt damned good. I enrolled at Embry Riddle Aeronautical and went to school. I bought an old truck and an old airplane—a Cessna 120 tail dragger. I loved that plane. I flew it every spare moment I could get in the air, and man could I fly that plane. Gary had turned over ownership of his drop zone to Bob Hallett and Tommy Piras. Tommy let me do what I wanted. I went to school for a year. School wasn't cheap, but it was good.

I would sometimes fly my Cessna over to a little grass strip called Bob Lee's. Now Bob was a crusty old dude and as mean as a rattlesnake, but he liked me and I liked him. One day he caught me down at the end of his runway where I was with a girl having sex. I flew in with my plane thinking I'd find some privacy. Well, you guessed it. Cagey old Bob snuck down in his truck—more for a cheap thrill than anything else. Well, from that moment on, we were best of friends. I did a few odd jobs for Bob, but mostly I worked for Tommy Piras in DeLand.

Just about this time, Bill Booth had come up with a rig he called the tandem rig. Now Booth wasn't the most courageous skydiver I've ever known, and even though it was his rig and he built it, he didn't like jumping it. The year was 1984. He'd bring his tandem rig to the drop zone and say, "You want to take a friend on a jump?"

Why hell yeah, I did. I took several friends to jump, including a 5 a.m. jump to watch one of the shuttle launches. I believe it was Columbia, the one that blew up. All in all, I took at least 75 people on a tandem jump without a drogue chute. I even took a little eight-year-old, Gary's little nephew called Wally.

Wally had been around skydiving since he was about four years old, and on this day he apparently said something to Gary about wanting to jump. Gary asked me if I would take him, and I said okay. I told Wally I'd take him up and we'd do the tandem out of Mr. Douglas, Gary's DC-3.

I put the rig on, put the harness on Wally, and away we went. We got to 10,500 feet which was as high as I needed. I hooked him up and carried him down the aisle between the two rows of seats with his feet completely off the ground. Now we're at the open door, each of my hands on the door frame. I leaned way out and the kid had the best view of the entire world for seven seconds or more.

Here's where I'm going with this. This boy was eight years old, a little Florida cracker. He was definitely not afraid of the jump. Not one bit. This is an example of how skydiving is 90 percent mental and 10 percent skill. This little boy hadn't had a chance to let the newspaper reports and the television media influence him. The news media blows the danger of the sport way out of proportion. Well, it's not. In fact, if you look at the reality of fatalities that happen in all sports, you will see that skydiving is ranked well below gymnastics, horse racing, and bull riding. Somewhere in the teens. The reality of it is that when a death does occur the media will often say the skydiver died because his parachute failed. Well, it's not the parachute that failed, but the person using the system improperly.

A parachute system includes a harness and two containers and two parachutes and that's it. When your main does have a problem, you have a way to detach it and get clear from it before opening the reserve.

Another factor in skydiving is that it's fast, very fast, and people lose track of time, but with this kept in mind, it's definitely not dangerous. It's really quite simple. All you actually do is jump out of the plane. Gravity takes hold and your role is to control yourself in freefall and pull your ripcord at the right altitude. Pretty easy, don't you think? I do, and I have done it about 9,000 times.

The most jumps goes to some guy in New England with 42,000, and he's still alive. Young Wally hadn't had all that propaganda shoved down his throat so society hadn't gotten him all messed up yet.

When I pull him back into the plane, Wally spits out this hillbilly accent and in so many words says, "We ain't gonna land in dat der water down there, are we?"

"Now Wally," I said, "do you think I'm gonna land us in the water?"

He replies, "I reckon not."

I tell him, "Okay, put your hands across your chest."

As he is doing that, I'm backing up to get a running start. When I reach the edge of the door, I dive head first in a superman like dive, head down and pointed to the ground. Then I relax and spread out to slow down and let him soak up a panoramic view of the world. We fall for 50 seconds and I pull.

The little guy squeals "Yahoo!" I smile and tell the kid, "Here, you steer for a while." He reaches up and grabs hold of the toggles. I think, *Damn, eight years old and skydiving. This tandem stuff is cool.*

Back on the ground, I stand Wally up and unhook him. A big cow lick on the front of his hairline and flashing his big buck teeth, he slaps me five and says thanks. I daisy chain the lines and walk back in. Wally rushes up to Gary to tell him about his jump, and Gary is grinning back. Wally finishes his story and climbs back onto the bike he was riding before the jump. He never said a thing to anyone unless they asked. No big deal to him.

Tandem opened new doors for the sport of skydiving, and since then has been used for a lot of applications. The only real change is that now a drogue chute is used to slow a skydiver down to a moderate speed prior to opening the main canopy. In the old days it was not uncommon to blow up the main canopy every one out of 10 jumps due to excessive speed.

One day I got a package in the mail from Adrian Warren, one of my first students from England. It had a BBC sticker on it with a return address in Bristol, England. I opened the envelope and read the cover letter:

"Dear Rocky, Hope this letter finds you well. I am working on a film documentary and want to know if you would be interested in helping me. Enclosed are pictures and details."

I pulled out a stack of pictures and read a little bit about Adrian's proposed expedition and film documentary. It entailed flying to the middle of the Amazon jungle to tandem jump onto the top of a giant rock monolith 4,300 feet above the jungle floor. We would camp on top for two weeks, climb down 1,300 feet into a large cave that ran clean through the mountain, explore and map the cave, climb back up, and then prepare to BASE jump off the mountain to the jungle below. After we landed we would collect our gear, hike to the Orinoco River, and take a dugout boat back to the town where we started.

*Gee, is that all he wants?* I thought. *Easy, right? Yeah, not right!*

The letter went on to say, "If you decide to go, I need you to find us a tandem rig that you think we should use. Along with that, help me choose a group of Americans that you think can handle the jobs that we need done."

Now this was no ordinary mountain. There was no mountain chain. It stuck straight out of the Amazon jungle like it grew there—4,300 feet high and pretty close to straight up. Adrian had just come back from there where he had chartered bush pilots to fly him 75 miles into the jungle and then fly over and around the mountain Autana, taking pictures. He then returned to England before contacting me. The pictures took my breath away.

A week or two went by, and another packet with more information and forms to fill out arrived. Along with that info was a short letter telling me that he would be on his way to see me within the month. He said that the top was loaded with these special carnivorous flowers. Sounded like something out of the lost world. The top of this thing was plenty big for landing—300 meters by 500 meters.

I talked to Booth about the expedition, and he didn't want anything to do with the jump. It scared him. Hell, it scared me. Not only a jump, but a tandem jump.

Then I started to look at what we had for outs if something went wrong. Forget it; there were none. You missed landing on the mountain and you were screwed. Down into the jungle. This was serious. That jungle had shit that would kill you in two seconds after you got bit, and shit that would eat you, including the natives. Well, maybe not, but that's what I was thinking. I imagined my head cut off, shrunk down, and traded for five or six cows. What a way to go.

Plus, this was cocaine country. You get caught walking around down there and those natives might figure you for CIA coming to bust their lab. They'd shoot you quick, take your wallet, your passport, and every other thing that they could get money for, burn your body and say good bye. Back in the 1970s, I knew a guy that bought a Lockheed Loadstar and plumbed it so it had a long range tank. He and two other guys went down somewhere close to where I was going to get a load of pot and never came back. One guy left behind a new wife and baby. A couple years later, I saw some pictures of them all shot up laying on top of the Loadstar. I knew it was them. The damn N number was the same. I knew that these people here didn't dick around.

Adrian came to town on holiday and we got together. He brought me an associate of his at the BBC as an AFF student. Adrian's buddy did well and went through the program in seven jumps. He also brought his two boys of seven and ten—the age for enjoying Mickey Mouse and Disneyworld.

This time Adrian was dead serious, a side of him I had never seen before. We sat at the airport bar and had a few beers, and he told me what he had in mind. Then he looked at me and asked the big question, "Do you think it can be done?"

I replied, "Yes. The skydiving part shouldn't be a problem." It was the rest of the details that put a question in my mind. First of all, this expedition was not only about landing on the mountain, it was a film documentary. "How are you gonna get that equipment on top of the mountain? Helicopter?"

"Why, no," he replied.

"Well, then how?"

I knew what was involved in film making from working with Liza Jones. She owned a movie studio at the Nautilus Center in Lake Helen, Florida. Once she got her AFF certification, I did nothing but one-on-one work getting her to do what no other skydiver had ever done—to close in eighth or later in a formation and get her SCS before her 20th jump. Well, she had all this on film. The filming required a lot of equipment, and it wasn't small stuff either. The cameras had a big cradle that would fit on your shoulder, plus car batteries to power them, and that was just the cameras. The sound recorder was big with a long staff with a mike on that. Hell, that was just a small part of what would be required. Helicopter? Out of the question. Why, if they wanted to do that, they would use it for us.

"Well, what?"

"Cargo parachute."

I said, "What? Out of what kind of airplane?" "

He smiled. "DC-3."

"Who you gonna get to drop the cargo?"

"British military."

"Okay, I'll buy that. But if you're serious, I've got our man and he's damn good. Solid, ya know what I mean?"

"Oh, yeah? What's his name"

"Mitch," I said. "Two time world champion. Smoke jumper, twenty-plus years. Been kickin' cargo most of those 20. I spent time with him at the Nationals plus a couple of Boogies. Know him good. Good enough to put my ass in his hands."

"Interesting," Adrian said. "What about Booth?"

"He's scared, and I don't want him. He'll get in the way."

"What about his rig?"

"I've jumped it. It's good."

"Do you know Strong?"

"Sure. He sponsored our 4-way team for years."

"What do you think about his rig?"

"Don't know, Adrian. Haven't seen it."

Adrian said, "I'm gonna go down tomorrow and check it out."

"Good," I said. "Get a hold of me when you're back."

That's pretty much how it went. Adrian came back with Strong's rig, but I really didn't like his canopies. I told Booth about the documentary and dangled it in front of him. Told him he would be on TV. He liked that a lot. He agreed to give us the rigs. This was no little quest - three tandem rigs and 10 sport rigs complete. And we needed them in three months.

In the meantime, I called Mitch and he liked the idea. I turned him on to Adrian and kept on Booth about the rigs. Adrian had a contract with one of the very best cameramen in the business, plus the guy was a big time BASE jumper. He had over 200 BASE jumps. He and his wife did it together. I hadn't done one, but I would have if I could check out the jump.

This mountain was high enough, that was for sure. The landing might be tricky. And still that was not my concern. It's not like being in the good ol' U.S.A. We were going to be in the middle of the Amazon jungle. If somebody got hurt, how would we get them out—that's the problem. No helicopter was a big concern. Seventy-five miles away from nothing. I tried to stay positive, telling myself all I had to do was tandem a guy on top and then jump off. Piece of cake.

As the days went by, I started to work out. I was in pretty good shape as it was. I was completely healed from the balloon crash and I had a part-time job working at the drop zone. And now old Bob Lee told me that I could live on the end of his runway and pay him nickels to stay there. I bought a used trailer and put it down on the end. It was perfect. I had my C-120 and then I bought a 1956 C-170B, the last year Cessna made the aircraft—only 1,600 hours total time and a top on the engine. Four seater, beautiful airplane. I decided to fly it to Michigan to see my mom.

I shot out of DeLand with just a compass and no radio that worked. I had an artificial horizon(AH) but not much more. I left in the afternoon and stopped at a little airport in Perry, Georgia. I left there in the morning and headed north. The clouds came in and I decided to climb. Weather said that it would be scattered on the way up. Hell, I kept climbing and climbing. I had 3/4 tanks on both sides. I kept grinding on and on. Nothing but white, just white. While I was climbing up through the clouds, I got vertigo bad. I could hear the plane diving, airspeed climbing in the yellow. I'd shake my head and look at my AH. Hell, it was all cocked sideways. I finally got control back and fixed on my compass. It said 180 degrees. That was the wrong way! I started to turn back north but then there it went again—goddamn plane diving, ball out of the center. Shit! I learned how to fly basic instruments before it was over. Later, I recalled Gary talking about vertigo and how it could kill you. One thing that sunk in was that you would swear that the plane was doing one thing, and it was really doing something else. He was so right.

I locked on a heading with wings level and air speed on. I made it to the top of the cloud bank at 13,500 feet. The little plane did all it could do to get me there. But I was there, thank God. But now I was lost, and my fuel gauges were rocking in and out of the "no take off" reading. I knew these gauges were good because they were mechanical—just an indicator on a cork float. I started setting up for a descent. The way I had it figured I was somewhere in Tennessee—somewhere in the Smoky Mountains.

I'm going to tell you this right now. I've been through some scary shit, but this time was the big one. I was not only scared, but scared for a long time. I knew the tops on some of the mountains in this mountain chain went up to six or seven thousand feet. As I was descending, the vertigo wasn't quite so bad. I still felt it but I knew enough to believe my AH. Down and down I flew. I tried to go slow because if I did hit the side of a mountain, I wouldn't be going 160 mph and maybe, just maybe, I would make it through the crash. I was descending through 7,000 feet in a slow spiral at 100 mph. Then 6,000 feet and I thought, *God help me, where am I? What am I going to do if this shit goes to 500 feet?*

I'm descending through 5,000 feet. I reach down and pull my seat belt tight. *Not tight enough.* I didn't want to smash my face on the dash. I grab the belt and reef down on it. It pulls tight. I'm good and snug. I look. I'm passing through 4,000 feet and still no bottom. I'm starting to feel sick, starting to think it's coming. I'm preparing for a crash. I look down. The white is starting to fade. Spots are showing through the misty scene.

Damn it! Damn it! I made it. I'm through it! I feel good. I'm out. Whew! I look at the fuel gauges—they're still bouncing in and out of the "no take off" zone. I'm now convinced that I'm going to land on that four lane highway. Yep. That's just what I'm going to do. I look again at the gauges. I know I'll have an extra five minutes or so once I hear the engine start to sputter. Gary taught me how to slip it and pick up the residual. I've done it before; I can do it again if I have to and I damn sure will. Rapid fire thoughts are running through my head. I know I'm going to jail. I've only got a student license. My airplane's out of annual inspection.

I have to land this plane. I'm flying above the freeway. I'm lost. I look up and around. The mountains are going right into the clouds. I'm in a valley—thank God. Down at 500 feet is a layer of scud but I can still see. I'm going to land on that four-lane road. I don't have a choice. I start to look at the cars looking for a break in the traffic so I can stick this plane in between the cars. I look again and spot an antenna rising up through the scud clouds.

I'm still following that road waiting for a break. I'll be goddamned ... a runway, or at least that's what it looks like. I get closer. Damn it. It *is* a runway. It's an airport. YES! I fly over and look for the windsock. Then I see it—a tower! It's controlled and I don't have a radio. What the hell? I don't care. I don't have any gas and I've got no choice. I start my downwind. I'm looking at the sock. It's 90 degrees to my runway and the damn thing is sticking straight out. I set up for final. I'm only giving it two notches of flaps. My foot is stuck to the floor and my wingtip is down. I'm over the threshold now and am good and straight. Thank God I knew crosswind landings. I set my gear down and keep it there till out of cross control. I fly the bitch to the end. The tail comes down and I pin her down. The runway is pretty long and my taxi strip is just ahead. I turn off and taxi up to the ramp.

There is an old black guy giving me taxi instructions. I pull up and he signals me to shut down. He chocks me and I sit for a moment, my seat belt so tight I can hardly undo it. I start to climb out and notice how stiff my legs are. I can barely walk. I limp up to the old black guy and say, "Top it off".

He says, "OK, sir. No problem." I look to the tower then back at the black guy. He's already fueling the right side.

"I'm sure glad to see you," I say.

"What's wrong, bud? Have a rough flight?"

I say back, "Yeah, kinda. Well I guess I should get a hold of somebody in that tower."

He says, "Why shoot, you ain't gotta worry 'bout that tower. Ain't nobody been in it for two years."

I said, "Come on dude, and let's have a coffee".

I sat around for a while and tried to shake it off. This scared me a bit—a lot.

After my coffee, I got back in the airplane. I had called weather and they said moderate VFR and clouds broken to scattered. I sat there for a few minutes, thinking about what I'd just been through. I guess there was a lesson to be learned but at that moment I had only one thought, *I'm not going to get lost again*. I pulled out my Tennessee sectional and fired up my airplane. As I was taxiing out, there stood the old black line guy slowly waving good-bye. I gave him a military salute and taxied down to the end. I put my sunglasses on because the sun was starting to break through. I felt good. The cocaine was starting to work. Downtown Knoxville was the name of the airport. In case you're wondering, I made it to Michigan and back again with no more emergencies.

* * *

Time was going by fast. Adrian's BBC expedition was starting to come together. Booth had decided to go. I think he liked the idea of being in a movie. My passport was expired so I got a new one. I got all the shots required for traveling. I worked out every day. Some people asked me about practice jumps. How many had I done? Practice jumps? I had done 8,300 jumps, or whatever. I had been practicing the last twenty years for this jump. I was more than confident, but think about this: three tandem rigs, 10 sport rigs, all of our gear, plus the film crew's gear. All of this headed down to the Venezuelan/ Colombian border in the middle of the Amazon jungle. There was good reason to be concerned.

The infamous "Mr. Douglas" sits grounded on the runway after an unauthorized skydiver played with the controls.

Skydivers exit from the rear of a Russian military aircraft. Next stop, North Pole.

JUMPING TO THE TOP OF THE WORLD

Chapter Seventeen

## NORTH POLE ADVENTURE PART ONE

I'll always be proud of what we accomplished on the Autana adventure, but I was so happy to be safe and sound back in the good ol' U.S.A. I went back to my little trailer and back to work with Bob Lee, the old man with the airport. For the next five years, I lived and worked for Bob, one hell of a man who taught me a lot of ways of life. He was a true aviator.

I started my own drop zone in Flagler Beach, Florida, in the next county north of DeLand, and ran it for 10 years. During this time I taught a lot of people to skydive. I made several trips to Europe to teach instructors how to teach Accelerated Freefall. I had a string of experiences worth remembering. One of them was landing a 67-year-old woman on the North Pole in a tandem skydive.

While I was operating my drop zone in 1996, I got a call from a friend who owned a skydive operation in DeLand. He asked me if I would be interested in taking his place to tandem jump a 67-year-old woman to the top of the world—the North Pole. I said, "How much does it pay?"

He told me, and I said, "Why not?"

I asked him when and he told me next month. This was March of 1996. Damn, the North Pole, why in the hell does she want to do this? He said that she had done two tandems at his drop zone. There was an expedition being planned in April and she wanted to be part of it. That was good enough for me. Now, 67 years old was no spring chicken, and I knew from my previous experience traveling and skydiving abroad that this would be more of a pain than fun. The pay would make the pain not hurt so bad, but it would still be a pain. Little did I know how much pain. I got her number and called. Her name was Louise. Hell, the name even sounded old. I called Louise and got to ask her some questions and just plain bullshitted with her and got to know her. She sounded nice enough and I asked her if she would do a tandem with me just to feel the old gal out. I agreed to meet her at my friend's drop zone in DeLand.

When I arrived, Bob went to find Louise. Between the time he left until Bob got back with her, I must have pictured a hundred variations in my mind of what this 67 year old woman would look like. Then I saw this frail and fragile woman who had one of those kind of smiles, like, "Hello young man, I am the woman that you're going to take to the top of the world."

I smiled back, stuck my hand out and said, "Louise? I'm Rocky Evans, three times National Champion, two times World Champion skydiver. Now let's get one thing straight. I hate to blow my own horn and hate people who do. I don't need the ego boost like some. I figure it's like this: I did all that I have done for two people. One is dead and I'm the other. And that's just plain it. I like what I see when I look in the mirror and that's where it stops. I use my credentials and my past achievements in my business to comfort the people that I give my services to. And that's it."

She said, "That's very impressive, Rocky."

I also blew some more smoke at her, letting her know that I had 8,000 parachute jumps, that I did a lot of the research and development jumps for AFF, and told about my expedition to the mountain, Autana. Then I said, "What do you do, Louise?"

She replied, "I'm a Sunday school teacher."

"Oh, that's a very good thing to do, to help spread the Word," I said.

But I thought, this is going to be more difficult than I thought—not only to take on this woman made of glass, but now I'll have to watch my language. I knew that sometimes swear words fly out of my mouth. I'd try to control it, but shit, I can't stop all of it. Some stuff just plain flies out. Well, I'm sure it won't be the first time the old gal has heard blue language, and before this trip was done, she was sure to hear it again.

I let Louise tell me a little more about herself and then I asked her, "How many tandems have you done?"

"Two," she said.

"With who?"

She said, "Mad Dog".

"Did you like them?"

"Oh yes, I surely did. But on the second one, Mad Dog did a back loop and I passed out."

"Oh my gosh, Louise. When did you wake up?"

She said, "When we were under the parachute."

"Oh, okay," I said.

"Did you stand up?"

"Yes, we stood straight up perfect," she said.

"Well, that's the most important part, Louise," I said. "Every landing you walk away from is a good one. Well, that's interesting, Louise. Would you make a tandem with me before our trip? I would like you to get some confidence in me because we will need that before we jump."

"Oh yes, Rocky," she said, "I'd very much like that," she said.

"Good. How about day after tomorrow? Is that good?"

"That would be great."

"That's a date young lady. Let's make it about 1 p.m. when we have some wind."

I said my good-byes, climbed in my C-182 and flew back to Flagler. Damn, I thought as I walked to the plane, the old gal looks like she is 90 years old. I'd heard it said, "dust to dust," meaning how we end up. She was as close to dust as I could imagine. I landed back in Flagler, put my airplane in the hanger, and went to my office. My chief instructor Danny was there. I called him Homeboy. He called me Big Daddy.

"How did it go, Big Daddy?"

"Shit, Homeboy. The old gal is made of glass."

"Damn, Big Daddy. That bad?"

"Yeah, she's a Sunday school teacher to boot."

"Damn, Big Daddy. You won't be able to say shit without burning her ears."

"At least I know I can stand her up. I'm going to jump her in a couple of days, and I'll need you to run this place."

"Okay, no problem. I can handle it."

"Good," I said. Danny was my best guy. I taught him all he

knew in skydiving, and he had all his ratings. I helped teach him to fly. Plus, he was a good looking boy who was brought up on the beach in Flagler and had been riding a surf board since he was old enough to stand. Blonde hair, blue eyes with a natural gift of gab.

Two days later I flew to Bob's drop zone in DeLand. I arrived early to get Bob's tandem rig checked out and get a good look at the wind. I figured it this way: I only had to jump this woman of glass two times, and then I would be done. At the DeLand drop zone I watched a video of her tandem. It looked like she did a good job as a passenger although there really isn't much to do on a tandem but avoid grabbing anything, cross your arms, and arch. I've taken paraplegics and quadriplegics before but I wanted to be on my toes for this one. After all, she was the lady made of glass.

After the video, Bob and I talked a good bit more about her. Bob is good about that and takes the time to give his customers that homey feeling. Then it was 2 p.m. and here Louise came like clockwork right on time.

"Okay, good," I said to her, "Let's go in here and we will talk a little about your jump."

"Okay," she said.

I ran her through the typical briefing for a tandem student scenario. I suited her up and put my rig on and we walked to the airplane. I had to help Louise in and seat her in the plane. I put her seatbelt on and mine too. The Twin Otter took off with ease. As we climbed to altitude, I got a good idea of what this lady was all about. She stood 5-foot-5, 115 pounds, hair the color of silver. Her eyes showed the signs of age as any 67-year-old would, with a smoky cover that glazed her eyes, and thin lips that cultivated a permanent Mona Lisa smile. Her hands again showed her age as the veins were raised and full of seasoned blood—the hands of a lady who chose to teach about God. I wondered how many times she had read the Bible. Her feet also showed her age. I could tell that she was the kind of woman that in her childhood was never athletic. Small and frail, lacking the strength needed for this type of expedition.

As we passed through 6,000 feet, I was pleased that Louise was expressionless, showing no signs of fear. At 10,000 feet, I again explained our climb-out procedure and exit. At 12,000 feet, I had her turn around and started to hook her to me. On a tandem jump, there are four points of attachment; two in front and one on each side of your waist. I wondered about how it would be in the sub-zero temperature at 9,000 feet over the frozen arctic.

At 13,000 feet, I walked her to the door. I looked out to make sure of the spot and climbed in the door. As I started to get Louise into position, she slipped and fell off the door. I really wasn't ready to exit when she slipped and fell, but when that happened I started to fall also. I held onto the inside bar that is used for support for skydivers with my right arm. My arm extended to the end and I felt something snap. It was my tendon on my right arm. The tendon goes from the bone to the muscle. The bicep was gone. The muscle sank down like an inner tube when you let the air out.

I'm in freefall now and wondering what had just happened. I'm thinking that I have just broken or dislocated my right arm. On a tandem parachute, along with the three normal handles like on a normal sport parachute system, there is a small parachute that you deploy by pulling it out of a pocket located at the bottom of the parachute container. When you leave the airplane and go into freefall, you try to leave in a controlled body position called stable. If you are not stable, then you try to get stable by arching. Once you are stable, then you pull this small parachute out of the pocket and throw it into the wind. The small parachute is connected to the center of the parachute container. Once this small parachute is inflated and starting to do its job, which is to create drag, then you as the tandem master, can relax along with your passenger and enjoy the freefall experience. The small parachute's primary purpose is to slow the tandem pair down for a solid deployment of the main canopy. If not, the main parachute can explode a high airspeed.

I'm just free from the Twin Otter and have never lost stability. Now this is again a time related occurrence. I know something is wrong. Exactly what is wrong, I don't know. I have either broken my right arm or I have dislocated it. Either way, I know that the sequence is to reach, locate, and throw out the small parachute. All this has to be done with my right arm. If not, I need to make the decision at what altitude do I need to pull my reserve ripcord to deploy it and hope that it will not explode because of our high air speed. I need my right arm to do its job to reach behind my main container, grab the small parachute and throw it into the wind. That's all. Just that little task. Simple, right? Yeah, simple if your arm is not broken or out of the socket.

So far, my arm was doing its job. But all it was doing was holding its own straight out and at a 45 degree angle to my heading. The moment, yes this *moment thing* that I have talked about in this book. The moment is short or it can be long, but it's no more than one second. The moment came and I reached for the small parachute. I grabbed for the plastic handle on the top of the small parachute. The pain was there of course but not nearly what I have dealt with in the past. I grabbed the plastic handle. I pulled on it to extract the small parachute. Nothing, nothing at all. I was stripped of all power in my right arm. Again I pulled. This time I could feel the small parachute start to move out of its secluded pouch. Again I jerked and finally it came free to do its job creating drag. *My God*, I thought. *What the hell is wrong with my arm? Broken? Dislocated? What?*

On the left side, at the bottom of the main container is where the real ripcord is located—this is what you pull to deploy the main parachute. This is a left arm job and my left arm works great. In freefall, everything was perfect. My only concern now was my ability to steer my canopy. With that in mind, I had only to wait until my opening altitude of 4,500 feet. At this point, my lady made of glass was not aware of my problem and never would be throughout our whole trip to, then on and off, the North Pole.

At 4,500 feet, I pulled the ripcord that would start the opening sequence of my main canopy. My left arm found the plastic handle and with one positive pull released the small parachute that was followed by the main. I was watching the parachute deploy as I had done thousands of times before. I had learned in the past to never trust my main as I have had dozens of malfunctions through my years of skydiving. As usual, the canopy opened with ease, comforting me in a time of need.

Once it was open and flying, I reached up to grab my steering loops. When I reached, I noticed that I had good motion with my right arm. I grabbed a hold of the steering loops and started my control over the canopy. Once in control, I screamed to Louise, "Are you Okay, Louise?" to make sure she had not passed out.

In a soft tone, she replied, "I am fine."

I thought, *I wish I was.* As I started my descent under canopy, I was testing my right arm. I released my right steering loop and rotated my arm trying to figure out exactly what could be wrong. I knew by then it was not dislocated or broken, but something was not right. I focused on Louise. She was doing what most tandem passengers do—looking and pointing to things on the ground. It is a very panoramic view at 4,000 feet and the most interesting part of a parachute jump is that you are not enclosed in anything. No structure, no basket, no cabin. You are suspended in a freedom as no other way could be. As close as possible to a bird in flight. When you are suspended under canopy, you feel the wind, you hear the wind. When you look straight down, you only see your legs and feet dangling in a motionless state. The view is awesome. And it's non-restricted—nothing but you. You and the parachute. When you hang from this life saving combination of nylon cloth and lines, you can tell yourself, "I'm sure glad this life savior worked." All around are miniature marks of mankind: roads, houses, and parking lots look as if they could be toys. The ground itself is a green that changes from dark to light in different areas, all determined by the location. Rivers and streams stand out like snakes that worm their path through the dark green vegetation.

The closer you get to the ground, the less you can see. The signs of reality start to come to you as the ground starts to come closer. At 1,000 feet, you are now able to make out people, dogs, cats, even birds that occasionally join you as if wondering what this descending non-birdlike thing could be—not nearly as graceful or showing the sign of effortless flight, like them.

Now I'm steering the both of us down to what I hope to be a stand up landing. Just like the mountain jump, you need a good flare for landing. This means a strong and definite pull on the loops down, down so far as you can go, no further. But now I have the lady made of glass in my front and I know she will be no help. I can't even ask her to help me flare the canopy. I never even asked her to grab a hold of the steering loops.

I set up for my final approach at 500 feet. I know she is still conscious because she responded when I shouted at her. You have to shout at tandem passengers because of the wind that is created from the forward speed of the canopy—kind of like driving your car at 25 mph and sticking your head out to hear the wind rushing past your ears. I'm close to landing and I start to flare. I feel the pain in my right arm shoot down to my hand but not once does it stop my coordinated flow with my left arm. Flop, we land, both standing up. My canopy deflates and falls to the ground beside me like a sheet that has broken free from the clothes line. One moment we're free in the wind only to flutter and fall to the prisoner of gravity. We all are nothing more than the slaves of gravity able to break free from it temporarily with our knowledge and our mechanical skills that have been passed down from our fathers. I hold onto Louise because some passengers experience vertigo and have a problem keeping their balance and sometimes fall over. I tried again to make my right arm work. It wouldn't. I unhooked her from me with my left and asked her about her jump. She told me that she had slipped on climb-out and thought that because of that we fell off the plane. I told her she was exactly correct and how important the climb-out would be for the jump on the North Pole.

We walked to the truck that would carry us back to the drop zone. On the way back, we discussed the jump in detail. I didn't want her to know how bad my right arm was. If so, she would have lost her confidence in me. Here I am three days from going to the North Pole. My right arm has had the tendon snapped from my bicep to the bone. It sags like a deflated balloon. My arm has full motion but I have lost half the strength.

Okay, now here is the deal. In the next three days, I went to three doctors including the doctor who works on the Orlando Magic basketball players. They can repair the arm with surgery, which is quite painful. Then you have six months of rehabilitation before it is completely healed. Or you live with what you are now and go through your life with the injury.

The lady made of glass has been planning this trip for one year. During my life, I have been injured a lot and now I suffer and carry on. I'm a pilot, skydiver, aircraft mechanic by trade. I have always worked because I have to. No subsidized assistance of any kind. My dad raised me to where you work until you retire and only then do you collect your Social Security.

I had to make a decision. Can I do this job safely? Yes, even though my right arm has been cut in half by snapping the tendon. When I get back, it will be too late for surgery my chances of full recovery are non-existent. If I do it now and don't go, I will ruin Louise's one year dream. Even if I stay and do the surgery, the Doc said eighty percent recovery at best. Not many people have stood on top of the world. I really want to go. I tested the arm over the next three days to see just how far it would go. By the second day, I knew what I wanted to do.

Now you just don't get on a bus and go to the North Pole. This is straight on top of the world. Hell, I told myself, I've already stood on top of a mountain that almost no one had *ever* been on.

I made arrangements to have a friend fly Louise and me to Orlando International Airport where we would start the journey. I loaded the Piper Seneca with my clothes and equipment. Then we flew to DeLand, Florida, to pick up Louise. I said my good-byes and we were off to Orlando. We checked our baggage and had a little lunch and talked about our upcoming adventure. We got on a 737, flew to JFK, and then on a 747 Jumbo to Moscow. In Moscow we met up with some other people who were on the expedition. We took a taxi to the hotel. Now this was the biggest hotel in Europe. Rossiya Hotel, 3,200 rooms. It was huge, but old, built in 1957. Back in its day, it was quite something. It was torn down in 2006. Our room had double beds, of course, and really was quite nice.

This is 1996 that I am writing about and the communist regime has just fallen. The Russian mafia was all over the hotel and we were warned to travel in groups. The word had it that the mafia would kidnap Americans and hold them hostage. The Russian Orthodox churches with their big domes were everywhere, and Red Square was just down the street.

Some Americans who were on the expedition traded dollars for rubles and got the old Russian money that was useless. So that got around quick. I knew enough not to exchange except from a bank. This was not my first time out of country.

The food sucked in the hotel and I had a big problem because I don't like fish. There were a lot of fish dishes on the menu.

Now the lady made of glass had a big problem—or I should say that I had a problem. She snored, and I mean loud. I would throw a pillow at her, and she would stop, but only for a few minutes. Then the snoring would start again. Eventually I ran out of things to throw at her. At that point I knew it was going to be a long trip.

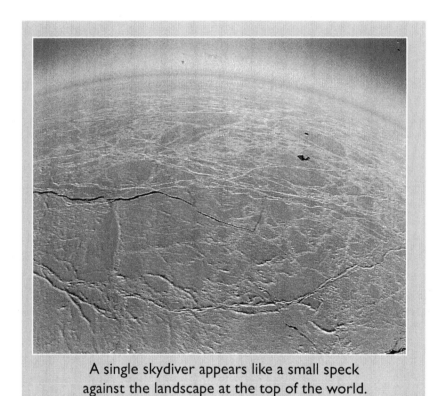

A single skydiver appears like a small speck
against the landscape at the top of the world.

## Chapter Eighteen
## NORTH POLE ADVENTURE PART TWO

O n day four at about 2 p.m. we all loaded busses that were to take us to the Ilyushin Il-76 aircraft. We didn't know where the base was located. During the regime, the military had bases all over Russia to hide their airplanes from any other countries that would be a threat. They said four hours to the base.

Man, I was hungry. On the way, we stopped at a Mickey D's and I got eight cheeseburgers. We had three busses of people and as we drove through the countryside, the signs of poverty were everywhere. The country was in a very depressed state. After about an hour of this, I got hungry. I opened my bag of Mickey D's cheeseburgers and brought me out two. They were wrapped great—perfect for my purposes. On the busses, the heat ran along the floor and up walls. I laid the two juicy burgers right on top of where this nice hot air was blowing. 15 minutes later, my Mickey D's cheeseburgers were hot and ready to eat.

After I ate the burgers, I just kicked back and enjoyed the ride. Aviation seemed to be a means of support for the widespread population of Russia—a lot of airports. I finally dozed off because of the boredom. When I awoke, it was dark out. And now I saw snow everywhere, so I knew we were a headed north. The drivers knew where this base was located, but nobody knew the name.

As we got to the entrance to the base, two Russian military guards in their brown uniforms stopped us for verification before they let us in. The gate opened and the three busses rolled through the gate. The dark was just plain impenetrable.

I looked out the bus windows and knew that MIG 29s were lining the parking ramp where the airplanes were tied down, but you just couldn't see them.

The road is full of pot holes and decaying asphalt. The winding road comes to a stop and so do we. I tell Louise to sit tight and I get my coat on and join some of the others outside the bus. When I climb out and walk around the bus, I join a small group of people. My ass was sore and it felt good to move. As I get a little closer to the group, I notice that they are pointing at something. When I turn my head, I see it. Tucked back into the woods, there it lay, in all its shining glory. The Ilyushin 76 Russian transport. The airplane range is 3,600 miles and can carry fifty tons. The back of the fuselage had a fold down ramp for loading and unloading tanks and trucks. The nose of the airplane is all glass. My God, I am in awe. I stand motionless gawking at the beautiful site, thinking this will work just fine. I walk back to the bus where Louise is waiting and tell her what I saw. This was about 8 p.m.

It's now 2 a.m. We are loaded in the 76 and taxiing to take off. Inside with us are 150 skydivers, two giant two-ton press machines, and everything else known to mankind—from Sony TVs to those machines to God only knows. I heard from one of the guys on the expedition that it would take us four and a half hours to get to Khatanga. Khatanga was where we were going to be based to go on to the North Pole. Khatanga is located to the northeast of Moscow in Siberia at the point where the land stops and the ocean starts. The population was 3,450 people and was established in the 17th century. 71 degrees 59 N. Khatanga was where they located three wooly mastodons frozen in the ground.

While I was there in 1996, I remember the local people talking about other artifacts—one being a saber tooth tiger skull, which I actually saw. So there was good reason to believe their stories about the mastodons, although for 85 percent of the people, the main diet was vodka.

The pilot kept one engine running all the time. This was used to power the electricity and heater in the plane. With everything tied down and when we were all loaded, the pilot fired up the other three. Still dark, we started to taxi and we were all ready to go. This was one massive airplane and you could tell it was loaded to the hilt. As we taxied, you could feel the plane rock back and forth as the taxiway wasn't real level. When we started to roll, it seemed like we would never lift off the ground. The airplane was Russian military and so was the pilot and crew. We had chartered it from the commander who was in charge of the base. After the government crumbled, the commander had free reign to do as he wished. He made all the money. The ride was five hours long. Not much to do after a couple of hours but to sleep.

On the way from Moscow to Khatanga, I discovered the Ilyushin 76 had three levels up front. This is where the bathroom was located on the very bottom floor. While using this bathroom, I looked around and at one point, opened a cabinet. There it was—a big jar full of vodka. Not for the pilots, but for the local ground crew who worked the airplane in Khatanga. Vodka is a way of life for them. Six months of the year, it is night. Snow covers everything. It is 25 degrees below zero most of that six months. That being the case, I guess I would stay drunk 24/7 too.

When we got to the base, the whole place was covered with snow and ice. Temperature was minus 25 below zero. The flight line was loaded with bi-wing airplanes and MI-8 helicopters. We unloaded and made our way to the building where we were to live for a week. I escorted Louise inside and located our room. Once I got her and our gear in the room, I went out to locate the bathrooms and showers. The place was poorly heated and the bathrooms just sucked. The commode especially sucked. The water was the issue. Only two of the four commodes worked. The showers were the same, and hot water was rare. The room had so much ice on the windows, you couldn't see out of them except for one small hole through the frosted glass. I put a beer on the inside of the window pane and it froze— inside the window. After we settled in, I went to a briefing to learn what was going on and then back to the room to report to Louise. She sat at the corner of the bed in awe as I told her about the bathroom facilities.

The lady made of glass was not in her usual soft environment. When she came back from the restroom, she was in shock. For me, I thought it could have been worse. At least we had occasional warm running water.

We had arrived just around dawn, so by the time we were all settled it was lunch time. The lunch hall was a small walk from our dormitory, probably 10 minutes. It was a cafeteria type serving. On the menu from day to day were caribou, salmon, and goat. Louise was a picky eater and I'm no better, so we both were a little hungry most of the time. When chicken was served, we took all we could and kept it on the window sill—we used that as our refrigerator.

On our third day, we were invited to go by helicopter into the Siberian tundra on a sightseeing ride. The ride would be in a MI-8 helicopter over the Siberian tundra. It also included two stops. The first was a trip into a Mongolian Indian village. The second was to an actual Eskimo village deep into the Siberian snow.

The Indian village was small with maybe 250 people. The houses looked to be old military bunk houses. All the houses rested on concrete blocks. The people had full electric and they also had TV. I saw some—maybe seven or eight and no more— with antennas for short wave or TV. They had snowmobiles that had one ski straight out from the center in front, instead of the two ski setup I was familiar with.

The small children were clothed totally with hides from wolves, beaver, or mink. Damn, they looked warm. Now these people knew what American currency was because I used dollars to buy some of their hats and coats for people back home.

The clothes and hats I bought from the villagers were all hand sewn and were so warm. The soft fur would keep a baby's heat inside real well. These people have lived in that environment for thousands of years. They know nothing else. I saw the biggest dog fight in my life while I was there. There must have been fifty or more dogs in a fight. There was one dog that for some reason pissed off the rest. At first, there were three or four fighting. Then the other forty-six or so jumped in. Good grief, I couldn't believe it! I figured with all that commotion, the end result would be that one dog laying dead. No way. The dog that got beat ran off, and the rest of them turned away like nothing happened. I had never seen anything like this so I walked over to where the fight ended and the dog hair was everywhere. Not only that, a great big chunk of hide had been torn off the ass of the dog they all ganged up on. A piece of hide 4 x 4 inches lay in the snow. The local people didn't blink an eye even though the fight lasted three or four minutes.

When that was over, the MI-8s took some of the expedition skydivers up to demonstrate for the locals. As I told you, this little Siberian town was small but not totally isolated. Apparently, the pilots were familiar with the village, and the locals knew about money, whether it be dollars or rubles. And they had TV and snowmobiles so they weren't that far out in the weeds. Not near as far as this next tribe I'm going to tell you about.

When the skydivers landed, they packed their parachutes and we loaded the MI-8's for the next stop. This time, I wore my hood with eye and nose holes cut out, my skydiving goggles, and my scarf. The MI-8 had porthole windows that would swing open to the inside of the helicopter. After we took off, I had my Walkman on and was listening to Pink Floyd. We are cruising at 100 to 200 feet over the tundra and I felt the helicopter roll left - right - left - right. I wondered what the heck was going on. And then, there it was, a Siberian timber wolf. The pilot was chasing it and this was cool. This pilot was no newbie— he could really fly. The wolf was doing everything he could to get away except turn around. The was pilot right on him as the wolf zigged and zagged. No one else on the helicopter saw it, and let me tell you, I will always remember that experience.

Either the wolf or the pilot tired of the chase, and we changed direction, heading deep into the Siberian snow. Way ahead, maybe half a mile, I could see a herd of caribou. Then a few at a time what looked like ice shanties came into view through my iced over goggles. Pink Floyd was setting the stage. I was listening to "Division Bell Keep Talking," and you couldn't ask for any better musical entrance. The chopper swooped in and let it be known they were having visitors. The pilot swung around in a hard right turn and settled in right by the caribou herd. The caribou stayed right there as if this happened every day. This might be an everyday kind of thing, but I didn't think so!

As the MI-8 settled, the whirling snow blinded my vision. After it was down and the snow settled, there they were— the Eskimos of 1996. No TVs, no snowmobiles, no money, absolutely nothing that represented the modern society of 1996. Nothing but caribou, ice shanties, and piles of beautiful salmon stacked like cord wood in a meticulous and perfect arrangement leaning on the side of each shanty. Outside were three heavily clothed Mongolian looking men covered with fur hides—they looked cozy. Not knowing the language, I just stood and watched as the pilot and the three Eskimos conversed. My focus was on the herd of caribou as they wandered like cows, not going any further than the shanties. Obviously they were part of the six shanty town.

We had two MI-8s full of skydivers that were jumping on the North Pole with the expedition. Most were occupied with how close we could get to the "reindeer." I thought Santa was going come on out of one of the six shanties to collect Christmas wishes, but that didn't happen. If it had, I would of put an order in for a thick T-bone, baked tater, sweet corn, salad, and a Corona. I was feeling pretty hungry.

After a bit, one of the men signaled for me to come with him inside of the shanty. I followed him inside and closed the door behind me. All I could do was stare. I had no words to define that moment. Straight ahead was a beautiful Eskimo woman maybe 22 years old or so. In her arms rested the cutest little baby, no more than six months old. It was wrapped in beautiful furs, with brightly colored beads of turquoise, red, and yellow, decorating the bare leather that supported his tiny body. Mother, child, father, and grandfather. There he sat. Quiet, polite, so shy but ready to protect. My hand went out to the old man. He reached out with his. Our two hands came together and we shook it up man to man.

A smile came over his toothless mouth and the same from me. At this point I saw him relax. As if to say, you are my brother. And me the same. Hell, you don't have to say a damned thing to any living being. It's a sense that is natural to all of us. This isn't the first time I felt this. My whole life I have always been a good judge of character, and this moment was no different for him or me.

I stood and took in all of this moment. The inside of the shanty was so small but held so many objects I would never ever see again. Despite the language differences I still wanted to be polite and try to communicate with the family. I continued to study their dwelling. On the walls hung paintings of animals. Who painted them? I couldn't tell you but they were very defined and colorful. Then my attention dropped to the floor covered with caribou hides. A small, tiny wood stove was burning and producing the most valuable resource—heat. The stove was so small it looked like it came out of a doll house. But it was more than they needed for the tiny home. In two corners were small sets of bunk beds. Set off in the middle was the most beautiful cradle rocker for the tiny baby. Nothing, I thought, nothing could be so minute yet so finely carved. Furs lined the inside along with a highly decorated assortment of beads. Finely tanned leather covered the rails to protect the child when it would pull itself up to look out upon its perfect life. The young man approached me with a small cup of what appeared to be tea. I reached out for the warm cup and sipped the warm tea. It tasted good and hit the spot. It is funny, not many words were said but that wasn't necessary. The emotion and vibes showed us the way for communication.

I finished my tea and motioned my thanks for their generous hospitality, turned, and walked out into the frozen arctic. Once I closed the door, I stood and stared out to the frozen nowhere and thought, *These people have it made.* No bills, no worries, no problems created by other human beings. All the food they wanted. When they wanted to move, the shanties had skis. They would hook a caribou to the shanty with a harness and pull it to wherever. I was jealous.

The MI-8s fired up with the demo skydivers on board. The day was perfect—sunny and cold. Wind at 10 mph. Kind of cold but perfect weather to jump. The turbine engine powered the spinning blades and created small tornados that danced on the snow, raising a blinding wall of snow. Up and away they went. All six of the shanties emptied. Louise was standing, camera in hand most of the time, trying to capture the moment. The power of the MI-8 showed as they made one small circle that took the skydivers to 9,000 feet. The Eskimos stood in awe, talking in some Russian dialect. I couldn't understand and never tried. They all herded up together like the caribou and pointed up to the MI-8s. The unmistakable rotor thump told me it was time for the skydivers to exit. Out they came. One, two, now six all hooked together. As they emptied the two choppers, the first out started to open their parachutes, and the colors of the nylon fabric shone more colorful than ever. The sky so blue, so pure, no clouds, nothing to spoil the solid blue canvas that was the background for the multicolored spectacle that was happening.

I'd been jumping for twenty-six years at this time, and I

had never seen the sky so clear and blue. The contrasting colors of the parachutes painted their way to the ground. When the last skydiver landed, the tiny town of Eskimos applauded and cheered. I'm sure they had never seen anything quite like this and had thoroughly enjoyed the display. The jumpers laid their parachutes in the middle of the half circle that the shanties formed.

I took this time to walk up to the herd of caribou. A few would scurry off but for the most part, they would just stand and wait for you to feed them. Their antlers were massive to the point where they are almost as big as the Eskimos. Luckily I had some carrots that I stashed from the mess hall. They knew what they were and would try to push one another out of the way to get to the newly presented orange delight.

When the skydivers got packed, we climbed back in the MI-8 for the long ride home. Our suits kept us warm and cozy. The whole time there I was amazed that my feet never got cold. I loaded Louise, the pilots fired up the MI-8s, and up and away we went.

When we got back, Louise and I got went to our room and shared our stories. When we were done, we went for supper. I was hungry and so was she. We sat down with some of the others. Man, the bullshit was flowing thick. I tried to eat my supper, but nobody knew what kind of meat was being served. Probably horse. Russians are known to eat it, but not me! Trigger was meant to ride, not to eat. I recognized the other food and ate it, and so did Louise. We were hungry and a long way from Mickey D's and we both knew it.

The time went by pretty slow and then we were waiting for the weather to break. Our weather at the base was great but on the Pole—3 and 1/2 hours away in the Ilyushin 76—it was a lot different. Indicated airspeed for the Ilyushin 76 was close to 600 mph, so even though we were already in Siberia, the Pole was a long way off—like flying from Florida to Canada. At this time of year there is no night. The sun shines 24/7. Louise and I got some cardboard to cover up our "refrigerator" so we could sleep. The next day in the morning, we got the news we had been waiting for: The Pole was ours.

Booth gave us our briefing. We all sat in the lobby. Booth started his spew. He had already been there twice. We all sat there like a sponge—at least I did. I wanted all the info I could get. Booth was placing emphasis on the polar bears and how you had to be careful that they wouldn't eat you. Come on now, do I look like some kind of dumbass or what? He did have some important stuff to tell us, like the wind direction and speed. The Russians had a first aid tent and two MI-8s already there and waiting on us.

He also explained how we would get back after our jump onto the North Pole. That journey would take almost eighteen hours of flying—from helicopter to turbine airplane to prop drive airplanes. Good grief, I thought to myself, I've got the lady made of glass to look after. Fragile, snorer, finicky eater, never smiles. Now what? Well, it's show time, and I can't dress this thing up. It is what it is, so hang on to your ass, Louise—ready or not, North Pole here we come!

At 4 p.m. we met in the lobby to get our last briefing on the weather on the North Pole. Everything was set. Our ground crew of two MI-8s and the first aid tent with heat was waiting for our arrival. Louise and I ran through an equipment check to make sure we don't forget anything. You leave gloves, facemask, goggles, hand and feet warmers behind, you will suffer to the point that we can't make the jump. Any bare extremities could result in frost bite. Depending on how severe, that could mean fingers, toes, nose and ears will be frozen. The temperature in freefall will be minus 85 degrees F. Even if it's only for forty seconds, that's enough to do the damage. The temperature on the North Pole before we left was minus 30 degrees F. The briefing called for terminal blue skies. The wind, 10 - 12 mph. The flight was four hours in the massive Ilyushin 76.

We were trucked out to the silent giant. There it stood. Like a massive bus that would give us a one-way trip to the North Pole. I helped the glass lady climb into the Ilyushin. We had already been inside the giant with wings. My mind went back to the story of Noah who was swallowed by the whale and lived to tell his story. Well, I can relate and this is my story.

Louise picked her seat, and I kept her harness with my parachute clipped together. It probably took one and a half to two hours before the pilot fired up the four engine beast and we started to taxi. I could feel that addictive adrenaline start flowing through my veins. Damn, there is something about that inner-body drugstore that makes me go up and beyond. I get one of those smirks that stayed molded to my face. The moment is now, and again it feels like I've been waiting so long.

My mind went back to the expedition to Autana and my performance under that stress. Then it crossed my mind, that wasn't shit compared to this. Then I had two good arms, and now my left was done and always would be. But it was only this time I had to worry about. One simple tandem. Just throw the drogue. That's all. Damn, the jacket felt like you were dressed as the Michelin man. So much bulk. I lived in Florida. It had been years since I had been back to Michigan, and Michigan was nothing compared to this. So here we were; the North Pole was waiting, and here we come, so hang on.

My mind went back to D-day and all our airborne boys riding to jump into hell. Well, at least there was no one trying to shoot us out of the air. I could almost put myself in the C-47s that carried our boys and feel the quietness that's injected into your soul when you think you could die on any given skydive.

That knowledge comes through at least once on every jump and I don't care how many you have or who you are. This is what keeps your ass alive in this business. No one is bullet proof and it's when you think that you are, then here he comes—Mr. Murphy with his big bag of surprises to dump in your lap. You had better be ready. If not, it could be terminal. Not only for one but two of us. So don't drop that guard.

I got Louise all seat belted in, and I stripped down to my arctic expedition bib overalls and went upstairs to the cockpit where the Russian crew was locking in flight plans and their final check lists. The chief pilot told me I could ride up front with the crew. He liked me.

With everyone seat belted in place, the captain fired up the other three engines and we started to taxi. Snow blind is the term used when the brightness of the sun gets magnified about half again. So bright that you have to wear some kind of sunglasses. I had some Maui Jim sunglasses that were polarized, and they really did the job. The 9,000 foot runway seemed endless as the Ilyushin slowly taxied, rocking back and forth from the weight of the massive wings. Finally we're there at the end of the taxi, rolling out for takeoff. I reach into my heavy coat and pull out my Walkman. I push the button and Pink Floyd Keep Talking fills my ears. My eyes focus on the captain as he calls out his commands in Russian. I can feel the power come up on the four turbine engines, and the true sense of the power overwhelms me. *My God*, I think, *what an airplane.* The co-pilot pushes the power lever forward. The plane starts to shake and we start to roll down the 9,000 foot runway.

Here I am standing in the cockpit of a Russian Ilyushin 76 with a Russian crew, jamming on Pink Floyd. Yes, this is where the West meets the East in a combination that's never been equaled. That permanent smirk covers my face. This giant airplane is eating up runway like a bitch. I'm not worried. These are cream of the crop pilots. They just don't let any newbie fly this plane. At 180 mph, the captain eased the yoke back and the Ilyushin pitched up and we were off. At an angle of best rate of climb, the 76 started the grind to cruising altitude of 32,000 feet. I was totally amazed at the vast snow covered ground below with no sign of life. Just the little town of Khatanga that rapidly disappeared behind us. As we began our climb, I started to see the value of an all glass cockpit. Again, I am semi blinded by the mirror affect projected by the sun and snow.

I walked back downstairs to check on the lady made of glass. There she sat, content as hell, Mona Lisa smile pasted on her face with her arctic snow suit on. I walked up to her and told her to take her coat off and relax. It would be four hours. I walked around and yucked it up with the skydivers on our expedition. The Russians had probably 25 of their own skydivers on board, ranging from static lines to tandems to solo. It was a long ride to jump, the longest I've ever been on. The ride to altitude was usually over in 30 minutes at the longest. This was three and a half to four hours.

The Ilyushin was pumping the heat in the cargo bay where we were sitting waiting for our jump of a lifetime. I was down to my long johns. I shed all my arctic expedition clothes and it felt good to be free of the cumbersome clothing that Louise had provided for the two of us. Our arctic clothes were the best money could buy, and I was very grateful that she had stepped up to the plate and bought us the best. Three and one-half hours into our flight, I went upstairs to find out our position. One of the pilots spoke English. I asked, "How long till we get to the Pole?"

He replied, "Thirty minutes."

I said, "Okay," and stayed there to look at the pure white snowy desert beneath us. The sky was a terminal blue and where the two met, it was hard to determine where one started and one stopped. It was as if there was no horizon—almost begging for vertigo to set in. No definition, period, a mystery of the arctic only an aviator who has experienced this picture could explain. The sun was 10 times brighter than most people could have ever experienced. Don't forget this is 10:30 at night. So time again is completely out of whack. If you didn't think of time and expect a horizon where the white and blue meet, then it's all relative and a skilled pilot could figure out where vertical and horizontal meet. When you could figure that, then you're okay. Unless that happened, you were going to crash your airplane.

Luckily, we were in the grand Ilyushin. The best of the best. In its day, it was one of Russia's biggest contributions to aviation—as big as our giant C5A, but in its own world, way more. The airplane was designed as a short field cargo carrier with a capacity to carry weights unheard of in the military aviation record books. Stocked full of the best technology Russia could stuff into the panel to do what it would take to fly in the worst conditions known to the aviation world. I was in seventh heaven just to be able to walk into it, let alone to skydive from it.

The curvature of the earth seems apparent in
these photos of the North Pole terrain.

## Chapter Nineteen
## NORTH POLE ADVENTURE PART THREE

Thirty minutes till we go on jump run. I take one last look into the crazy world where blue meets white and walk down the stairs to find the lady made of glass and prepare for our jump. Down the last step, I walked back in the cargo bay where the air was thick with bullshit and anticipation. There she sat, just as I had left her, soft, shy, fragile. Waiting. As I got closer to her, she turned her head to look at me. Her eyes smoky with the years, her lips cast in that Mona Lisa smile. I could read her expression asking "Now?" She didn't have to say a word because I beat her to the punch.

"Okay, Louise. Let's suit up. It's show time!"

This was the first time I had ever seen that smile change from the Mona Lisa to one of, *I'm ready, Let's go!* I helped her get her arctic suit back on. She had most of it on except the bottoms. I helped her with the small jacket made of polyfiber and then the puffy coat that would keep her from freezing in the sub-zero environment that we were about to subject ourselves to. Double check. Boots tight, coat, gloves, ski mask, ear muffs, hand warmers, camera. Oh, yeah. Don't forget the pictures. Who's going to believe you when you tell them you jumped onto the North Pole? No one. Unless they knew you from the past and even then, good luck. I always looked at that like this: Why even tell people what you've done or where you've been? Even if they believe you, they seem to get bored quickly and immediately try to tell you one of their stories to better yours, so why bother? I've never been one to try to impress people. Why even try? I'm all about looking at myself in the mirror, you know, and when I do, I smile. I'm feeling that my mom and dad and the rest of my family would be proud of me. I guess it all boils down to *Good job, Rocco.* Either way, I don't puff it all up and think I'm way better than everybody else; on the contrary, I feel sorry for people who don't get out and broaden their horizons and seek out the real things in life. But I'm not trying to figure their shit out—that's their business. All I know is that Louise wants to jump onto the North Pole, and I'm going to do my best to see that she gets the chance. That's why she hired me.

15 minutes until jump run. I had Louise all ready. I triple checked her to make sure the lady made of glass was totally protected from the elements that the cold environment of the North Pole can inflict on a human being—not only that, but a human being in a freefall environment subjected to minus 85 degrees below zero. Satisfied everything is ready, I wait.

Now on a jump run at 3,500 feet, the door opens. The door on this Ilyushin 76 is a ramp big enough to drive a full size army tank up and into the belly of the Ilyushin. When the door starts to open, there is a red signal located next to the door that lights up, and one of the loudest horns I've ever heard sounds off. The first time this horn sounded off, I damned near jumped out of my skin. My ears were penetrated with this vulgar noise to where I had to put my hands over my ears to cushion its piercing sound.

Standing on the edge of the open ramp were four Russian airborne soldiers dressed in military uniforms covered by the extra clothing that it took to survive the frozen piercing wind that came through the door as the giant Ilyushin slowed down to 130 knots. That was as slow as the old girl could go without falling out of the sky from a stall. Anything with a wing can stall and when that happens, the wing loses lift. The four young Russians could not have been any older than 21. During the 3 and 1/2 hour flight, I got the chance to yuck it up with all of the 179 skydivers. So even thought I didn't really converse with these young Russian airborne soldiers, I could tell what they were made of.

At this point in time they didn't even know what their job could be. Don't forget - this was at a point in history that will never ever be forgotten. The Russian communist rule was done. Now they didn't know how it would all shake out. Everything was in flux—government, military command. Nothing was settled. Everything was a big question. A question of what lay ahead in the future.

But this was now. When they were standing on the edge of the Ilyushin at 3,500 feet, the only thought in their mind was, *I hope my parachute opens on this jump!* Four young men as disciplined and as tough as nails, but with sphincters still drawing tight with thoughts of *what if.* I could only relate that moment to my first parachute jumps in Austin Lake, Michigan, Rick and I standing on the edge of the doorway ramp looking at each other with that smile. You know the one. The one that would always grow on my face, as on his, when the adrenalin gets pumped into your veins—not from any syringe but from your brain.

I know these four Russian young men felt like Rick and I, but they never showed it by the expression on their faces. And again maybe they didn't encounter that thing called fear. I know that I did! Encounter, recognize, and overcome. That's the point when you know that you are in control over the adrenaline. Their jumpmaster gave them the go signal and away they went. Here one second, gone the next. Then four more. Gone. And then four more gone. Then that damn horn and the ramp came closed.

I went back to Louise. I told her we were on the third pass. That meant when they were through with the static liners, the airplane would climb to 13,000 feet and would make however many passes of 25 jumpers it would take until empty. I started to suit up for our jump. Yes. Showtime! Okay. Tighten boots. Secure my bib pants. Insert chemical warmer in my boots. Next my coat. Draw strings tight. Scarf around my neck. Hooded ski masks. Gloves—two pair, liners and then the outer cover. That was only the left hand. On the right, I only had the liner. Too hard to find my handles with all that bulk. The last was my goggles. They were the most important. Without goggles, your eyeballs would freeze, minus 30 degrees without the wind. With the wind, imagine minus 120 degrees.

Louise was all dressed sitting on the bench that ran on the inside of the plane all along the fuselage. They went almost thirty yards. I waited now, waited to empty the plane of the first two passes of 25 skydivers. Then it was our turn. Louise sat there patiently, again with that Mona Lisa smirk, no more in question, only one of soon. Two more times the repulsive horn blew. When the second pass was empty, it was time.

I told the lady made of glass to stand and turn. I brought her body back to mine as close as I could. I grabbed hold of the connectors that would connect us. Carefully, I snapped the top two. Once snapped, I inserted the pins that kept them from failing. Then the two bottom ones. My good friend Trey stood beside me while I hooked Louise to me. Next the bottom snaps. Trey checked to make sure that no material from our bulky arctic clothes were in the way of a solid close of the snaps. Then Trey pulled tight on the harness that made the two of us one. Then he stowed the excess harness away after a solid, firm connection. Anything hanging out and blowing in the wind shouldn't be anything but my drogue handle. I knew of one tandem that bounced pulling on the excess strap all the way to the ground. All the way till they died. Not me! No way! Double check me, Trey. And he did. Cool.

There we stood, two as one. Perfect. This was what I wanted. Now our turn was only minutes away. Again my mind went back to Gordon and myself. This time I'm going to make sure that this lady made of glass has those goggles on all right.

The giant plane circled, coming around for our turn. There we stood, two as one, united as no one knows but skydivers who have a tandem rating. My attention is focused on the other 23 in our group. There we stand in formation as if standing in front of the executioner, waiting for our destiny. I could feel the Ilyushin bank around for our turn as the wallowing airborne beast gracefully rolled out of its last turn to come onto jump run. No more did skydivers have to spot. This was all done with GPS. On every pass made, once the skydivers left, the ramp would close until the next pass of jumpers. Here I was as thousands of times before—adrenaline juices flowing, pumping, filling my veins with power. My friend. My savior. The reason for my existence. That little bit of extra that goes along with what they call walking the edge. Standing, waiting. I can only wonder what lay behind the folding ramp. No windows inside the Ilyushin. I could only wonder what the North Pole would look like. I've seen only the pictures from Admiral Byrd, the first on the Pole. It changes all the time. No picture is the same.

The horn comes screaming out. Goddamn, the thing is loud. At this point, the folding door opens to give me my first look at the majestic North Pole! *My God! There it is! WOW!* What a way to see this. It took my breath away. I saw a path of broken ice rivers. Some small, some as big as the Amazon. I watch one big crack in the snow with at least 25 smaller ones running alongside parallel to it. Looking down from the plane, this place looked like the moon's surface. Jagged mountains of ice formations spotted the frozen sheet of ice. Giant rivers of dark blue snaked through the spotted ice.

At this point, now and not before, my arm comes to mind. My suit is so big, so bulky. Can I get my arm to work? Just this time. Just one more time. I knew I could do it. I did it one hundred times or more on the ground. Hell, I even made it work at the Russian air show. But that was on the ground with no arctic suit. All this bulk and the lady made of glass on my front. Well, this wasn't the time or the place to entertain doubts. Fuck it. I just put on that smile. You know the one. The one that comes on with that clean hard shot of adrenaline.

I've got 10 people in a line in front of me. The horn went off. Booth said that when that goes off we need to be exiting the airplane. Well, the horn went off and no one did shit. No movement, no nothing. They all stood as if to be locked up. I couldn't believe it. Yeah, maybe one or two—but not all 10! Well, I screamed "Go!" Nothing. Again, "Go!" Again, nothing. My turn, I moved forward with Louise's help and pushed the guy in front, and away he went.

We start to roll off the ramp and Louise is doing her job. Her head is back, arms across her chest. The moment has come, and now I'm finally in my environment. This is where I shine. We roll off the giant Ilyushin at 150 mph. This was the fastest exit speed I ever had to deal with in my skydiving career. Hell, the fastest Louise and I would be falling was 115 mph. I hit the wind perfectly. My left arm is working fine, as stable as a rock. I look up over my right shoulder. Other jumpers are scattered all around me, and most of them are every which way but stable. I can't throw the drogue now; it will tangle up with the out of control skydivers.

One guy was on his back fighting to get control. He looked like a floundering turtle, his neck all stretched out, arms flailing. *Christ*, I thought, *all he has to do is relax and arch*. The high airspeed can be your friend if you know how to use it. I looked over my left shoulder. Someone else was doing the same flailing thing. All I can do is wait. Five seconds into my jump, I hear my airspeed start to slow down. I look around. There I was, 12,000 feet above the North Pole. The panorama was unbelievable. Cracks in the ice everywhere. Some are miles wide. Ice mountains growing up from the heavy pressure of the ice crashing together. I looked again over my right shoulder. Again a skydiver who is flailing and fighting the high airspeed of the Ilyushin. Get smart dude—relax and arch.

Now I'm starting to slow down to my terminal velocity. You can hear and feel it when you are as experienced as me. Now I'm 10 seconds into the jump. I look one more time in the direction I have to throw the drogue. At last the skydiver over my right shoulder is in control and looking at Louise and me. My right arm swings back to grab the handle that's hooked to the small drogue parachute. I grab a hold and lock onto the handle.

Before we left, I made a point to make sure that on my right hand I had one glove only. And I knew that it would get cold. On my left hand I had two pairs. A wool glove and then a leather shell. On my right, a single tight leather glove—enough to keep frostbite from freezing my hand. In the pocket of my $2,000 arctic expedition coat is another wool glove. Once I open my parachute and get it in control, I can unzip and dig into my pocket and put the glove on for my canopy control. It's minus 85 degrees in freefall. It takes only seconds of exposure to freeze your flesh. Once this happens, there is nothing you can do except cut it off. The frozen meat will turn black and start to infect your body, and then you've got big problems. I have a solid grip on the handle of the drogue that will slow our freefall down to under 115 mph. By this time, the speed of the airplane has dissipated and my forward trajectory has bled off and now it's all vertical. If I don't throw the drogue, my airspeed could increase to over 130 mph.

I look again one last time to check the airspace over my head to make sure that I don't throw it into a skydiver. Good. Clear. Now. I pull and throw. I feel the drogue inflate. As it inflates, I fall away from the dragging anchor. With that part of my job done, I can relax and enjoy my freefall. I lean to my right and give the lady made of glass a panoramic view of the icy desolate frozen arctic that lay 9,000 feet below. I can only hope that Louise doesn't pass out. She did it on her first tandem.

Nothing I can do now but ride out the moment. My right hand is starting to burn. You know when your fingers start to ache when the feeling passes from cold to burn. I pull my arm in to bring my hand just below my chin out of the wind.

Now I'm starting to feel the icy cold of the North Pole. I look to my left where my altimeter is carried on every jump. It's like a big giant wrist watch. I look and see we are passing through 5,000 feet. I want to ride this skydive out so I don't spend so much time under canopy. When you're hanging under your parachute, your arms reach high above your head to where your steering toggles are located. When your arms are up and over your head, the blood starts to slow down in circulation because your heart only pumps at a given pressure and it's a long way to travel up to your fingers. So the circulation isn't as good when your arms and hands are above you. This wasn't the first time that I had jumped in a snowy icy environment. In the early years of my skydiving career, don't forget, I learned to jump in Kalamazoo, Michigan. Through the years, I made many skydives in the winter. So I had experienced what it was like to skydive in the cold, icy environment that winter brings, although this was in a league of its own.

Again I look at my altimeter, now passing through 3,500 feet. I reach to the bottom of my parachute container where my ripcord lay waiting. My arm goes down and behind me. I grab a hold and pull it out and away. As I start to fall away from the staged deployment of the canopy, I see the bag that holds my folded parachute appear. The lines start to tear free from the rubber bands that keep the shroud lines nice and neat. When the last stow is released, the mouth of the bag opens, setting my canopy free into the 100 mph wind. Finally, my parachute is starting to blossom out and fully deploy. Now open, I reach for the steering toggles that are located above my head. I grab them and get my canopy in control. When I did that, I screamed down to Louise.

"Louise!" No response. Shit. Did she pass out?

"Louise," I scream a second time louder than the first. No response.

Now I am really yelling, "Louise!"

She finally replies, "Don't yell at me."

Laughing, I say, "Get your camera out and let's take some pictures."

205

I feel her start to move as she fights to dig her camera out. I tell her to give me the camera. I steer my canopy right and left in 360 degree turns to locate the actual point of the North Pole. The Russians we hired were already there with two MI-8 helicopters and the first aid station that would be waiting for us when we land. The first aid station was a military tent 10 feet by 10 feet with a propane heater inside. They used GPS to find the exact location of the North Pole, where they stuck a long pole with a long skinny strip of yellow crepe paper for a wind direction. They had also marked the pure white snow with an M-18 smoke grenade.

As I turned my canopy right 360 degrees, I couldn't locate our drop zone. *Shit*, I thought. *Where in the hell is the drop zone?* I started my left turn 360 degrees. About 180 degrees into my turn, bingo. There it is. The red smoke had saturated the pure white snowy ice. I looked down and saw the parachutes landing from the first three passes. I pointed my canopy in the direction of the drop zone and let go of my steering toggles. My right hand was burning from the cold and the left was starting to burn also.

"Give me the camera, Louise!"

Slowly she raised her arms over her head, camera in her hands. My right hand was beyond the burning stage to the point of numbness. I grabbed the little yellow box and was careful not to drop it. The camera was the only way to prove that you had really done this jump on the North Pole. I had to fight to hang on and make my right hand grip the small box. I turned the camera and pointed it directly at Louse and me. Smile, Louise! Click.

I brought the camera back and grabbed a hold with my left hand. I fought to hang onto the little box. I wound the small wheel to take the next picture. I only hoped that the sub-zero temperature wouldn't snap the film while I advanced it. Once more I yelled, "Smile, Louise!" Click. Again I advanced the camera for the next picture.

I looked down. I was almost to the drop zone. I turned my canopy 180 degrees to face into the wind. I looked to my altimeter. Two-thousand feet. *Good. I've got time.* I handed the camera back to Louise. "Take some pictures!" I yelled. "I have to steer now."

"Okay," came the soft frail words from that Mona Lisa

mouth. My hands were now beyond the burning point. I looked over my right shoulder and down to the big red smudgy streak that grew wider as the wind blew the smoke away from our drop zone. Again I dropped the steering toggles. I let my arms drop. I could feel the warm blood fill my frozen fingers with heat. I let them hang down as long as possible. My canopy flew straight ahead. I had a good one that came from Performance Design. Trimmed perfectly. Performance Design makes the best square canopies. I can remember when John and Billy were making canopies in a garage in DeLand. Now they were the biggest canopy manufacturer in the world.

I reach back up for my steering toggles. I'm now at 1,000 feet, getting ready for my downwind base to final approach. Again I look over my right shoulder to locate the drop zone. *Okay, there is the wind streamer.* I pull down on my right steering toggle. The canopy starts to turn to the right. I'm going with the wind bleeding off my altitude. I can see my ground speed increase and my canopy starts to fly with the wind. We shoot past the wind streamer. How far to go is the question? This is where more than 8,000 times of doing this falls into place. I've always been good at my canopy control, and I was confident that I could put the lady made of glass dead smack on the North Pole.

"Okay Louise, here we go!"

I pull down hard on my right steering toggle. The canopy rocks hard and banks into a sharp right hand turn. My timing has to be perfect. Now I let up on my right steering toggle. Perfect. Dead ahead lay the exact location of the North Pole. Closer, closer, closer. Now! I pull both of my steering toggles down to my sides. The canopy responds and starts to pitch up. My airspeed starts to slow down. Slower, closer, slower. Just as we touch down, I am next to the pole that holds the wind streamer and marks the exact location of the North Pole. Plunk. Louise and I stand. The two of us. Motionless. My canopy still fully inflated flies above our heads. It hangs motionless for a moment as if to have the last gleaming moment of our final destiny.

I watch as it starts to turn and slowly deflate into the snowy arctic snow. My hands ache. I try to unhook Louise but my hands are too cold. I tell Louise to wait. My hands are so cold that they won't work. I look up. The clear blue sky is decorated with colorful parachutes. Plunk. Right next to me, my friend Trey.

"Yahoo!" he yells.

"Trey," I call out. "Help me unhook, my hands are frozen."

Trey peels off his gloves and unhooks Louise. She falls to her knees. Finally, I unzip my coat and dig deep into my bib snow bottoms. My hands are so cold. I push them down deep into my groin. I bend over to cover them with my body heat. Damn it, do they hurt.

As I stand and warm up my aching hands, my eyes lock onto the lady made of glass as she starts to dig into her pocket in search of something. What is she looking for? At last she pulls out empty zip lock sandwich baggies. She singles out one and starts to pack snow into it. My hands are starting to warm up. Louise fills more bags. What is this woman doing? I unhook my parachute harness. Once free I let it lay in the snow. I ask Louise, "What are you doing?"

She replies, "Why, I'm taking back some of the North Pole."

"What?"

She tells me that she's going to take some of the North Pole in baggies of snow, and when the snow melts she will pour the water into small bottles and place them on a plank along with a picture of her on the North Pole.

"Why?"

"To give to my Sunday school kids."

"Well, whatever." I walk away and leave her to her work. I walk to the first aid tent to warm my hands. I open the canvas door and walk in. There sits a young Russian boy, a large gash on his cheek, blood trickling down.

"Damn, what happened to you?"

He couldn't understand a thing I was saying. I watched as another Russian stood over him, needle and thread in hand. The young boy gritted his teeth while the older one started to shove a needle and thread through his cheek. I watched and warmed my hands while the boy, not making a fuss, sat patiently while the older one sewed up his gash. I knew that must hurt. Nothing deadened the pain as the sharp needle passed through the young boy's flesh. Seven times the makeshift doctor sewed through the boy's cheek.

My hands now warm, I went back out to collect my parachute. There was Louise still packing snow into baggies. I told her to go and get warm in the first aid tent, and that I was putting my gear away.

"Okay," she replied.

I had two beers stashed in the pockets of my coat. Many of the 179 jumpers on the top of the world were screaming and opening champagne bottles with the frozen liquid bubbling up and out of the bottle. You would get a mouthful of slush and swallow it. Just like the frozen drinks you can buy at the 7-11 back home.

I heard someone call my name. I turn and it's Smitty.

"Come on, let's smoke a joint," he said.

I wandered over to where he stood with the crooked joint in his mouth.

"Fire it up, Smitty." I wondered how many people smoked pot on the North Pole. We were probably the first. I helped Smitty finish and wandered back to find Louise. She had finished packing snow into baggies, and I suggested we go into the tent and get warm. Inside, I took my two cold beers from my pockets and set them on the propane heaters. Louise and I talked our jump over. I told her that she did a great job. And she did. I told her to let me see her camera. I inspected the little yellow box to determine the status of the film. Good. The film didn't break.

The heat felt good, but my hands still were cold. I opened the flap door to the tent. There they were, our ticket out, the two MI-8's sitting on the ice—bright yellow single rotor helicopters ready to go.

I told Louise to hang out there and take some pictures. We were going to be on the first helicopter out. I drank my beers and went back out in the minus thirty degrees to get a look around. I wandered out behind the tent to see what the North Pole looked like. I walked about a hundred yards out. There were big chunks of ice everywhere. Some were small, the size of cars; others were as big as a three-story building, snow covered and hard like rocks. I circled back to the drop zone.

I had to pee and I noticed a clear spot on the ice. This was perfect. I unzipped my bib coverall and pulled out my shriveled up penis. I really had to go. I hadn't peed since I was in the Ilyushin. I started. A heavy stream started to flow as I wrote my name in the snow. R O C K. When I got to the K, I was running out of liquid. I had just finished the K, and that was it. I shook my penis dry, put it back in my bibs and zipped up. I stood back to look at my masterpiece. Perfect. I did it just like I said I would and felt satisfied both ways—relieving myself and doing what I said I would do.

On my way back to the first aid tent, I went by a different route and stopped in amazement by the most magnificent piece of ice. Almost as big as a house, it caught the sun like clear blue glass, blue as an ocean. It sparkled like a diamond. I walked closer to look at this giant piece of blue ice. The older the ice, the more it turns blue I was told. The air bubbles that get frozen into ice start to rise up and out. Eventually the bubbles all leave leaving the blue color. This piece must have been millions of years old. My God. This was so cool.

I again started to walk back to the warmth of the first aid station. As I got closer, I saw the remnants that marked the desolate, isolated North Pole. In front of the tent and all around scattered were beer cans, champagne bottles, parachutes and people running around like idiots. I just stood and looked. The giant red residue from the red smoke M-18 stained the pure white of the North Pole. I felt sad for a moment. I could only hope that those crazy ass skydivers had enough respect to pick up their trash before the last one left.

When I found Louise she was stumbling around snapping pictures. I heard someone scream and looked over my shoulder to see this crazy ass skydiver running around naked. He scurried into the first aid tent. What in the hell was he doing? Apparently a few skydivers had found an open crack and were jumping into the icy water.

I arranged to have Louise and me on the first chopper out. I told Louise to get herself ready to go. I had brought with me a gear bag to put my rig in when I was done with the jump. I jammed my parachute in my gear bag and started toward the MI-8 helicopter. I loaded my bag on board and walked up to the cockpit where our pilot was preparing to start up the big yellow airborne bus for our journey off the North Pole. The pilot asked me to be in charge of the first load out. I said okay.

My first responsibility was Louise. I walked back to the first aid tent to get the lady made of glass. The snow was knee deep and not easy to walk through. I made my way back and told Louise that it was time to go. It was probably 50 yards to the chopper. She was huffing pretty good by the time I got her inside and belted down. Once that was done, I went back to the drop zone and put the word out that the first load off would leave in 20 minutes sharp. I wanted to get going. I knew it was eighteen hours back. Three and a half up and on the pole, and eighteen hours back. It was now one o'clock in the morning Russian time and the sun was just going in circles across the arctic sky. One by one the skydivers loaded into the MI-8. Now full with 18 passengers, I gave the North Pole one last look. Still littered with beer cans, wine bottles, paper bags, and skydivers, I waved good-bye and closed the door.

I went up to the cockpit and told the captain that we were all loaded. The turbine engines had been running to keep the heaters running. Now the rotors started to swing. The M-18 started to shake the normal way all helicopters do. I stayed up front to get one last look at the North Pole as we began the long journey home to Khatanga. The rotors up to speed, the pilot slowly started to lift off. The rotors pitched from flat to the angle we needed for lift off. When he did that, the snow surrounding the chopper rose up, and our visibility went to nothing—like being in a blizzard. Suddenly we were above the ice hovering about 20 feet high. The pilot did a slow 360 degree turn to give us one last look at the North Pole. The chopper pitched forward and we were on our way back to Khatanga.

I went back to my seat next to Louise and belted myself in. There I sat. I sighed in relief. I thought to myself again about my father. *How about it, Dad? How about that?* "Good job, Rocco!" I had tandem jumped the lady made of glass onto the North Pole and landed exactly where I wanted. That should have been good enough to hear those simple three words. Wouldn't you think? I'll never know. He's dead now. I'll never know. I can only guess, but I thought so. I closed my eyes and went to sleep, satisfied I had done my job. Not only had I done my job, I had done it perfectly. Even with a snapped bicep in my right arm.

The ride was four and a half hours till we arrived at the airport where our next aircraft, an Antonov 24, sat waiting for us. The Antonov 24 was a high wing jet with two turbine engines located on the high wings. The porthole windows of the chopper were all frosted over and you couldn't see out. I awoke to see Louise still sitting, still sleeping. I unsnapped my seatbelt and made for the cockpit. Once up front, I saw the pilot point off in the distance. There she was. The red and grey stood right out in contrast to the pure white of the snow. We flew over the top of where the 24 lay, and our pilot swung the MI-8 around in a hard banking turn. He sat the MI-8 down next to the 24, just far enough away not to disturb the plane with rotor wash. Again we were blinded by the blizzard created by the rotor wash of the helicopter blades. When the snow settled, there was our new taxi.

I had never seen an airplane quite like this. The Antonov 24 had a ramp that retracted, two turbine engines mounted on the high wings capable of hauling at least twenty-four people. Inside were fifteen 50 gallon drums full of Jet A fuel. They had to be unloaded, so I helped so I could get Louise back to the comfort of civilization. I knew that this type of lifestyle was me! Never again would I get the chance to mingle with the Russian military and join them on a mission.

Once the fuel was unloaded, I loaded Louise and myself. The others followed. The 24 taxied on the ice where the falling snow had been plowed off. We hadn't even taken off yet, and Louise was sleeping. I wasn't far behind. The sun still circled above us at 5 o'clock in the morning. The Antonov 24 was off and flying in a short distance, and I was off and sleeping.

Five hours later, I was awakened by the shock of the jet engines at reverse thrust, full power. This was a short field Russian aircraft and that was how it was to be flown. The Russian pilots did just that, proud to show their aviation skills to their American passengers. Their demonstration got my respect. Every move was polished and smooth. I knew. I don't really think anybody else took note but Trey. Trey was a perfectionist in his aviation activities as I was, and I know that he knew that he was aware of the Russian skills exhibited.

As we taxied down the asphalt strip, I knew we were getting close to Khatanga. At least we were back on solid ground, and I was glad. Now 48 hours into this expedition with only small periods of interrupted sleep, exhaustion was starting to take its toll. Poor Louise was withering away from all the traveling. Not only that, but her fourth skydive ever was on the North Pole. The 24 taxied up to a big twin engine airplane. No jet engines on this airplane—an Antonov 24 transport aircraft capable of handling 36 people. This ride would be our last, six more hours to take us to our final destination. I was ready.

We loaded the 24 and I got Louise and myself a nice seat

that reclined. As soon as I got Louise in her seat and her seatbelt snapped I saw her eyes start to fade, her lids dropping like blinds. I walked to the cockpit to see the layout of the Russian plane. Pretty much the same controls and layout I was familiar with, but everything written in Russian, of course.

I wandered back to my seat, sat down, and snapped my seatbelt closed. The twin started its roll down the runway rocking to and fro. Once we got to the end, the pilot started to push throttles forward, and I could feel the power in the turbine start to come on. Our take off taxi was a lot longer than the 24, but this airplane was built as a transport aircraft and the 24 was built for a short field. As the airplane launched from the ground, I faded to sleep. At least this airplane was far more comfortable and didn't smell like Jet A turbine fuel.

Six hours later, we were finally back at Khatanga. We taxied up next to the Ilyushin that had carried us to the North Pole. After the pilot landed he shut the engines down. I opened the airstair door. It swung down and stopped just above the asphalt ramp. I woke up Louise and guided her down and out of the 74. Finally back! I knew the return trip would take a while but hadn't anticipated this. I helped Louise, and then I got my rig and went in to take a shower.

I finished my shower and went down for a beer to relax and wind down. One of the skydivers on the expedition was from Spain, and I had known him for some years. Bruno and I had a few beers and then a few more. Then there were no more, and I was pretty drunk. And I was tired.

Bruno said, "Hey, Rocky. Stay here and I'll be right back."

I said, "Okay."

When Bruno came back he had another 24 beers. We drank it all, and I finally went to bed. It felt good not to have any responsibility, and I slept for 22 hours straight.

When I woke up, Louise was getting ready for our trip back. I ran into Trey and asked how his ride back was. He told me it took the same as us—about 18 hours. He also told me while he was there that two Twin Otter helicopters had come full of wealthy people who had chartered them to fly to the North Pole.

When they got there, they climbed out to see probably at least one hundred crazy skydivers running around, wine and beer bottles everywhere, and a great big red stain in the virgin white snow. I laughed and so did he and we agreed, it's a small world.

The trip back to Florida was pretty much uneventful. Louise was happy, and I had a great experience under my belt. My arm is still messed up to this day. One day I won't be able to use it, but I guess it goes with the territory.

Russian MI-8 helicopters made the trip off the North Pole a little easier than the flight there.

Above, a women's skydive team was almost lost when Rocky's Cessna 206 blew its engine. Below, an example of the Cessna 206 Rocky flew. Introduced in 1962, it is still being made today.

Chapter Twenty

## A Fortunate Son

Adventures like landing the "lady made of glass" on the North Pole come along rarely, but in my life with flying and skydiving there were very few ordinary days. And danger was often close at hand. The years running my drop zone in Flagler Beach were filled with days I won't forget.

In 1994 a girl from New York had been at the drop zone for the three days waiting for training. Because my partner Rich Fenimore (known to most friends by his nickname Fang) was in Daytona Beach taking his written for his commercial pilot's license, training was left to me. We had completed the first jump ground school but couldn't get in the air to jump because it was too windy. I was getting a little antsy. I hadn't been in the air myself for three days.

At 2:30 in the afternoon I decided to fly to Palatka where they were hosting an 80-way attempt—80 people holding grips to create a formation. I told John, my chief instructor, to keep the girl there at the drop zone because I knew that the wind would die. I climbed in my Cessna 206 and headed for Palatka. I took off and stayed at 1,000 feet. I like this altitude because I can see the ground well. Palatka was 20 minutes from Flagler by air. My C-206 would cruise at 143 mph so it didn't take long. I rolled in and taxied up to the drop zone. When I got out of my airplane, the place looked a little shy on people.

That lasted only a matter of minutes. I could hear airplanes grinding to altitude. I looked up to see the formation: two DC-3s and two D-18 twin Beeches. The round motors powering the airplanes make a sound all their own. I could see real well because there was a high layer of clouds above them. They circled the drop zone until they reached their altitude. At 15,500 feet, here they came on jump run. The formation tightened as they got closer to the exit point. I had pretty much figured out where it was. The sound died down and out they poured, building their formation as they got lower and lower. At about 9,000 feet, you could see them clearly—maybe forty or so hooked up with the other forty waiting. The base was pretty solid but the other forty had a few that were low and a few circling. I could see that this attempt was not going to work.

At about 6,000 feet, the 40-way was now 60-way and starting to wobble. This is a critical time when building large formations. If one side gets higher than the other, the low side will go under the high and steal the wind. At this point, the whole damn thing will come crashing down into each other and then it's every man for himself. With eighty people in the same place, if they all pull in the same area, the potential for a collision is quite good. So as taught in the AFF program, you bring your hands to your sides and straighten your legs into what jumpers call the track position. This gives you vertical and horizontal separation, creating a clear area to pull. At 12,500 feet, a skydiver in the track position can go horizontal for one mile. They all looked like small darts gliding across the sky.

I watched the failed formation coming apart and between 4,500 and 2,500 feet, the skydivers started to deploy their canopies. At this point, I saw all of them open but one. I know what 2,500 feet looks like and it was damn sure lower than that.

He appeared to be tumbling and was already down to 1,000 feet. I wondered if he had an automatic opener—it should have been deploying his canopy. I was still watching him fall. Yes, he was tumbling and well below 500 feet. *This guy is going to bounce.* It looked like his impact point was directly on the main runway. *My God, he is going to really bounce.* Right then I heard a noise like I have never heard before. Crack! The noise sounded like a shotgun blast. He had just landed on the runway and it was gut wrenchingly loud. I watched his mangled body bounce back into the air, his helmet and head exploding. I had seen this before but never this graphic.

The people on the ground were screaming. Most were in

tears. *Damn it,* I thought. Within minutes, sirens were blaring and heading to the site of impact. "What happened?" I heard someone say.

I said, "It looked like he was unconscious."

When all the skydivers got back, they began trying to figure out what had happened. This was a good time for me to leave. I climbed back in my C-206 and flew home to Flagler. The wind was down. I landed, got out, and told John to get the girl who had waited three days ready to go skydiving. I didn't say a thing about what I had just seen. John and my staff would find out soon enough.

This girl we were training seemed a little flakey. I mentioned to John to be on his toes and watch out for anything. John and I took her up on a Level 2 jump and she did great, to my surprise. I talked her down with the radio and she landed perfect. Stood right up. She had surprised me. I learned the hard way to never trust a student. Most of the time, I'm right when I sense one who might give me a hard time. But sometimes I'm wrong. On this jump, I was wrong, and was grateful for it.

The wind was perfect right then for student jumpers, but we were running out of daylight. I told John to take her back up on Level 3 with Rick in my place. I would stay on the ground.

Fang's friend from California, who wanted to learn to skydive, was coming to check us out that day. He was called one-eye Tom for the simple reason that he had just one eye. As John and Rick were getting our student ready for her next jump, here came Tom. I introduced myself and told him to get in the jump truck. I had modified a truck with seats in the bed that we used to pick up the skydivers. As for me, I was done flying and jumping for the day.

We drove to the center of the airport where I had built the landing area along with a 10-meter pea gravel pit and watched my C-206 take off with the three on board. As the plane ground to altitude, I explained to Tom how our program worked and that we would give him a price break because he was friends with Fang. After about 15 minutes the jump plane was about to start on jump run.

I pointed to the sky and said, "There it is. Can you see it?"

One-eyed Tom squinted and said, "No. Where?"

I pointed again and said, "Right there."

He had his dark glasses on, so I don't even know if he was

looking in the right direction. I heard the engine cut back and out came the jumpers. Four seconds later, I could see the three-way piece quite clearly. I pointed again to the sky even though I knew it was hopeless.

I was thinking that they should be letting go from the formation soon. In the new AFF training scenario, the instructors released the student at 6,000 feet or above. I saw Rick release her at 9,000 feet. She looked like she was good and stable, which she needed to be for a good release of the reserve side. Rick moved away while John remained in close, good and tight. The girl continued to lay stable. I asked one-eyed Tom, "Can you hear them?"

He said, "Yes. Yes, I can."

Next, John released. The girl lay stable. Then it happened—and quick. She bent at the waist and her knees came in. Immediately she was upside down and spinning. Rick closed in and tried to grab her spinning leg. She was going too fast. She started to wobble. This was starting to get bad. John tried next. He shot in and rolled up on top. And then the two tumbled. John let go. She started to go into a violent spin. By this time, they were going through 2,500 feet. Again, Rick shot in and again he couldn't hang on. By now, they are falling through 1,500 feet.

Again John started to close. I could hear one-eyed Tom scream, "I see them! I see them!" *My God*, I thought, *I have never seen anyone fall that low and live.* My mind flashed back to the scene earlier at Palatka. *Christ, not four in one day.* Then her equipment worked exactly like it was supposed to—the automatic opener fired off. The square reserve was open by 1,000 feet.

I saw Rick pull his ripcord at 800 feet as John turned 180 degrees to the track. He opened his parachute somewhere around 300 feet. I could not believe what I was seeing. Pilot chute came first and lines started to slowly unstow. Then came the bag, and after what felt like forever, the canopy started to deploy. As it started to inflate, the slider came down the lines. It made it about three quarters of the way down. John hit the ground exactly at that moment.

Fang rolled up on his motorcycle and said, "What just happened?"

I said, "John just bounced. I'm talking this girl down. Go out and find John."

As the student approached the ground, the ambulance, the fire trucks, and the airport manager were rushing out to the spot where John had gone in. I landed the girl and said to Tom, "What do you think?"

"Did that guy mean to open that low?"

"No, not really," I said.

I drove the truck over and picked up the girl. When I got to her she was collecting her canopy. I asked her "Did you have a good skydive?"

She said, "Yeah, but I think I'm going to have to repeat that level."

I told her we'd go over the jump on the debrief and helped her into the truck.

I took her back to the drop zone and went back out to get John. I met Fang half-way and asked, "Did you find John?"

"No," he responded.

"Well, let's go find him." As we drove out I kept running through the day's events in my mind. I could not believe it. I parked the truck and went out to where the airport manager, fire trucks, and ambulance were parked. I stepped out of the truck and started into the woods.

I had made it about 50 yards when I saw Rick walking out. "Where is John, Rick?"

He said, "I don't know. I think over that way."

I went the way he pointed and was totally startled by what I saw. There was the airport manager and John walking out. John was not being carried out—he wasn't even limping. He was just walking as if nothing had happened. The only thing I noticed that was different was the look on his face, a look as if he had just seen God.

As I got closer to him, I could see his face a lot clearer. Written all over his face was the look of a man who was sure he was going to die but didn't.

I went up to him, inches from his face, and asked, "John, did you have a good skydive?"

All he could say was, "Wow."

* * *

I sometimes marvel at the fact that during all my time in the air—skydiving and flying—I never lost a student or passenger, or was severely injured myself. But believe me, I tempted fate many time, especially as a pilot. Most people fly thousands of hours and never have an engine failure, but not me. In 3,500 hours, I had four—three on takeoff.

The first was when I was just out of the burn hospital and had just soloed in a C-150. I didn't have much money and couldn't afford gas for flying. I pushed the little Cessna up to the pumps and put in three gallons and figured that would be enough. I cranked up the airplane, taxied down to the end of the runway, and went through my checklists. As I pushed the throttle, the little C-150 started to roll down the 6,000 foot runway and began to lift off. After I retracted the flaps, I established a good rate of climb. Things were as they should be. I was thinking, *This is so nice not to have an instructor sitting next to me watching my every move.* Just after reaching the end of the runway, the engine started to sputter.

I was too far down the runway to land straight ahead. If I did, I would have crashed into the houses that bordered the airport. I knew that wouldn't work. All those nights listening to Gary talk about flying were about to pay off. I remembered him saying don't lose your airspeed or your airplane will stall. There are only two ways to do it: Power, which at this point I didn't have, and angle of attack. Well, I had no power so I pushed the yoke in a forward position, dropping the nose of the airplane. This is where that phrase "seat of the pants flying" comes into play.

I never looked at any of the gauges. I could feel and hear the wind of the gliding airplane. I very carefully started a slow right hand turn. The airplane responded well. As I was turning, I was focused on an open part of the airport that bordered the adjacent runway to the one I took off from. This runway was closed but the city, which maintained the airport, kept the grass mowed. I set up to land just on the edge, in the grass. The little C-150 was doing its job now as a glider. At this point in my flying career, I don't even think I had 25 hours. Scared never entered my mind; I was too busy flying the airplane. I could see that I was going to make the grass. My only concern was a hole or real rough ground that my landing gear would fall into. I had no power, so whatever would be, would be.

The ground was coming up fast. I pulled back on the yoke and the airplane responded. The nose started to pitch up. I could feel the 150 wanted to stall. *I'm too damn high.* I eased the yoke ahead to get a little closer to the ground. This also gave me a little more airspeed and I needed that. Again I started to pull back, and this time I was at the perfect height for the flare. The little 150 started to mush into the ground. Crunch, I was down. I sat in the seat and said, "Thanks again, God. You pulled my ass out of another one."

Another close call came flying a plane ordered out of a catalog while I was working with Bob Lee. Part of my job was to test fly the airplanes that we worked on. Before we could return the airplane to service, we had to test fly it. I had been working on an Ercoupe, a little two seat airplane from the Sears and Roebuck catalog. I put a new engine on this airplane and did a little work on the airframe. I put a Cleveland brake conversion on it and a stainless steel firewall to separate the engine from the front part of the airframe. I got the little plane done and told Bob I thought it was ready to test fly.

We put fuel in the tank, located behind the new firewall I had just put in. I took the airplane out of the hangar and started it for the first time. She fired right up. What a weird airplane. It had no rudder pedals. The rudder and nose wheel steering was integrated into the yoke. This was quite a bit different from what I was used to because every other airplane I had flown had rudder pedals.

I filled up the fuel tank and talked to Bob about "engine out" procedures. This was a new Continental 0-200—100 horses. He got a field approval from the FAA to install the engine. He and I talked about how he wanted me to run the engine, rpm's, and airspeed. He also said to stay over the top of the field in case the engine quit.

With all this in mind, I climbed in, started it up, and taxied down to get ready for takeoff. The 0-200 engine was doing the job and before I knew it, I was in the air. I got my airspeed up and then started my best rate of climb. Up we went, almost 200 feet per minute. Pretty good for a little plane. I wrote the information down on a little notebook I had brought with me. As I started my circle pattern around the airport, I noticed that the engine was working perfectly; temperature for the oil was in the green as well as my cylinder head temp. I started a gradual climb up in altitude, monitoring my temps. Again, this was a strange airplane, and you flew it like you drive a car—by the steering wheel, or in aviation terms, yoke. The Ercoupe was developed in the 1950s and marketed to the average middle class family. I really don't know what it sold for but it was inexpensive. Besides you could buy it out of the catalog. What more could you ask?

Well, I got a couple of hours under my belt and thought I should land and take a break. I landed and taxied up to the club house where Bob was waiting in the shade of the small overhang that sheltered the picnic tables, the place where all the oldtimers would hang out and tell stories of their time flying, as they all had done, present and past. Most were grounded because they couldn't get their medical renewed for one reason or another.

I reported to Bob that it flew pretty good, although the no rudder thing was a little weird. The 0-200 engine we installed had been flawless. After some talk and a Doctor Pepper, Bob, being the guy he was, insisted on hooking up the wing fuel tanks that would supply fuel to the hopper tank, the standard fuel tank in front of the fuselage of the airplane. Once that was connected, I went up on another test flight. I was thinking that anytime that you bring change into a formula, it will bring new questions into the picture, but I taxied the airplane after the wing tank installation and everything worked perfect. I taxied the little Ercoupe down to the end of runway 270, the runway I preferred to take off from because it was clear of trees. It was a pasture for horses and a few palmetto bushes. I felt a little leery of this flight because of the new tanks.

I reached the point where the Ercoupe was starting to lift from the ground. I kept it there for only a moment as I was questioning my fuel. These wing tanks could have some kind of debris in them, and I hoped it would show up then. Now was the time to increase my angle of attack. As I rotated, the little Ercoupe started its climb as it had done before. I started to see the tops of the pine trees below me, and then a larger panorama began to spread out before me—a distant picture that only altitude can give. Closer and closer I got to the end of the runway—the point of no return. This is where you are too far, too low to come back to the safety of the runway. If your engine quits then, you have no choice but to glide straight ahead. The 0-200 was working hard as it had done ten hours before.

Suddenly it came. The engine started to sputter. *Shit, I knew it! Damn you, Bob! Shit!* I knew what was happening. This was no strange noise to me. The goddamn thing had run out of gas. But I knew that wasn't it—I filled them, all three: hopper and the two wing tanks. This was the noise I had heard when the C-150 quit. It was out of gas, too. It also was a 0-200 engine.

So now I was in a glider again, but this time with nowhere to go but straight ahead. Trees on the right, houses on the left. I thought maybe I had just enough room this time to stick it back on. I had some airspeed and I damn sure was going to need it. I dropped the nose down; the Ercoupe responded. I only needed 500 feet and it looked like I had enough. As I lowered the nose, I could hear my airspeed increase. Airspeed, wind—it's all the same, an aviator's friend, or in some cases, foe. In this case, I needed it.

My visual picture changed from blue sky to green ground. The ground came up fast, and I mean fast. If I started to pull back on the yoke too soon, I would glide off the end of the runway. If I pulled back too late, I was going to crash into the runway and possibly burn.

I could feel the pressure on the yoke as I had so many times before. The lighter the pressure, the less response. The heavier, the quicker the airplane responds. The wind is created from the forward speed of an airplane. The more wind you hear, the faster it is going past the airplane's structure. The quieter it gets, the less you have going past the airplane. Well, when you put the two together, it just adds to the rest of your piloting skills. I knew I had to stick this plane in, and that's just what I did. As I pushed the yoke in, the airplane came diving into the ground. At the very last moment, I started to ease the yoke back. The airplane started to level off, and all three of the landing gear touched the ground. Perfect. Just perfect.

But it wasn't over. My ground speed was still fast, and I was coming to the end of the runway. Closer. Closer. *I sure hope these Clevelands hold.* I reached for the hand lever that operated the brakes. I knew better than to jerk the handle as the airplane would go up on the nose. I started to slowly pull the handle up, and damn if I wasn't right. The airplane coasted to a stop. I was probably ten feet from the fence when I stopped. I climbed out on the wing and stepped onto the ground and looked at the little Ercoupe. This was a lesson in life—go with your gut feeling. Don't listen to others. Later on, Max congratulated me on my flying and told me he thought I was a goner.

In March of 1991 I flew to Sacramento, California, to buy a C-206 with a bad engine. I put a brand new engine in and flew it back to Flagler Beach, Florida. It was a long flight as the 206 would only cruise at 145 mph. I was running my own drop zone then, along with a small flight school and a maintenance facility. Along with my partners—Fang, who was later killed in an airplane crash, and Terry Warby—we agreed to buy the airplane. We would use it for flying skydivers.

Fang and Terry negotiated a contract for our company, Flagler Aviation, for 500 jumps with a four-way all girl competition team sponsored by Coca-Cola. I had flown the girls in our new C-206 for about two hundred jumps. The airplane performed well, and the engine was running perfectly. I did all my own maintenance inspections and had already put 160 hours on the engine.

On one summer morning in April, 1991, I had all four of the girls plus their videographer in the plane as I had done two hundred plus times before. They would usually jump six times a day and this particular time was the first jump of the day. I loaded them in, climbed into the pilot seat, and started the C-206. I taxied down to the threshold of runway 240, turned into the wind, and ran through my checklists. I called on our communications system, Unicom, that I was taxiing into position for takeoff. With all traffic clear, I pushed the throttle in and the 206 shot down the runway. I always took off with 20 degrees of flaps as this helped me get off the ground quicker and lengthened the life of the tires.

As I picked up my ground speed, I could feel the airplane wanting to lift. I eased back on the yoke and then into the air. As my airspeed increased, I started to gradually retract the flaps. I kept the airplane close to the runway as I built up my airspeed. I knew that you can trade airspeed for altitude if needed. I was now up at 50 feet, and my airspeed was around 150 mph. Full power, I started to rotate and noticed the small swamp that goes into Gore Lake off the end of runway 240.

As I started to rotate to my best angle of climb, I heard a noise that I had never heard before. A noise so solid, so definite, one that screamed that something was really wrong. It sounded like a firecracker but 100 times louder. An explosion. My mind was racing—*I knew it would come! The one that you read about! Catastrophic! Your engine has just exploded*!

By the book, you try a restart. I'm watching the goddamn prop spinning like a ceiling fan. I go through emergency procedures, boost pumps on. *For how long*? I don't want to saturate the engine with fuel for fear of a fire. There was no way I wanted to burn again. After a few seconds, I shut the pumps off and gave up on a restart.

I knew that now I was back in a glider. Time slowed long enough for me to make a decision—abort my takeoff. Now what? Straight ahead wasn't an option; that would take me and my passengers into either the swamp or the lake, and neither one was good. My concern wasn't focused on me, but on my passengers and the airplane.

I had a plan and a good one. On my left was a runway that ran perpendicular to the one I took off from. It was disused and had a lot of mowed grass like the DeLand airport. I had 150 mph of airspeed that now I transferred to altitude. As I started my climb, I eased the big flaps on to 40 degrees, full flaps. Then I started a gradual left turn and set up to land on the grass that separated the disused runway and disused taxi strip. Those four girls and the videographer were screaming for dear life.

I was busy trying to get the plane down in one piece and trying to avoid killing all of us. The airplane did as I asked. A shallow turn to the left and I was set up on my final in between the runway and taxi strip. I flew the Cessna to the very end. Plunk. It settled right on target. I had the yoke back as far as it would go and more. The plane started its roll at a high rate of speed despite the brakes being on. The damned thing wanted to roll into the palmettos that lay ahead. I couldn't do anymore. I had the brake pedals as far forward as they would go.

The screaming didn't stop until the airplane stopped six feet short of a single palm tree. I opened the jump door and told the girls, "Get out fast!" I didn't have to say it twice. They got out faster than any exit they had ever practiced for their competition. Then it was my turn, and I was out as soon as I could. No way would I burn again. There we stood, all six of us staring at the lifeless airplane. I wasn't even shook up. By now, this was a way of life. My life. The girls all took their turns saying what a good job I did. They all kissed me on the cheek, all but the videographer. He and I shook it up and shared a well-earned smile.

On another day flying skydivers at my drop zone in Flagler

Beach, I was forced again to prove my skills when another engine gave out. I had the usual five skydivers and was climbing to altitude over the Flagler airport. I had just taken off and was starting my circle around the airport on my climb. I learned from my previous experience to stay within gliding distance to the airport.

It was a winter day in Florida, and the sky was crystal clear. I was at 1,700 feet coming up on 2,000 feet when the engine just plain stopped. Again, I went through my engine out protocol. No luck. I wasn't that high, and I was at the border of gliding safely back to the airport. Everyone in the airplane thought I had chosen to return for some reason other than engine failure. I had a few previous experiences with the engine out scenario when flying jumpers. When that happened, the engine runs and slows down, runs, slows down. You could get about another five minutes if you pushed the rudder pedals down to the floor. The residual fuel would go to the wing root opposite the pedal you were pushing. I did this while gliding down.

I called on the radio and told the control tower my intentions. Luckily, there was no one in the pattern, and I had a clean shot for my final approach. As I crossed the threshold, I lowered my flaps. *Squawk* was the sound I heard, telling me that we were down and safe. I had enough ground speed to taxi up to a tie down. I told everyone, "Don't take your gear off," and directed them to the second 206 we had purchased as the business prospered. In this situation, it paid off.

We climbed in the second plane, and as I taxied, I thought *these God damn airplanes are going to kill me yet*! My mind was still on the blown cylinder and the sudden stop of the first engine. I taxied into position and announced on the radio that I was taking off. I pushed the throttle in as far as it would go, still concerned that all could go wrong, and began my climb to 9,000 feet. I started to relax with the C-206 climbing strong. All my temperature gauges were in the green, and my passengers were enjoying the climb to their "experience of a lifetime." I had an AFF Level 1 and a tandem student student on board. Both fresh to the sport. I thought to myself that if they only knew what had just happened, they probably would have never gotten back in another plane after climbing out of the other lifeless 206. I put all that aside, relaxed, and began to enjoy my flight to altitude. The sky was crystal clear. The Atlantic Ocean was only five miles from the airport. As soon as the plane took off, it was very visible. On this morning, the ocean was smooth as glass. The temperature was probably 70 degrees on the ground, perfect for the performance of the engine of the 206.

I leaned back in my seat and could see Cape Canaveral in the distance. I was thinking to myself how good life really was and what a lucky man I was to see the world in this way. My mind jumped back to all the bullshit I had been through in my lifetime, and I thought *I'm an awful lucky guy to be here.* And again I thought, *I'm sure glad I had such a great dad who raised me to go out and seek the new challenges of life, but made sure I knew to keep my guard up.* My focus returned to the present and this latest episode in my life. Dammit, every time I turn around, something was always going wrong. Yeah, but then again, maybe everything is going just as it should.

Flagler Beach drop zone partner Fang lands
a tandem jump with Rocky's brother Mike.

Chapter Twenty-One

## ANOTHER TRIAL BY FIRE

There are a handful of people in my life who I've really looked up to, beginning with my dad. Gary Dupuis, who taught me to fly, was another. Then there was Bob Lee. When I worked for Bob Lee, every day was a new lesson in life. This old man had character. He was tough, and if he had to say something, he would say it. Never once would he hold back. He was mean as a rattlesnake and not afraid to show it. And he liked me. Bob was like a second dad to me. His airport was like no other, full of old hangars built with salvaged material from torn down houses, with A-frame angles for the roofs. The only thing he paid for was cement for his concrete mixer.

The place was a mess, with hangers full of Piper Cub parts and pieces from every other kind of airplane imaginable. Other hangers held old vintage airplanes and makes—PA-12s, Tailorcraft, Stearman, C-150s, Aeronica Champ, and so on. They were all mine to fly. Bob liked it when I would fly. His grass strip was perfect: 3,000 feet long and plenty wide.

Bob was no dummy even though he came across as pretty gruff to some people. He went to the University of Wisconsin where he met his wife, Claire—a lovely woman, one who bore six children and who stood by Bob's side through thick and thin.

I loved living at Bob's—my own runway, my own airplane parked in front, and a shop to work on all my airplane maintenance. I loved running my drop zone in Flagler, but I had it made during those four years with Bob Lee. I had so many good times at Bob's. One thing we had in common was doing what we wanted without worrying whether anyone approved. I could tell a long list of stories. For instance, right next to Bob's runway was a spring fed pond, which led me into one of my favorite adventures while I was there—diving without a parachute from 50 feet up out of a Hughes 360 helicopter into that 45-foot deep crystal clear pond.

In 1999, I divorced from my second wife of 10 and 1/2 years. I really can't blame anyone but myself. I had so much pain from my injuries in my skydiving career that like a lot of people, I got addicted to pain medication. This was a time period of going from up to down. The shock of the divorce threw me into depression and further into my addiction. It took me from being a world champion skydiver to a total drug addict. I knew if I kept up on this downward plunge, I would end up in jail or worse, prison. At this point, I went into my own recovery. Like any addict or alcoholic, you need to choose which path in life you want to take. It's your own choice.

So in 2003 I made my way back to where I needed to be to start over. Again I chose to go to my father—the father who took over for my real father—Bob Lee. Now at age 84, I asked Bob if I could come back to his airport to help him and work for him for a little bit of money. Of course Bob said, "Yes, come here with me. I could use your help."

I went back to Bob's and had a nice apartment above the clubhouse located right on the runway—full kitchen, shower, stove, everything that it would take to live. Thirty-seven windows facing north, east, and west made up the walls and provided a fantastic view of the runway. In his earlier years, Bob was an air traffic controller in WW II stationed in Louisville, Kentucky. He told me stories of 500 Boeing Stearman airplanes, used as a primary trainer in WW II, all in the air at one time. It felt good to hang out with the old man. There was a majestic charisma that seemed to follow him around. He was smart and still sharp at 84. I loved him like a dad. A true aviator.

If my life has taught me anything, it is to not get too comfortable. One night during the summer I was watching TV in my upstairs apartment when I noticed a big orange glow on the windows. At first I really didn't pay attention. Finally I stood up and looked down the long row of hangars. I couldn't believe my eyes. Orange flames were pouring out of the hangar No. 12, shooting up at least twenty feet above the roof. I immediately ran down the stairs and on down to the road toward 12—no shoes and just boxers. I was on it. The road that paralleled the hangar was probably 150 yards long. As soon as I got through the door of the clubhouse, I could see Rich, Bob's youngest son, lying on the ground. As I ran to him I thought he had been blown up by something. He was a welder and a damn good one.

When I got to him I said, "Richie, Richie, what happened?"

"Electrical fuse box shorted and started the fire," he said. "Get the water hose and start putting water on the roof."

"Did you call 911?"

"Yes," he replied.

The pump wouldn't work because it was hooked to the junction box in the burning hangar. There we sat helpless with all the fire extinguishers used up.

"Come on Rich," I said, "let's start pulling these planes out just in case it all burns."

"Okay," Rich said.

We start in front where the fire is. The wall partition is on fire as we start to pull out a Cessna 172. We drag it out of the way and then go back for a Taylorcraft. We pull it out and away, too. We pull two more out. The sounds of sirens fill the evening dusk as Rich and I bust our guts to pull yet another plane out and free from the gutting flames. It is just dusk when I first noticed the fire.. We've been at it about an hour, so now it's probably 8:30 p.m. Dark is starting to bleed in. Soon it is dark and the whole infrastructure is burning.

In the chaos, I lost Rich. I found out he was trying to get the fire department of DeLand to put out the fire. They had 2,000 gallons of water being held in a big tank that they could have used to put the fire out. Right next to Bob's, within 50 yards, was a mobile home park with fire hydrants right there. In the past Bob was known to have issues with the police department or any fire fighters and equipment. He would just plain tell them to get off of his property.

*What next?* I've got the time to pull out one more plane. The plane was the silver bullet, Bob's baby. *Is she going to burn? No way,* I thought.

I'm in my bare feet, boxer shorts, no shirt. I am running alongside burning hangars. As I run, I am trying to recall what hangar the silver bullet is in. I run through an open hangar and there she sits. I rush to the tie down ropes and start to untie them. Good. All three ropes are clear. As I run to the front of the airplane, I grab on to the prop. As I'm trying to pull the Cessna 150 out of the burning hangar, chunks of burning debris are falling from the roof onto the silver bullet's wings. My mind races back to the balloon crash. If one of those tanks blows, I'm cooked. This thought gives me extra strength to pull the Cessna to where it wouldn't be harmed by the fire. I brush the hot glowing embers off the wing. I look back. Shit, it's to my place now.

I turn away from the saved Cessna and run to the clubhouse. The bottom level is still solid. I rush up the circling spiral staircase to the top. As I stand up my head is engulfed with smoke. I drop down on my hands and knees. The smoke is solid down to four feet above the floor. I crawl to where I kept my parachute, my leather jacket and Bob's 22 rifle his dad had given to him as a boy. I was using it to shoot nasty squirrels that were living in the hangars and chewing the insulation off wires. I threw most of the stuff down the spiral staircase, all but the rifle. I went back again and got a handful of clothes. No shoes, nothing. My pictures, my wallet, everything I owned, up in smoke.

I ran down the staircase as the wall started to roar with flames. I hustled everything I had rescued out to the runway, a safe distance from the last bit of timber left to burn down at Bob Lee Airport. I laid what I had down onto the grass and sat down next to it to watch my golden clubhouse and my apartment burn to the ground. As I sat there and watched sixty years of work go down the drain, I just felt so sorry for Bob. This was his whole life. Everything. I started to sob. Why? Why? Why did the fire department stand there and do nothing? Not one drop of water came from those fire trucks. Not one. We begged them. Is the politics that bad? My God.

Then I came out of my frenzy and looked again at the flames now consuming all my personal belongings. First thing I thought of was all my clothes. There I sat on the grass runway with only a pair of boxer shorts on. My feet cut and bleeding. *I don't have any shoes*, I thought—*my passport, wallet, all my guns, my whole life, gone.* Gone. I looked to my side. *I'm OK.* I got my parachute, my leather flying coat draped over my rig, a pair of Levi's, a couple pair of socks and a pair of underwear. That was it. That was all I could save of my own.

Now my the clubhouse was full of flames, and the glass windows were starting to fall. I could hear the glass breaking as the fire set them free to fall and explode into tiny jagged pieces. The noise of breaking glass seemed endless. Again I started to think back to Bob. My God. My guts ached. All those years. Those glorious years that so many people had shared. The good times, the bad times. All those years.

My mind drifted away from the gruesome present. I remembered my first time at Bob's. I flew into Bob's strip in a Cessna 120 I owned, a young aviator and highly skilled skydiver hungry for knowledge in aviation. The old man, 72 years then, was sitting under the overhang on the picnic table built by him and his boys. I taxied up and spun the tail wheel around so my airplane faced the runway. I shut her down and climbed out. I could see Bob squint. He had cataracts and his vision wasn't that great.

"Rocco, is that you?"

"Sure is, Robert. How you doing?" I replied.

"Come over and have a Dr. Pepper," he said.

"Sounds good, Robert." I walked proud, proud to have flown my own little tailwheel airplane in at Bob's and be greeted by the "Grand Dragon," the nickname I had given him. I sat across from the old man.

"Rocco, how is the airplane running?" he asked.

"Like a scolded dog," I replied.

"Good," Bob said.

Then here it came like it did from that day on—the history of my airplane and the conception of my Cessna 120. Bob knew it all. Hell, he was my age when the damn thing was built. I sat across from him and sucked in every word that came out of his mouth. And when he was done I was speechless, and thankful—thankful to be around a man who was what I aspired to be: A true aviator.

Well, eventually our conversation drifted to women. Bob always was a bit of a cocksman, as he called it. And he told me I was one, also. I guess he was right. I never disagreed. I took it for what it was and left it at that. We chatted for an hour or so, and I told Bob I was going back up and fly. This is the best time. The air was real stable. Good for a nice flight.

"Okay, Rocco. Come on back!" he shouted.

My thoughts again were shaken by the breaking glass and

falling timber. I could see the glowing embers chase each other skyward. I saw the Bob Lee Airport sign I had found in a corner of a hangar covered with dirt just now starting to burn. We had cleaned it up and hung it on the front of the clubhouse to snazz the place up a bit. It was a final blow. There I sat on the grass strip. Head in hand watching the Bob Lee Airport sign slowly burn, the last bit of wood to burn in the long line of hangars that ran along the dirt road.

I don't know how long I sat there, and I didn't care. I was still in disbelief. When the clubhouse burned down to nothing, I stood up and walked down the dusty road that paralleled the hangars. My God. I couldn't believe what I was seeing. The whole infrastructure was now nothing but golden embers laying in strange patters. The skeleton outline of burned airplanes lay in sagging pieces melted from the intense heat of the fire. I knew every one of them. The only ones that made it through the fire were the ones Rich and I pushed from the burning hangars. We saved eight of twenty aircraft. Trucks, road grader, tractors, cars, everything—and I mean everything—was burnt to the ground. Hell, I didn't even manage to push my own damn toolbox out. I lost everything. Everything gone.

The radios from the fire trucks pulled my mind back to the truth of what just happened. Still barefoot and in my boxers walking slowly down the dirt road next to the decaying hangars of glowing embers, a fireman ran up to tell me to get away. I didn't even hear him in his worthless helmet, fire coat, and fancy boots. I slowly walked up to Bob's house. Friends and some family were there to comfort Bob. There he sat in his special chair as always, surrounded by old canes. I squeezed the aluminum door handle and walked in to where he sat.

As I stood in front of him, he looked up and asked, "Did any planes make it?"

In a long sigh I answered, "Me and Rich pushed out eight, Bob."

"Good boy, Rocco. How about the silver bullet?"

"I got her on my own, Robert."

"Good."

"How about your stuff," Bob asked.

"All my shit burned up too. Everything except my parachute, your gun, my leather flying coat, and a handful of clothes. No shoes."

"Damn," Bob replied. "How's the clubhouse?"

I looked back at Bob and replied, "Gone. Nothing left."

Bob could only hang his head and slowly roll it back and forth.

"What's the fire department doing?"

"Not a damn thing," I snapped in a stern but controlled way. "Do you think they let it burn down because they got a thing about you?"

"Hell yes, I do," Bob replied.

And I knew also. The fire department didn't like to answer to Bob Lee.

Richie showed up with streaks of soot on his face like Indian war paint. Bob asked him what was going on. Richie told Bob the same thing I did. After a few minutes, I told Richie that I was going down to the runway to get what little I had left. He asked me if I wanted to stay the night with him.

"Sure," I replied. "My house just burned to the ground. I'm gonna need a place for a couple of days."

I looked at Bob, his head hanging down, looking as if the whole of life had been sucked from his soul.

"Robert," I said.

His head popped up and turned to me. He said, "Yeah, Rocco."

"I'll see you in the morning."

"Okay," he replied.

I turned and walked out the door I'd been through so many times before. But never, ever had I walked through it like I did that night. I was devastated. Still no shoes, no shirt, just boxers covered my bare ass. I had fought, fought hard, harder than most would have. As I walked down the dusty dirt road between the now glowing pile of embers, I was still in disbelief. Everything gone! Gone! The worthless fire department was still there. Not one drop of water was put on the fire. Again another fireman approached me. As he got closer to me, I turned to him.

He said, "Sir, I told you, you can't be here."

With a firm but positive tone I replied, pointing to the piles of glowing embers and the small flames that were still burning, "This was my home, my livelihood. I strained my guts out and saved eight airplanes from burning to nothing, pal. What were you doing?"

The fireman's head fell as he turned to walk back to his

crew and bright shiny trucks that did absolutely nothing. Again I started my walk down the dusty road. My mind again back on poor Bob. He had no idea yet of the devastation and total destruction.

The soft sand felt good on my bare feet. I knew that they were cut up but I never felt them. I walked out on the runway where I had laid the only material things I had left. I sat back down on the spot from which I'd watched my apartment and the clubhouse burn. Head in hands, I sighed and thought, what next? What will Bob's next move be? I already knew he'd try to clean up the mess and move on. The man was 84 years old, but still tough as nails and never one to give up. Yes, and I would stand by his side until we got to where he wanted to go with his dream. I was there for that old man thick or thin.

A couple days later, I moved in with Bob. I had my own bedroom and was free to come and go as I wanted. It took a year to clean up the wreckage. The payoff came one evening when we were finished with work. The old man and I were on his golf cart. Bob turned to me with a look I'd never seen come across his 84 year old face. His eyes watered with a tear or two.

"Rocco, you're one hell of a man, and you are my best friend." The words rolled out of his mouth and his hand reached out to me. A big lump came into my throat.

I looked into his eyes and said, "Robert, you've been like a dad to me. The feeling is mutual." We shook hands and that was that.

Then we started back up the old dusty dirt road as Bob pointed at the concrete pads—the only things that made it through the fire—like gravestone markers where all the wooden hangars had stood. "We'll build a new hanger here where No 12 stood. That's where we'll start," he said.

I listened to his words but knew in my own heart that this was all that would ever be in Bob's lifetime.

I left to work in an airplane factory some time later. Bob knew it was my time and supported me. I came back to visit from time to time. He made it to 91 years old when he died. I went to the funeral and made my own peace with the old man.

I had now lost two fathers, two men whose approval has been so important to me, both of who loved to call me Rocco. They were gone, but I still had work to do. The Flagler Beach drop zone was in my rearview mirror, and running another drop zone was no longer in my thoughts. I was determined to follow my dream of developing an alternative AFF training program. That would be my focus now. It would not be easy but if there was one thing I had learned from my father and from Bob Lee, it was to never give up.

## ABOUT THE AUTHOR

**IN ROCKY EVAN'S OWN WORDS**, he is an "expert and professional skydiving enthusiast, competitor and instructor with a lifetime spent in the air."

This book tells his life story, from humble beginnings in Michigan to the British expedition into South America, and landing "the lady made of glass" onto the North Pole as part of a Russian expedition. Rocky is a former national and world champion sky diver and has also been a licensed pilot and aircraft mechanic. He knows the private aviation business from the top down and the bottom up.

Working with other highly skilled sky divers, he continues to develop new training programs to make the sport safer and more enjoyable.

*Flying High, Living Free* is his second published book.